Modern Folk Guitar

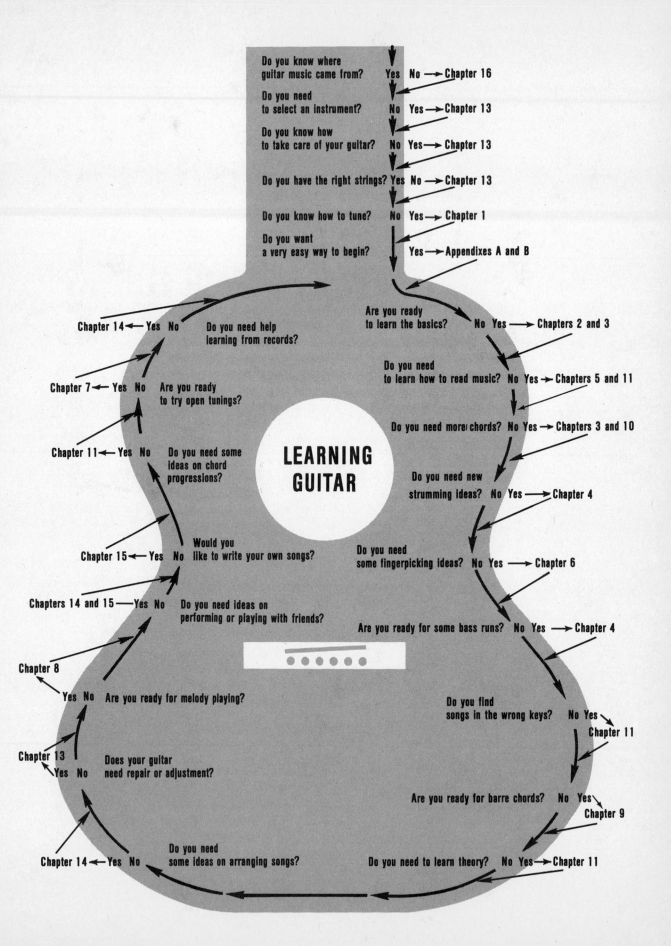

Do you know where
guitar music came from? Yes No ──→ Chapter 16

Do you need
to select an instrument? No Yes ──→ Chapter 13

Do you know how
to take care of your guitar? No Yes ──→ Chapter 13

Do you have the right strings? Yes No ──→ Chapter 13

Do you know how to tune? No Yes ──→ Chapter 1

Do you want
a very easy way to begin? Yes ──→ Appendixes A and B

Chapter 14 ←── Yes No   Do you need help
learning from records?

Are you ready
to learn the basics? No Yes ──→ Chapters 2 and 3

Chapter 7 ←── Yes No   Are you ready
to try open tunings?

Do you need
to learn how to read music? No Yes ─→ Chapters 5 and 11

Chapter 11 ←── Yes No   Do you need some
ideas on chord
progressions?

Do you need more chords? No Yes ─→ Chapters 3 and 10

LEARNING
GUITAR

Do you need new
strumming ideas? No Yes ──→ Chapter 4

Chapter 15 ←── Yes No   Would you
like to write your own songs?

Do you need
some fingerpicking ideas? No Yes ──→ Chapter 6

Chapters 14 and 15 ──→ Yes No   Do you need ideas on
performing or playing with friends?

Are you ready for some bass runs? No Yes ──→ Chapter 4

Chapter 8

Yes No   Are you ready for melody playing?

Do you find
songs in the wrong keys? No Yes ↘
Chapter 11

Chapter 13

Yes No   Does your guitar
need repair or adjustment?

Are you ready for barre chords? No Yes
Chapter 9

Chapter 14 ←── Yes No   Do you need
some ideas on arranging songs?

Do you need to learn theory? No Yes ──→ Chapter 11

Modern Folk Guitar

Terry Lee Kuhn
and
Harvey D. Reid

McGraw-Hill, Inc.
New York   St. Louis   San Francisco   Auckland   Bogotá
Caracas   Lisbon   London   Madrid   Mexico City   Milan
Montreal   New Delhi   San Juan   Singapore
Sydney   Tokyo   Toronto

MODERN FOLK GUITAR

First Edition
     6 7 8 9 MAL MAL 9 9 8 7

Library of Congress Cataloging in Publication Data
Kuhn, Terry Lee
   Modern folk guitar.
   Includes indexes.
   1. Guitar—Methods—Group instruction. I. Reid,
Harvey D. II. Title.
MT582.K85   1984   83-22253
ISBN 0-07-554461-X
Cover Photograph by Doug Moore
Cover Design by Laury Egan

This book is printed on acid-free paper.

Contents

Preface

This book was written to provide a self-contained, comprehensive coverage of guitar accompaniment skills. The performance techniques it emphasizes include basic chords, strumming, fingerpicking, open and simulated tunings, traditional melody playing, and barre chords. It also treats holding and tuning the guitar, arranging, and performing and writing songs. Other chapters on history, owning a guitar, notation, scales, chords, keys, capos, transposition, and hints on learning from records and song books make this book a compendium for guitarists at all skill levels.

A number of songs have been included to facilitate the learning of various skills. Many of the songs contain strumming and/or picking suggestions for multiple-player arrangements. The songs are then usable in classes that may contain different levels of players, or they can be used as teacher-student duets in a private teaching situation. In classes more advanced students can be working on different skills while playing the same songs with beginners.

Most of the songs in the text are in the public domain—that is, they do not lie under the copyright jurisdiction of anyone and are the common property of all. Due to the nature of the copyright laws and the fact that the music of this instrument has emerged relatively recently, much of the music that people typically play on the guitar cannot be included in this text, mostly because copyright owners have refused to give permission for such use. Nevertheless, you are encouraged to play material that is meaningful to you. Printed versions of popular songs can be obtained from any number of commercially available song collections and folios. Since many of these collections are not arranged specifically for guitar, Chapter 15 contains helpful information on how to devise playable arrangements of popular songs.

The structure of this book is intended to help you learn to play the guitar and to understand its music. Each chapter is written with skills and conceptual material sequenced from easy to more difficult, and chapters are arranged in progressive difficulty within parts. However, the chapters—which cover left- and right-hand playing skills, theory, and special topics—are intended to be studied concurrently rather than in order. This strategy assumes that whatever you learn first will facilitate the learning of topics subsequently studied and that theoretical and background knowledge will enhance performing skills. The need to know something at a particular moment may be the determining factor for the order in which you study this book. Remember, too, that many of the skills presented in a few pages may take months to master. Take a moment to look at the Table of Contents and consider the many things there are to know about *Modern Folk Guitar*.

Acknowledgments

We would be remiss if we did not acknowledge the insight we have gained from our students over the years. The members of each class have continually shared new ideas on playing, performers, and music. Wendy L. Sims deserves special credit for her astute observations about the manuscript: many of the book's finer points are attributable to her comments. Liz Kuhn fed, housed, and generally gave moral support to the authors, typists, and readers through days of toil. Lisa Kuhn was a faithful typist and proofreader, bringing the manuscript into final form. Roth Wilkofsky's professional judgment and analytical sense as editor has been most helpful.

We also would like to thank the following reviewers for their helpful suggestions and comments:

Alan Schmidt, *Erie Community College*
Nels Leonard, Jr., *West Liberty State College*
Ronald J. Crocker, *Kearney State College*
Carole J. Delaney, *California State University, Sacramento*
Randall S. Moore, *University of Oregon*
Dorothy McDonald, *The University of Iowa*
C. Nelson Amos, *Eastern Michigan University*
Patricia Flowers, *University of Texas at San Antonio*
Martin Shapiro, *California Polytechnic State University*

To the Teacher

Every instructor who teaches a guitar class assumes responsibility for organizing content, instructional procedures, and grading of students. The order in which material is presented will depend on the purposes of specific instructional settings, the students' backgrounds, and the experience of the instructor. Given these qualifications, Figure 0.1 represents one way in which some or all of the chapters in *Modern Folk Guitar* might be covered. There are four columns, one each for courses which are one quarter, one semester, two quarters, and two semesters in length.

Each column is divided into left-hand skills (Lh), right-hand skills (Rh), and theory (T) or special topics (S). Some class periods may be devoted entirely to one idea, a guest performer, or performances by members of the class. More typically a class period would be organized around the review of previously learned skills, presentation of a new skill, introduction of a theory or special topic, intensive practice on the new skill, and a review of the day's activities. In such a plan approximately 50 percent to 60 percent of a typical class period is spent in performance.

Typical class period	Approximate % of class time
Playing review	10
Presentation of new skills	10
Theory or special topic	40
Practice of new skills	30
Review of day's activities	10

Teachers are encouraged to study Appendixes A and B for two alternative approaches to beginning the study of executive skills.

Week	One quarter Lh	Rh	T-S	One semester Lh	Rh	T-S	Two quarters Lh	Rh	T-S	Two semesters Lh	Rh	T-S
1	*		1	*		1	*		1	*		1
2	2		13	2		13	2		13	2		13
3	3	4		3	4		3	4		3	4	
4	3	4		3	4	5	3	4	5	3	4	5
5	3	4	5	3	4	5	3	4	5	3	4	5
6	3	6	5	3	6	5	3	6	5	3	6	5
7	3	4	11	3	6	11	3	6	11	3	6	5
8	7	6	12	3	4	11	3	4	11	3	4	5
9	9	6	15	3	6		3	6		3	4	11
10	review				6	12	review			3	6	11
11				7			3	4		3	4	
12						14	7	6		7	6	
13				9			9		12	7	4	12
14				10		15	9	6		9	6	
15				review			8	6		review		
16							8			8	5	
17							8		15	9		
18							8			9	5	15
19							10		16	8		
20							review			8		
21										8		11
22										8		
23										8		
24										10		11
25										10		
26										10		
27												14
28												15
29												16
30										review		

Key

Left hand	=	Lh
Right hand	=	Rh
Theory	=	T
Special topic	=	S
Chapter numbers	=	1–16

FIGURE 0.1   Suggested Course Content by Weeks

*Appendixes A and B contain material especially suited to beginning classes. Some teachers may prefer to begin with Chapter 2 if all students in the class have had previous experience with guitar. Other teachers may prefer to begin with Chapter 5 on playing melodies and single note reading.

PART I
Playing the Guitar

The guitar has become the dominant instrument in the musical culture of the United States and is employed by nearly every cultural segment of our society as a means of expressing its musical energy. It is found as a rhythm instrument, providing the pulse for dance music; as an accompaniment to poetry, stories, and political statements; and also as a melodic solo instrument on the concert stage. The fiddle, bagpipes, and accordion have their place in other cultures as the instrument of choice, but there is something about the guitar that represents and personifies a common spirit in this country.

Part I will introduce you to various aspects of playing this ubiquitous instrument. Holding and tuning your guitar are explained in Chapter 1. Chapter 2 and Appendixes A and B present very easy skills to enable you to start playing immediately. Appendix A in particular presents a new approach to beginning guitar that is readily accessible to adult beginners, young players, and even handicapped individuals. It also forms a transition between having no skills and the material presented in Chapters 2 and 3. Chapter 4 is intended to be studied concurrently with Chapter 3. Such concurrent study combines the left-hand chords you learn in Chapter 3 with the strumming techniques you learn in Chapter 4. Chapters 2, 3, and 4 often require several months to master, so don't be in a hurry. Read other parts of the book as you keep mastering one skill at a time.

Music reading of melodies, the transforming of visual symbols into sound, is presented in Chapter 5. Many folk guitarists play for years without formally reading music while others find the reading of music a great aid in learning new songs from books. Whether you intend to play "by ear" in the folk oral tradition or to play from written materials, you will most likely profit from studying Chapter 5.

Fingerpicking patterns presented in Chapter 6 add variety to the strums given in Chapter 4. Some songs will sound better when played with a fingerpicking accompaniment.

Many guitarists enjoy the unique sounds created by the open and simulated tunings found in Chapter 7. If you can play the basic chords without hesitation, using interesting strums and fingerpicking patterns, then you are ready to study Chapters 8 and 9, which cover Carter- and Travis-style melody playing and barre chords. These chapters are generally considered to be intermediate-level materials. Chapter 10 will start you playing scales, a necessity for eventual melody playing and improvisation. The second part of Chapter 10 will expand the number of ways you can play chords.

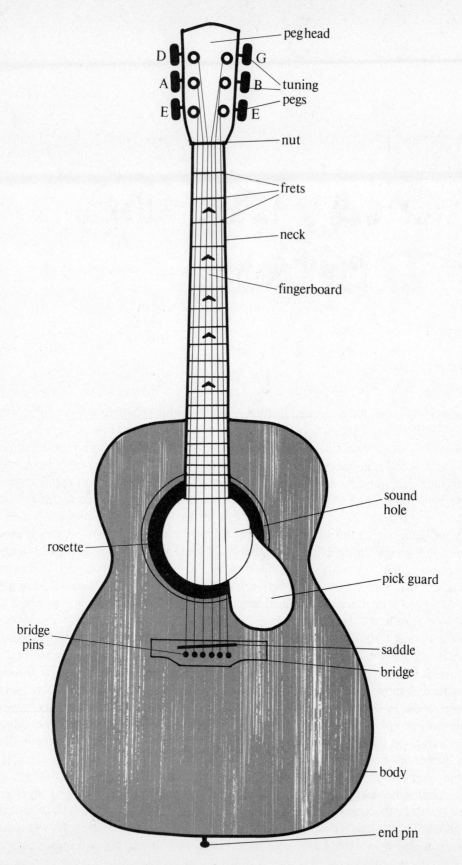

peghead

D

G

A

B

E

E

tuning
pegs

nut

frets

neck

fingerboard

sound
hole

pick guard

rosette

bridge
pins

saddle

bridge

body

end pin

FIGURE 1.1 Parts of the Guitar

chapter 1
Holding and Tuning the Guitar

PARTS OF THE GUITAR

The names of the parts of the guitar are shown in Figure 1.1. The *peghead* is sometimes called the head or headstock, and the *tuning machines* are called tuners or tuning gears. The strings rest on the *saddle*, a small piece of plastic or bone set into the *bridge*, and on the *nut*, which is on the peghead. Some guitars have a slightly elongated neck with an added fret where the nut is usually placed. This "zero" fret then produces the open-string pitch, and the nut serves only as a guide for the strings as they curve toward the tuning pegs.

Inlaid markers on the fingerboard are called *position dots* and are usually found only on steel-string guitars. The circular inlay around the *sound hole* is called the *rosette*.

The names of the strings from bass to treble are E, A, D, G, B, and E. These strings are numbered 6, 5, 4, 3, 2, and 1, respectively.

HOLDING THE GUITAR

The guitar should be held in such a way as to maximize the player's ability to produce good tone with maximum agility. Classical guitarists have been studying the issue for centuries and generally agree that a position such as the one shown in the upper right of Figure 1.2 is effective. The left leg is raised six to eight inches above the floor, usually by means of a small footstool, the peghead is at about the height of the guitarist's face, and the right wrist is gently arched away from the top of the guitar.

Folk, blues, and country players have a number of ways of holding the guitar, all of which depend a great deal on the playing ability and style of the players. Many singers stand, and wear a neck strap to hold the guitar, while others sit on chairs or stools. The more accomplished steel-string guitarists tend to use body positions approximating the classical position, although perhaps because they often play much bigger guitars, they often rest the guitar on the right leg when seated. The guitar must be supported in such a way that both arms are free to play, and this support is offered by the legs or the strap. It is a

3

FIGURE 1.2 Holding the Guitar

good idea to watch different players, especially those who are proficient in any of the various ethnic styles of playing, and observe how their body position and method of holding the instrument reflects the technical demands of the style. Figure 1.2 shows some examples of other common ways to hold the guitar.

HINTS FOR LEFT-HANDED GUITARISTS

The guitar is a two-handed instrument, and theoretically it should not make any difference whether it is played left-handed or right-handed. Many left-handed people have learned to play in a right-handed manner without complications, yet some players still feel more comfortable playing left-handed. If you are considering that option, you should weigh the following two points:

1. If you simply play the guitar upside down, you can use a normal instrument, but none of the instructional material available will work and you will probably have to

invent your own fingerings for chords and scales. It is not uncommon for players to do this and offers some new musical possibilities not available to right-handed players, but it greatly complicates the learning process.

2. You can purchase a left-handed guitar or have a right-handed guitar converted. The latter alternative is better in that it allows you to use normal instructional materials, but it limits you to being able to play only on left-handed instruments. A guitar is not totally symmetrical, and a right-handed instrument can never be completely converted to a left-handed one without changing the bracing, bridge, and nut and perhaps reshaping the frets. Expensive instruments should not be converted, but on a student model, a repair person can change the nut, saddle, saddle slot, and pickguard and refile the frets for a reasonable fee, and provide a workable left-handed guitar. Some large music stores stock left-handed instruments, and these guitars can be special-ordered from any manufacturer. All of the instructions in this book assume that the guitar is held and played in the normal right-hand manner.

RIGHT-HAND POSITION

There is disagreement among guitarists as to what the "correct" right-hand position is. The hand position that works for a jazz player may not work for a country player, and each of the many styles of guitar playing seems to have its own hand positions. The only thing that makes one way of playing "right" and another "wrong" is if the first way allows you to do something that the other does not. If your goal is simply to strum chords, then there are several different effective ways of doing this. Likewise, a right-hand technique for playing melody must allow you to play smooth and efficient scale lines. The more demanding the skill is, the more precisely you may have to study and perfect your hand position and muscle control. You can strum chords slowly with all sorts of techniques, but if you want to strum very quickly, you will need an efficient hand and arm movement that is controlled well enough to give the right attack to the motion of striking the strings. There seem to be certain basic ideas about right-hand technique that are common to all styles of guitar.

If you are using the right-hand fingers to pluck the strings, either in pattern-style fingerpicking or melody playing, then you will need a right-hand position that allows the fingers freedom of movement and easy access to the strings. Most finger-style players feel that the whole right arm is involved and that the arm should be relaxed. Shake your arm from the shoulder, and let it fall limp; then drape it up over the guitar, still limp, so that the first three fingers lie directly over the three treble strings of the guitar. This will put your arm in a state of maximum relaxation with respect to the guitar, and should allow you the most muscular control. The forearm should not rest on the top of the instrument, and the wrist should be bent in an arc. Your wrist, hand, and fingers should have maximum mobility in this position, although it takes a good deal of practice and muscular training to develop the ability to strike the strings with some force while still maintaining a relaxed arm and hand. The more forcefully you strike the strings, the more careful you have to be to have a hand and arm position that allows you to play smoothly without tightening up the muscle.

Placing a finger, especially the little finger, on the top of the guitar is done by a lot of players, but this limits the mobility of the hand. The "free hand" method is recommended, since it allows the thumb to move to a treble string or the fingers to the bass strings if necessary. The same thinking applies to the placement of the forearm. If it is laid flat on top of the guitar, then the strumming and picking movements will have to come from the wrist only. If you are playing electric guitar, you may not need a lot of force to strike the string, and this may work fine. In most cases lifting the forearm up and suspending it from the top edge of the guitar will allow the necessary arm movement for the proper strumming and picking of the strings.

There are a number of specialized right-hand positions associated with different styles of playing that sometimes violate these rules for specific purposes. If you use a right-hand muting technique similar

Classic

Flatpick

Fingerpicks

Muted bass (damping)

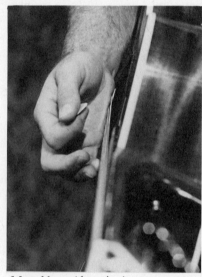
Muted bass (damping)

FIGURE 1.3 Right-Hand Positions

to the one popularized by Merle Travis and Chet Atkins, you will have to place the heel of the right hand on the strings just before they cross onto the saddle (Figure 1.3). This limits the mobility of the right-hand fingers but produces a unique sound. Flamenco players use a variety of exotic strumming, clapping, and tapping techniques for percussive effects associated with the style which require special hand positions.

LEFT-HAND POSITION

The guidelines for "proper" left-hand position are the same as for position and body position in general in that the more refined the skills are, the more refined the technique must be. The left-hand fingers will have more mobility if they are arched above the fingerboard, as shown in Figure 1.4. This also allows the tips of the fingers to depress the strings and gives maximum strength. If the left-hand thumb is placed behind the fingerboard, it offers maximum mobility and strength to the hand and fingers, although it may seem awkward to beginners, who may be more inclined to wrap the thumb over the edge of the fingerboard. At times the left-hand thumb may be used to dampen or fret notes on the bass string, although it will normally return to its position behind the fingerboard immediately afterward. Circular shapes tend to have the greatest structural stability, and athletes find that bent arms give stronger punches or baseball swings. Likewise, if the arm, wrist, hand, and fingers assume circular shapes you will have the best mobility and strength.

Building Strength

To play guitar you need to develop strength and dexterity: you need the ability to hold down a note or a chord for a sustained period; you need to move quickly from one fret to another; you need to be able to hold some fingers still while moving others in opposite directions; and, finally, you need the ability to impart a great deal of force onto the fingerboard in a very short time such as when hammering-on. You can work on endurance just by holding a finger or chord position on the fingerboard for as long as you can. This is how you master barre chords. You simply do it for as long as possible, usually only a few seconds at first, gradually building up your endurance. This takes up very little time, much like isometric exercises.

Scale drills are the traditional way to gain musical knowledge while acquiring hand strength and mobility. Andrés Segovia, the great classical guitarist, when asked whether scale playing was essential, replied that, no, you could do it other ways, but it is the most direct way to overcome the greatest number of obstacles. If you have never played scales for fear they would interfere with your enjoyment of guitar, you will no doubt find that some regular and concentrated scale work will do more for your playing than you ever could have imagined.

The ability to stretch long distances up the fingerboard and diagonally across strings to higher frets is essential for any guitarist and is another of the purely physical things that can be improved with practice. When you first pick up a guitar, just to stretch three frets is difficult, as in trying to play a C chord. A reach of four frets is essential for playing scales and anything beyond basic chord strumming. The closed-position scale patterns given in Chapter 9 make good practice material for this skill.

The fourth finger of the left hand is clumsier than the others, and it takes a good deal of work to get it so that you can depend on it in different situations. The important thing to remember about your little finger is that its mobility is controlled by the thumb. If the thumb is curved over the top of the

FIGURE 1.4 Left-Hand Positions

fingerboard, then you will not have the necessary mobility in the little finger. Although there may be times when you will want to dampen or even fret the bass E string with the thumb, learning to keep the thumb in the back of the neck will greatly increase your reach and mobility, especially with regards to the fourth finger. It requires more strength to keep the left thumb on the back of the neck, and most guitarists probably wrap the thumb around the neck because it gives them a stronger grip. But getting the thumb in the back and doing some work every day to build the new hand strength needed to play this way will pay off in added flexibility and control.

Callouses

Callouses on the fingers are certainly a part of playing a stringed instrument, and some knowledge about the building, maintenance, and repair of callouses should be learned by every guitarist. The primary role of the callous is protection of the fingers: the first time you try to fret a guitar string you will probably experience some pain, since a certain amount of pressure is required to obtain a clear tone, especially from a steel-string instrument with medium- or heavy-gauge strings. Almost all beginners have had a practice session shortened because their fingers were too sore to play another chord. Callouses are essential to playing acoustic guitar.

In order to apply enough pressure to the string to obtain a clear, strong sound when it is struck forcefully with the right hand, you must press hard and will probably need good callouses to do so. If you don't believe this, try fretting the G string at the third fret and—still applying pressure—sliding up to the seventh or eighth fret in such a way that the upper note sounds clearly. This is a common guitar technique; but if you have normal string gauge and normal string action, you will not be able to get the proper tone unless you have good callouses.

The next most important thing to having good callouses is caring for and preserving them. If you wash dishes or swim regularly, you may have trouble keeping good callouses for guitar playing and may have to limit your practicing to periods when your hands are dry.

Playing a slide on a wound string with a wet callous can cut a groove in your fingertip that can remain for a week. When you have such a groove in your callous, the skin begins to flake and peel around it and the strings will snag on your fingertip in unpredictable ways. You can file down the whole callous to smooth out the rough spot, but unless you have really deep callouses this can make your fingertip very sore and perhaps even worse off than with a groove in it. However, many pros (Chet Atkins for one) recommend filing down callouses, claiming that if they are too thick, they will interfere with the touch and sensitivity of your fingertips. This probably applies more to guitarists who play on classic and lighter-gauge steel strings because those instruments require less force in general.

TUNING

Guitarists are responsible for tuning their own instruments. This is not always an easy thing to do. Basically, the tuning process consists of nothing more than adjusting the tension of the six strings with the tuning pegs until the pitch of each string matches a standardized pitch. For the most part, tuning is a scientific and a mechanical process. However, certain crucial elements enter into the realm of personal taste and judgment. There are numerous physical problems with instruments, strings, and climate conditions that can greatly affect the tuning process, and there are also numerous methods of comparing the pitches of the guitar strings to the standards. The comparison of guitar pitches with the standard has always depended on the ability of the guitarist to discern pitch differences, although there are now commercially available several electronic tuning devices that are extremely accurate and that can be used to tune a guitar correctly independently of the ear of the guitarist.

Tuning is an essential element of guitar music, and it is not something that is only learned once, at the beginning of the study of the instrument. A beginner can learn to tune the guitar satisfactorily in a few minutes; yet entire books can be written detailing all the intricacies of tuning. Beginners

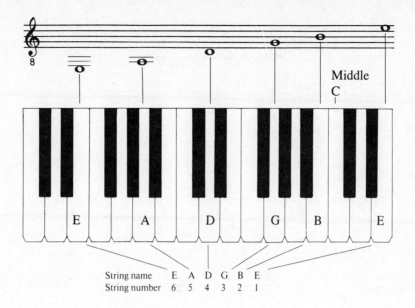

String name   E A D G B E
String number 6 5 4 3 2 1

FIGURE 1.5 Open Strings of the Guitar Shown on the Keyboard

usually have problems with the purely physical aspects of tuning: turning the tuning pegs in the correct direction and comparing the notes to each other. Some beginners do experience difficulty and must resort to pitch pipes or electronic tuning devices until their listening skills improve enough to hear the finer discrepancies in string intonation. More advanced players find that as their ears improve, they can hear smaller discrepancies in tuning, and consequently spend more time tuning, even though they are more skilled in its execution. Several methods of tuning are given here.

Tuning to Another Instrument

If there is another tuned guitar available, then that instrument can be used as the standard against which to tune, but it is advisable to tune to an instrument that is more likely to stay in tune. A xylophone or accordion is an excellent source of tuning pitches, since neither of these instruments needs tuning adjustments. A piano is more likely to be available; and although pianos are not often in perfect tune, they can offer some very reasonable "ball park" notes for tuning the guitar. The piano keyboard is shown in Figure 1.5, with the strings of a guitar indicated. The guitar sounds one octave lower than piano music is written.

The lower-pitched E string, the A string, and the D string are referred to as the bass strings, and the other three strings are the treble strings. The guitar strings are often numbered: the treble E string is the first string, and the bass E string is the sixth. It is important to remember this, since the string nearest to the player is not the first string, but the sixth. In naming and describing pitches the words *high* and *low* are often used and always refer to pitch. (Even though the bass E string is higher off the ground than the treble E string, it is called the low E and the treble string the high E. Playing "higher" on the neck means higher in pitch, and thus farther up the fingerboard toward the body of the guitar.)

The naming system for musical notes uses seven letters of the alphabet together with symbols called *sharps* (♯) and *flats* (♭). Because of the nature of the naming system, which is described in detail in Chapter 5, there is a sharp or flat between successive letter pitches except between B and C and between E and F. Thus, the first fret of the E string gives the note F, and the second fret gives F♯—or G♭, as it is sometimes called. The third fret is G. The lower portion of the fingerboard is shown in Figure 1.6 (see page 12). It is not necessary to understand this system of naming notes at this time, but it is presented in order to elucidate the tuning process. The sequence of notes is

A	A# B♭	B	C	C# D♭	D	D# E♭	E	F	F# G♭	G	G# A♭

Relative Tuning Methods

The three tuning methods given here are used to tune the strings of a guitar in relation to each other. For these methods to give a correct pitch, an initial reference note is needed. A reference note can be obtained from a piano, a tuning fork, or an electronic tuner. The tuning fork is as accurate as, and more convenient than, other ways of obtaining a reference note.

Fretted-String Method

1. Tune the A string of the guitar to a reference pitch.

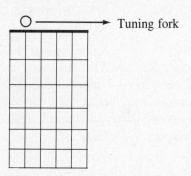

Tuning fork

2. Tune the bass E string fretted at the fifth fret to the open A string.

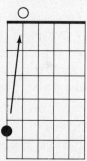

3. Tune the D string to the note produced at the fifth fret of the A string.

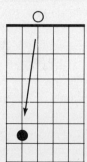

4. Tune the G string to the note produced at the fifth fret of the D string.

5. Tune the B string to the note produced at the fourth fret of the G string.

6. Tune the high E string to the note produced at the fifth fret of the B string.

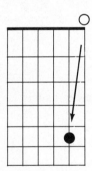

The fretted-string method is the simplest tuning method and is sufficient for most beginning guitar situations (Figure 1.6). The drawback to this tuning method is that it is prone to an "accumulation of error." Small pitch imperfections of the lower strings are carried over to higher strings.

Tuning with Harmonics

While a string is vibrating its full length, it also vibrates in fractional lengths of ½, ⅓, ¼, ⅕, and so on. Each length produces a distinct pitch, but the pitch produced by the full length of the string is the loudest and is called the fundamental. The fractional vibrations are softer and are referred to as harmonics. On a guitar these softer, flutelike harmonics can be made to sound clearly without the fundamental being present by lightly touching the string at a *node*. Nodes are the points on a string that divide it into its fractional vibrating lengths. Figure 1.7 pictures the string vibrations of a fundamental tone and the first three harmonics.

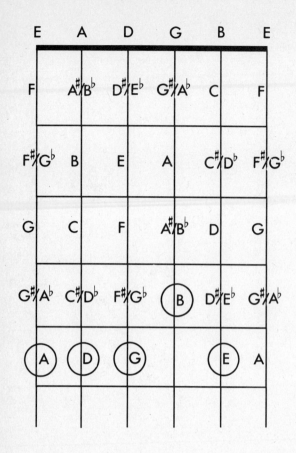

E	A	D	G	B	E
F	A♯/B♭	D♯/E♭	G♯/A♭	C	F
F♯/G♭	B	E	A	C♯/D♭	F♯/G♭
G	C	F	A♯/B♭	D	G
G♯/A♭	C♯/D♭	F♯/G♭	(B)	D♯/E♭	G♯/A♭
(A)	(D)	(G)		(E)	A

FIGURE 1.6 Tuning the Guitar: Fretted-String Method

FIGURE 1.8 Playing Harmonics

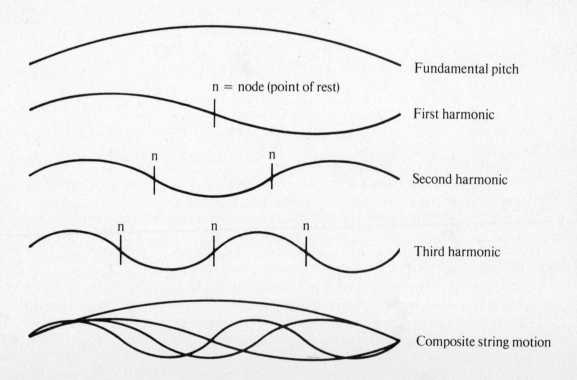

Fundamental pitch

n = node (point of rest)

First harmonic

n   n

Second harmonic

n   n   n

Third harmonic

Composite string motion

FIGURE 1.7 Fundamental and Overtones of a Vibrating String

Pitch of open string

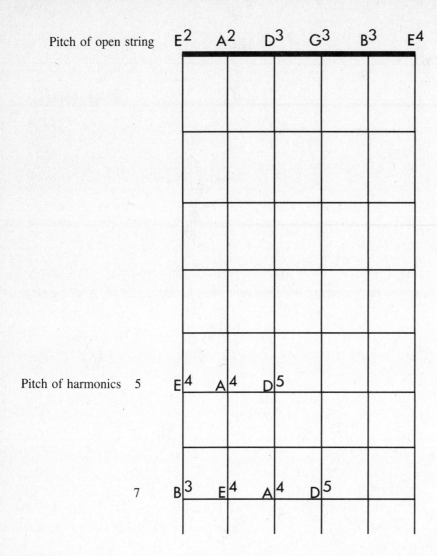

Pitch of harmonics   5

7

FIGURE 1.9 Notes Produced on the Open Strings and Selected Harmonics

To produce a good, clear harmonic (see Figure 1.8), put the tip of the fretting finger *directly over the fret*, not slightly behind the fret as you would do to fret the note. Do not press the string to the fingerboard but merely graze it as lightly as possible with the fingertip. Pluck the string forcefully with a pick or thumbnail close to the bridge.

When you can obtain clear-sounding harmonics on each string at the fifth and seventh frets, then you can use the following tuning method. Figure 1.9 shows the actual pitches produced by the open strings and by selected harmonics. Since all the pitches in various octaves carry the same letter name, numerical subscripts are assigned to each. C_1 is the lowest-pitched C on a piano keyboard; C_4 is middle C; and the notes in the octave above middle C are subscripted 4 through the next C, which is C_5. The bass E string pitch is E_2. This exact pitch notation will help you understand tuning with harmonics.

It is easier to compare harmonics than open strings, since they are higher-pitched, and the tuning pegs can be adjusted while the harmonic note is still sounding. However, this tuning method, too, has its drawbacks. Old strings can produce faulty harmonics, and so can guitars that are warped or poorly adjusted or constructed. Harmonics are untempered pitches, and the frets on the fingerboard are placed in a tempered system. The slight disagreement between the two is a symptom of the overall slight "out-of-tuneness" of the Western musical system. (See "Hints on Tuning" in this chapter.)

1. Tune the A string to the tuning fork or the reference pitch.

Tuning fork

2. Tune the fifth-fret harmonic of the bass E string to the seventh-fret harmonic of the A string (E_4).

3. Tune the seventh-fret harmonic of the D string to the fifth-fret harmonic of the A string (A_4).

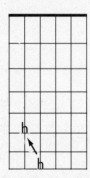

4. Tune the seventh-fret harmonic of the G string to the fifth-fret harmonic of the D string (D_5).

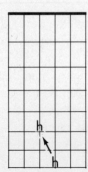

5. Tune the open B string to the seventh-fret harmonic of the bass E string (B₃).

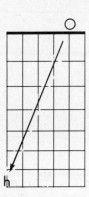

6. Tune the open treble E string to the fifth-fret harmonic of the bass E string.

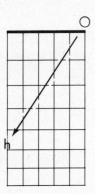

Tuning with Octaves

Due to the discrepancies in the construction of guitars and strings, the problems of comparing pitches, and the differences between pure (untempered) and tempered intervals, the fretted-string method and the harmonics method may not tune the guitar satisfactorily. A more accurate but more complicated tuning method uses pitches an octave apart on different strings to achieve the relative tuning. An initial reference note is needed, and then the successive strings are tuned in the following sequence.

1. Tune the open A string to a tuning fork or other reference pitch.

Tuning fork

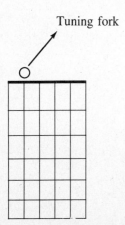

2. Tune the second-fret A of the G string to the open A string.

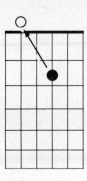

3. Tune the third-fret G of the treble E string to the open G string.

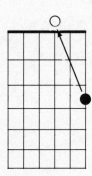

4. Tune the third-fret G of the bass E string to the open G string.

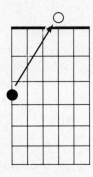

5. Tune the second-fret E of the D string to the open treble E string or to the open bass E string.

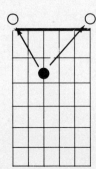

6. Tune the third-fret D of the B string to the open D string.

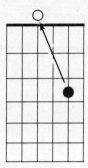

This method of tuning seems to allow for more of the individual variations in guitars, players, and strings.

HINTS ON TUNING

Tuning a guitar can be difficult for beginners. Here are some things you can do when learning to compare and adjust pitches.

1. *Get help*. Have someone who already knows how to tune a guitar assist you until you understand what to listen for and what to do. Remember, too, that temperature and humidity changes affect the tuning of a guitar. Old strings, too high action (height of strings above fretboard), warped necks, and tuning gears that turn unevenly also make a guitar difficult to tune.

2. *Make sure you have a good reference note*. Tuning forks (Figure 1.10) are inexpensive and produce an accurate pitch. They are sufficiently loud if the handle is placed on the bridge. To create additional resonance, six-string guitars should be kept at normal pitch (A = 440 cycles per second) but twelve-string guitars should be tuned one step lower to the pitches D, G, C, F, A, and D. This practice lessens the tension on the neck, makes the strings easier to fret, and generally improves the tone.

3. *Listen for beats*. If you are in a quiet place, you can hear if two notes are in tune by listening for beats. If two pitches are close to being in tune, they will form pulsating combination waves that will "beat" at a certain rate. The slower the beats, the closer the two pitches. The pitches have to be within a reasonable degree of closeness before you can hear the beats (five to ten cycles per second), and eliminating the beats is a good way to "fine-tune" the strings.

4. *Listen for sympathetic vibrations*. If one string is tuned to another string, playing a pitch on one string can cause the same pitch to vibrate on the other string. So if the bass E is tuned with respect to the A string, fretting the fifth-fret A on the bass E string will set the open A string in motion. Sympathetic vibration only occurs if the strings are very close to being in tune, and this is a good method of comparing open strings to fretted pitches.

5. *Make sure your tuning knobs are working*. Be sure that the strings are connected to the correct tuning pegs and that you are turning the correct peg in the correct direction. It is easy to get confused and to break strings accidentally.

6. *Investigate electronic tuners*. Electronic tuners that give extremely accurate readings are increasingly available from many reputable companies (see Figure 1.10). More expensive models give chromatic (referring to the twelve tones of the octave) readings in many octaves, and special guitar tuners are available that just give the six guitar pitches. These are reasonably priced and can allow you to be in good tune under

FIGURE 1.10 Tuning Fork, Strobe Tuner, Electronic Guitar Tuner[*]

any condition. If you have trouble tuning or have to tune in noisy environments, these can be extremely helpful. However, the placement of the frets and the slightly erratic vibration of strings, especially bass strings, mean that even a guitar tuned precisely to an electronic tuner may sound slightly out of tune. The bass E string often has to be flatted (lowered in pitch) so its fretted pitches are in tune; likewise, when a bass guitar and a normal guitar are tuned electronically, the bass may have to be flatted.

7. *Don't get discouraged. All guitars are slightly out of tune.* Tuning is difficult even for professionals. Heat, cold, sunlight, humidity, air conditioning, old strings, new strings, and countless other factors can make guitars hard to tune. The Western musical system which dictates the placement of the frets on the guitar neck with respect to the strings is designed to make each note, chord, and key equally and slightly out of tune. If you tune one chord so that it sounds perfectly in tune, then other chords will sound sour. On the guitar this is most easily apparent if you compare a G chord and an E chord. The B string as tuned for a G chord will sound flat when you play an E chord; likewise, if you tune it for the E chord, it will sound sharp in the G chord. The *tempered* system places the B string between those two so that neither is completely right or wrong. It takes a good ear to hear these differences, but you should try to use the tuning systems rather than tuning to a particular chord. Many players will slightly change the tuning of their instruments when they play in different keys to "sweeten" the sound of the important chords in that key, although this will make other chords sound unnecessarily out of tune. Instruments themselves may not be capable of producing musically correct pitches, and if you find yourself unable to tune satisfactorily, check out your guitar. (See Chapter 13.) As you progress in your ability to discern pitch differences, you will be able to tune more accurately and will also be able to hear more easily when you are out of tune. Remember that enjoyment and intelligent use of your time may require you to avoid perfection.

---

*Strobotuner Division, C.G. Conn, Ltd., Elkhart, Indiana.

chapter 2
Reading and Playing with Two Basic Chords

Chapter 2* contains information essential for playing the guitar. This includes the left-hand skills required to play the D chord and the A7 chord, as well as sections on reading chord-fingering diagrams, strumming, and lead-sheet notation. It is important when learning new skills to keep practicing them until they can be performed with ease. In the early stages of learning guitar this means that you should not try to learn too many chords too quickly. In general, you are ready to move on to a new chord when you can change from one chord to another smoothly and without hesitation. Most teachers advocate playing many songs that use a limited number of chords and right-hand techniques until students have command of them, then moving on to a new chord or right-hand skill. You will attempt to learn skills that seem impossible to accomplish; but soon those skills will become easy. By steadily and persistently practicing a few minutes each day, you will progress quickly. You can accomplish much more in six ten-minute practice sessions spread over six days than you can in one sixty-minute practice session occurring on the weekend.

Reading Chord-Fingering Diagrams

The chord diagram or fret diagram in Figure 2.1 consists of vertical and horizontal lines, small circles, Roman numerals, and letter names of pitches. The chord diagrams are drawn to represent the guitar the way it would appear if you were looking at the fingerboard with the body of the guitar pointing toward the floor. The bass strings of the guitar are always at the left. A summary of the basic open chords presented in Chapters 2 and 3 appears in Figure 3.1. Some of these chords have more than one acceptable fingering; what seems to be the most popular way is given in the figure. The vertical lines represent the strings, and the horizontal lines represent the frets. Small circles tell you where to put your left-hand fingers. An X above a string indicates that the string is not sounded in the chord.

*If the class contains some students with little experience, the instructor may prefer to begin with Appendix A. This appendix presents an entirely new approach to beginning folk guitar using the Third-Hand capo. The approach allows students of differing abilities and experience to learn effectively in the same class. Appendix A has also been found to be effective with young beginners and handicapped individuals.

Chord name: D

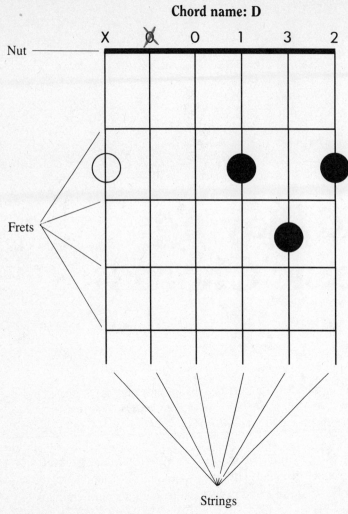

Explanation of Symbols

1 = Left-hand index finger

2 = Left-hand middle finger

3 = Left-hand ring finger

4 = Left-hand little finger

O = Open, unfretted string

X = String not sounded

● = String pressed (fretted) with finger

○ = Optional

Nut

Frets

Strings

FIGURE 2.1 Reading Chord Diagrams

THE D CHORD

Play the song "Frère Jacques" using only the D chord and strumming once on each beat, as indicated below.

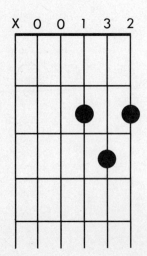

D	D	D	D		D	D	D	D
Are	you	sleep-	ing,		Are	you	sleep-	ing,
D	D	D	D		D	D	D	D
Broth-	er	John,			Broth-	er	John?	
D	D	D	D		D	D	D	D
Morning	bells are	ring-	ing,		Morning	bells are	ring-	ing,
D	D	D	D		D	D	D	D
Ding	dong	ding,			Ding	dong	ding.	

Strumming

You need to develop a few simple right-hand strumming techniques to play the songs in this chapter. Try strumming or brushing across the strings toward the floor with a downstroke (D) or toward the ceiling with an upstroke (U). Downstrokes and upstrokes can be combined in different patterns to produce different kinds of rhythmic feelings. Start with the suggestions given, and then experiment until you find a strum pattern that feels best to you. Sing the song and tap the beat of the song with your foot. All of the songs in this chapter have beats that occur in groups of two, three, or four. The beat grouping is shown at the beginning of each song as the upper of two numbers written at the beginning of the first staff. These two numbers are called the *time signature*. In $\frac{4}{4}$ time each beat grouping, sometimes called a "measure" or "bar," contains four beats.

Tap your foot at a *steady* pace and count

1	2	3	4	1	2	3	4	etc.

Strum once for each beat, stressing the 1 of each measure.

1	2	3	4	1	2	3	4
D	D	D	D	D	D	D	D

Strumming twice, down and up, on the second and fourth beats can make the sound more interesting.

1	2	3	4	1	2	3	4
D	D/U	D	D/U	D	D/U	D	D/U

In fast tempos it may be effective to leave some beats silent.

1	2	3	4	1	2	3	4
D	—	D	—	D	—	D	U
D	—	D/U	D/U	D	—	D/U	D/U

Likewise, in $\frac{3}{4}$ time you can try different D and U patterns.

1	2	3	1	2	3
D	D	D	D	D	D
D	D/U	D/U	D	D/U	D/U

See Chapter 4 for more ideas on strumming.

Lead-Sheet Notation

The music published for each instrument takes on a format that makes it easy to present visually the sounds produced by that instrument. Piano music uses the grand staff, clarinet music uses but a single staff, and organ music is often notated with up to three staffs. Classical guitar music is usually written on a single treble staff or sometimes on tablature. Popular, rock, and folk music intended for guitar players are most often written in *lead-sheet notation*, which is the practice of notating the melody, chords, and words of a song on a single treble staff. The verses and chorus of the song are sung to fit the notated melody. The chord symbols, which are written above the staff with letters and numbers such as D, A7, Em, and Am7, contain only a suggestion as to how long they are to be played or the rhythm in which they should be played. The rhythmic interpretation must be supplied by the performer, and the number of beats that each chord should be played is suggested by the placement of the chord symbol over the staff. Most chords change at the beginning of a measure, and a few change on accented beats within a measure—for instance, on the third beat in ¾ time. Here is an excerpt in lead-sheet notation:

CHORD SYMBOLS:

MELODY ON STAFF:

WORDS OF SONG:

Notice that the underlined syllables in the words of the song correspond to the first (stressed) beat of each measure. This underlining makes it easier to follow the melody in the succeeding verses of a song, which are usually printed as poetry at the bottom of the page of music.

HINTS ON CHORD PLAYING

1. Use the tip of the fingers whenever possible.

2. Make sure the nails of the left hand are trimmed. The right-hand nails need not be trimmed.

3. Be sure to press the string to the fingerboard *just behind the fret toward the nut* and in the space between the frets. If your finger is directly on top of the fret, you will hear only a dull, muted sound; and if you are too far below the fret, the string may rattle and buzz.

4. Make sure you are applying enough pressure to hold down the string. This should not be a problem on a nylon-string guitar, even for beginners. On a steel-string guitar, especially with relatively thick strings, this can cause a problem. Thinner strings and adjustments to the guitar to lower the height of the strings above the fingerboard can help solve this. The process of building up callouses is necessary and can be painful. (See Chapter 1 on callouses.)

5. Good left-hand position can facilitate chording. The fingers should be arched, and the palm of the hand should be away from the neck of the guitar. The thumb should be behind the fingerboard since this greatly facilitates the dexterity of the fingers. It is hard at first to play with the thumb in the back, but it can become a bad habit if you allow it to wrap around the neck. (See Chapter 1 on left-hand position.)

6. Be sure that each note of the chord is sounding clearly. Check each string, and pluck it individually. It is very easy to accidentally touch a string with a finger not intended for that string.

7. Holding the guitar correctly can help facilitate the chording. The tendency at first is to turn the guitar to see the fingers, and this makes it harder to reach around the neck to form chords.

8. Make sure that your guitar is tuned properly. Tuning methods are discussed in Chapter 1.

THE A7 CHORD

The A7 chord can be played with either the first and second fingers or the second and third fingers. If fingers 2 and 3 are used, finger 3 should slide from the second fret to the third fret in changing chords. If fingers 1 and 2 are used, they should be moved in a single motion when changing between D and A7.

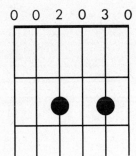   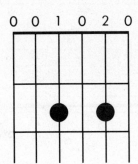

Playing the D and A7 Chords

Play the following chord progressions until you can change from the D to the A7 chord and back to the D chord without hesitation. As soon as you can do that, try the songs in the remainder of this chapter which use the D and A7 chords.

Chord progression 1 (strum once per chord)

D	D	D	D	D	D	D	D
A7	A7	A7	A7	A7	A7	A7	A7
D	D	D	D	D	D	D	D
A7	A7	A7	A7	D	D	D	D

Chord progression 2

D	D	D	D	A7	A7	A7	A7
A7	A7	A7	A7	D	D	D	D

Chord progression 3

D	D	D	D	A7	A7	A7	A7
D	D	A7	A7	D	D	D	D

Chord progression 4

D	/	A7	/	D	/	A7	/	(/ means repeat the same chord)
D	/	A7	/	D	/	/	/	

Tom Dooley

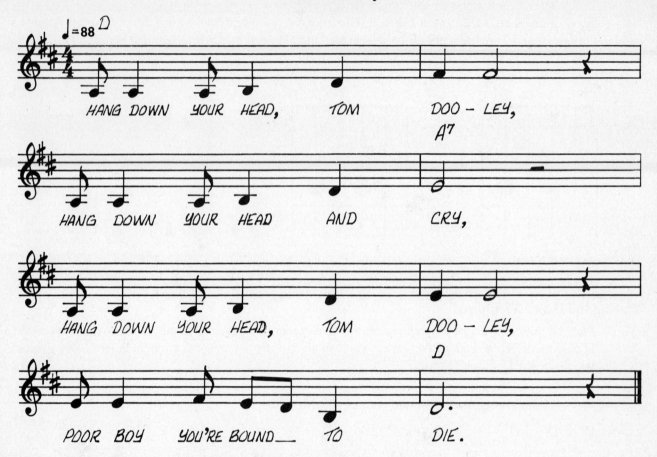

HANG DOWN YOUR HEAD, TOM DOO – LEY,

HANG DOWN YOUR HEAD AND CRY,

HANG DOWN YOUR HEAD, TOM DOO – LEY,

POOR BOY YOU'RE BOUND__ TO DIE.

2. Hand* me down my banjo, I'll pick it on my knee,
   This time tomorrow night, It'll be no use to me.

3. I met her on the mountain, I swore she'd be my wife.
   I met her on the mountain, An' stabbed her with my knife.

4. This time tomorrow, Reckon where I'll be,
   Down in some lonesome valley, Hangin' on a white-oak tree.

5. I had my trial at Wilksboro, And what you reckon they done?
   They bound me over to Statesville, And that's where I'll be hung.

6. The limb a-bein' oak, boys, The rope a-bein' strong,
   Bow down your head, Tom Dooley, You know you're gonna be hung.

*The first syllable of each measure is underlined as an aid to the performer. The underlining denotes rhythmically stressed syllables, normally those falling on the first beat of a measure.

Polly Wolly Doodle

1. OH, I WENT DOWN SOUTH FOR TO SEE MY SAL, SING-IN'

2. Oh, my <u>Sal</u> she is a <u>maid</u>en fair, Singin' . . .
   With <u>curl</u>y eyes and <u>laugh</u>ing hair, Singin' . . .
   (*Chorus*)

3. Oh, a <u>grass</u>hopper sittin' on a <u>rail</u>road track, Singin' . . .
   A <u>pick</u>in' his teeth with a <u>car</u>pet tack, Singin' . . .
   (*Chorus*)

4. Be<u>hind</u> the barn, down <u>on</u> my knees, Singin' . . .
   I <u>thought</u> I heard a <u>roost</u>er sneeze, Singin' . . .
   (*Chorus*)

5. He <u>sneezed</u> so hard with the <u>whoop</u>ing cough, Singin' . . .
   He <u>sneezed</u> his head and <u>tail</u> right off, Singin' . . .
   (*Chorus*)

Suggested strum: D D/U D D/U.

Down in the Valley

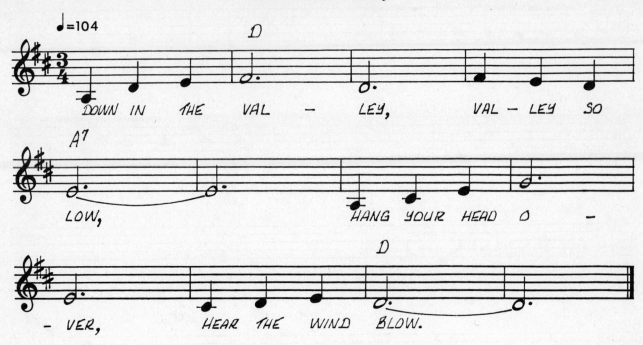

2. Hear the wind blow, dear, hear the wind blow, ___
   Hang your head over, hear the wind blow. ___

3. If you don't love me, love who you please, ___
   Throw your arms 'round me, give my heart ease. ___

4. Give my heart ease, love, give my heart ease, ___
   Throw your arms 'round me, give my heart ease. ___

5. Write me a letter, send it by mail, ___
   Send it in care of Birmingham Jail. ___

6. Birmingham Jail, love, Birmingham Jail, ___
   Send it in care of Birmingham Jail. ___

7. Build me a castle, forty feet high, ___
   So I can see her, as she rides by. ___

8. As she rides by, love, as she rides by, ___
   So I can see her, as she rides by. ___

9. Roses love sunshine, violets love dew, ___
   Angels in heaven know I love you. ___

10. Know I love you, dear, know I love you. ___
    Angels in heaven know I love you. ___

Suggested strum: D D/U D/U.

There are many songs that can be played with only D and A7 chords. A large number of these songs appear elsewhere in this book, and suggestions for other two-chord songs appear in the Two-Chord Song Index.

The songs in this chapter are all notated in the key of D. Because of this, the singing pitch for some of these songs will be comfortable for some people but may need adjusting for others. The overall pitch level of a song can be moved or transposed by using a normal capo or a Third-Hand capo with all of the discs facing down (see Appendix A and Chapter 12 for a more detailed explanation of capos and their use in beginning guitar instruction and transposition). Once your facility in playing the D and A7 chords is established, begin learning more basic chords, as presented in Chapter 3.

chapter 3
Learning More Basic Chords

Chapters 2, 3, 4, and 6 are aimed at developing the skills necessary for accompanying a wide range of music. For ease of learning the skills are separated into those for the right hand and those for the left hand, since it seems to be difficult to concentrate on both hands at the same time during the learning process. The motor skills involved in guitar playing are different for each hand. When the focus is on learning the basic left-hand chords, the right hand is expected to play only very simple strums. When the chords have been learned to a point where they do not require conscious effort to execute them, then more advanced right-hand strumming and picking skills should be attempted.

Chapter 3 continues a presentation of the basic open left-hand chords starting with the easier chords and keys and progressing to the more difficult ones. At least one song is given to illustrate each new skill; however, you are encouraged to apply each new skill to several other songs.

Chapters 3, 4, and 6 have been designed to be studied concurrently, although for purpose of clarity of presentation they have been arranged sequentially by content. Thus, by the time you reach the songs and chords at the end of Chapter 3, you should have already studied many of the right-hand strumming and picking skills from the later chapters. Then, as new right-hand skills are developed in Chapters 4 and 6, the songs in Chapter 3 can be used as examples.

Preceding each song is a Song Performance Guide containing helpful information on how to play the song effectively and giving the starting singing pitch. For clarity the entire first measure of the song has been shown along with any "pickup" notes. The singing pitches are given in guitar tablature. The strumming and picking ideas are given in right-hand tablature, with the bass strings at the bottom as they appear to the player. If the suggested strumming pattern is such that it detracts from concentration on the left-hand chords, a simpler, one-strum-per-beat rhythm may be substituted. The strumming ideas have been carefully selected to reflect an effective and simple way to play the song.

The songs in this chapter have been chosen to illustrate certain guitar techniques. For this reason the singing pitches of the songs may not be suited to your vocal range. The songs may either be transposed to other keys or played with a capo (see Chapter 12).

READING TABLATURE NOTATION

Tablature depicts the six guitar strings from bottom to top, 6–5–4–3–2–1, with the bass E string (6) lowest in the diagram. The TAB signature means tablature, a six-line staff, each line representing one guitar string.

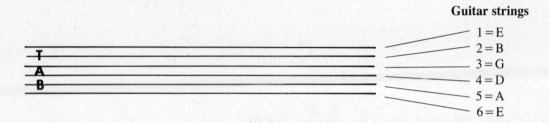

Arrows on the TAB indicate the motion of the pick, thumb, or fingers of the right hand across all or some of the strings and show pitch direction. For instance, an arrow that points to the top of this page is showing that the strum moves from the low E string across A, D, G, and B through the high E string. In terms of the direction in which the hand moves, this motion is downward, toward the floor.

Strums and fingerpicking patterns are pictured in TAB notation in order to maintain the student's orientation to the guitar. To help identify where each beat should be felt in relationship to the strum, the beat numbers are labeled in the Song Performance Guide.

Two or more strums of fingerpicking patterns are given for each song in this chapter. The different ways of playing the right-hand accompaniment patterns are labeled "Player 1," "Player 2," and so on. It is possible to play the different parts simultaneously; however, the song will sound fine if any of the player's parts are performed alone. Beginners should concentrate on the left-hand skill that is introduced and use the "Player 1" accompaniment. More advanced guitarists can use the "Player 2" or "Player 3" accompaniments.

Numbers placed on the TAB show that a particular string is to be fretted a certain distance above the nut (or capo, if one is used). A 1 placed on the third string would tell the performer to play the first fret of the G string with the left hand; an O indicates that the string is then played open or unfretted. Tablature does not show the duration of the notes. That information must be obtained from the standard notation.

Basic Right-Hand Strumming

In this chapter the focus is on the left-hand chords, but first the right hand needs some guidance. Each song in the text is coded with an indication of the simple strum that will keep the beat of the song but allow maximum concentration on the chording. Strumming can be done with the side of the thumb, with the nails of the fingers, or with a flatpick.

The strumming should be done with enough force to sound all the strings clearly but not so hard that the strings rattle or buzz. It takes a swift, smooth motion to strike all the strings in a chord in such a way that they all sound at once rather than sequentially. Although different guitarists will strike the strings at different places along their length for varying tone colors, it is generally considered best to strum over the sound hole about four to five inches from the bridge. Keeping the strumming hand relaxed will help you obtain a good sound, and you should strive to find a way to position your body, hands, and guitar so that the strumming motion is not impeded. (Right-hand position was discussed in Chapter 1.)

If you are using a pick, be sure to hold it very loosely. Picks come in many sizes and shapes, but a medium pick is best to use at first.

When fingerpicking, it is sometimes necessary to indicate which finger of the right hand is supposed to play a given string. This instruction is usually given below the staff with the letters *T*, *i*, *m*, and *r* being used to identify the right thumb, right index finger, right middle finger, and right ring finger, respectively.

THE A CHORD

There are several acceptable ways to play the A chord. Make sure you get a clear sound from all six strings. The 2–1–3 fingering allows for a direct connection to E^7 by sliding the index finger from the second to the first fret on the third string.

"Row, Row, Row Your Boat" has only one chord in it, which makes it a good song on which to practice an A chord.

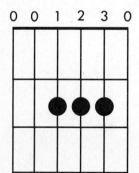
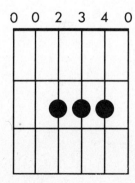
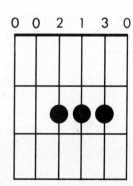

Song Performance Guide

CHORDS IN SONG: A

SINGING PITCH:

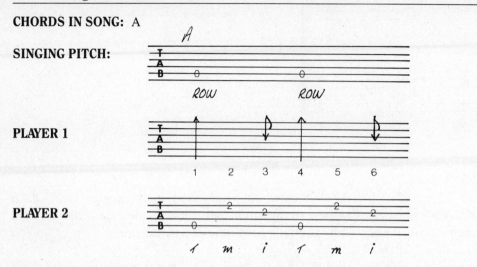

Row, Row, Row Your Boat

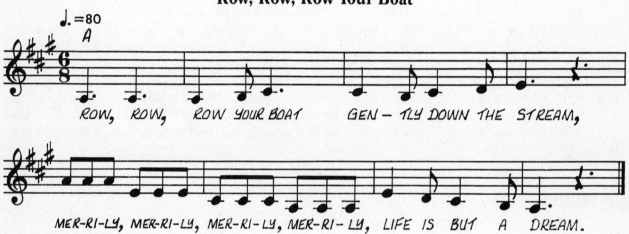

ROW, ROW, ROW YOUR BOAT   GEN – TLY DOWN THE STREAM,

MER-RI-LY, MER-RI-LY, MER-RI-LY, MER-RI-LY, LIFE IS BUT A DREAM.

THE E7 CHORD

Practice the A–E7 change. These chords have the same musical relationship to each other as do D and A7. Play each of these pairs of chords, and listen for this sound.

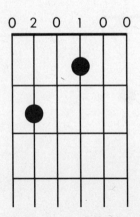

Practice the A–E7 change in "He's Got the Whole World."

Song Performance Guide

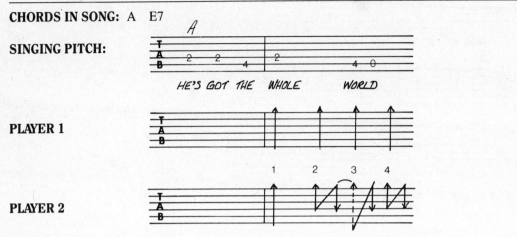

CHORDS IN SONG: A   E7

SINGING PITCH:

PLAYER 1

PLAYER 2

He's Got the Whole World

2. He's got the <u>wind</u> and the rain <u>in</u> His hands.
3. He's got the <u>little</u> tiny baby <u>in</u> His hands.
4. He's got <u>you</u> and me, brother, <u>in</u> His hands.
5. He's got <u>you</u> and me, sister, <u>in</u> His hands.
6. He's got the <u>stars</u> in the heavens <u>in</u> His hands.
7. He's got the <u>whole</u> world in His <u>hands</u>.

"Frankie and Johnny" is an old ballad that uses three chords. It has a bluesy feel and should be played with a crisp, accented shuffle rhythm.

Song Performance Guide

CHORDS IN SONG: A   D   E7

SINGING PITCH:

FRANK-IE AND JOHN-- NY WERE

PLAYER 1

PLAYER 2

Shuffle

The shuffle rhythm is written in $\frac{4}{4}$ meter but is played with uneven beats. Instead of each quarter note dividing into two equal halves, it divides into triplets, thus giving an unevenness to the division of the beat.

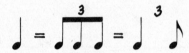

Frankie and Johnny

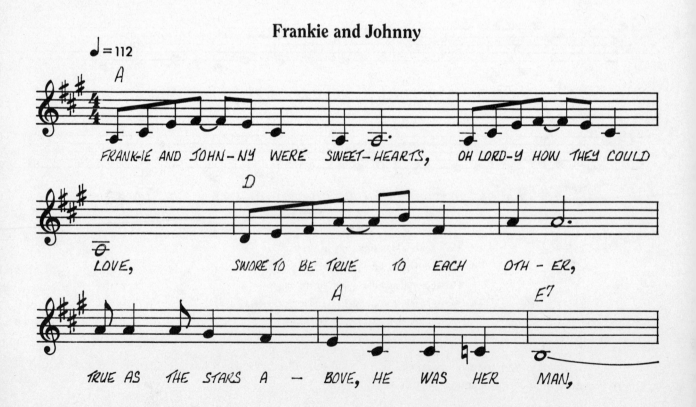

FRANK-IE AND JOHN-NY WERE SWEET-HEARTS, OH LORD-Y HOW THEY COULD

LOVE,   SWORE TO BE TRUE   TO   EACH   OTH - ER,

TRUE AS   THE STARS   A — BOVE,   HE   WAS   HER   MAN,

AND HE WAS DO-ING HER   WRONG.

2. Frankie and Johnny went walking, Johnny in his brand new suit,
   "Oh, good Lord," says Frankie, "but don't my Johnny look cute."
   He was her man, ___ and he was doing her wrong. ___

3. Johnny says, "Frankie I got to leave you, baby, But I won't be gone for long."
   "Honey, don't you worry about me, Or miss me when I'm gone."
   He was her man, ___ and he was doing her wrong. ___

4. Well, Frankie went down to the corner bar, To get herself a cold beer,
   And she said to the fat bartender, "Has my man Johnny been here?"
   He was her man, ___ and he was doing her wrong. ___

5. "I ain't going to tell you no story, And I ain't gonna tell you no lie,
   I seen your man Johnny about an hour ago with a woman named Nellie Bly,
   If he's your man, ___ I believe he's doing you wrong." ___

6. Frankie went down to South Twelfth Street, She did not go there to have fun.
   Underneath her long red dress she carried a forty-four gun.
   He was her man, ___ and he was doing her wrong. ___

7. Frankie went round to the back door, Looked in the window so high.
   There she seen it was Johnny just loving up Nellie Bly.
   He was her man, ___ and he was doing her wrong. ___

8. When Johnny seen Frankie a-coming, He jumped and started to run.
   She said, "I caught you red-handed," and she pulled out that forty-four gun.
   He was her man, ___ and he was doing her wrong. ___

9. He got down on his knees, Lord, She said, "Praying won't do you no good."
   Rooty toot toot and she started to shoot and he fell like a stick of wood.
   He was her man, ___ and he was doing her wrong. ___

10. Police took Miss Frankie downtown to the can.
    Said, "We got to book you, darling, 'bout killing your good man."
    He was her man, ___ and he was doing her wrong. ___

11. The judge he says to Miss Frankie, "What you doing up before me?"
    Looks like you got yourself in a heap of trouble called murder in the first degree."
    He was her man, ___ and he was doing her wrong. ___

12. Well, the foreman of the jury, He says, "Mr. Judge we can't decide.
    Some of us think she was guilty, But them on the other side,
    They say he was her man, ___ and he was doing her wrong." ___

13. Oh, Frankie and Johnny were sweethearts, Oh, Lordy, how they could love,
    Swore to be true to each other, True as the stars above,
    He was her man, ___ and he was doing her wrong. ___

"Banks of the Ohio" also uses only the A, D, and E7 chords, but it has a different mood than "Frankie and Johnny." The strumming should be softer and more flowing. Other songs included elsewhere in the book that can be played with these chords are "Red River Valley," "Silent Night," "Gold Watch and Chain," "Irene, Goodnight," "Roll in My Sweet Baby's Arms," "Jesse James," "Down by the Riverside," and "The Gambler."

Song Performance Guide

CHORDS IN SONG: A D E7

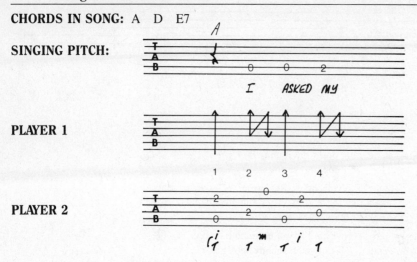

Although notated in $\frac{4}{4}$, this song may actually be played with the feeling of two beats per measure. This often happens when the tempo becomes so fast that the half note begins to be felt as the beat. The tempo shift places a heavy stress on the first and third beats, thus producing the feeling of twoness.

Banks of the Ohio

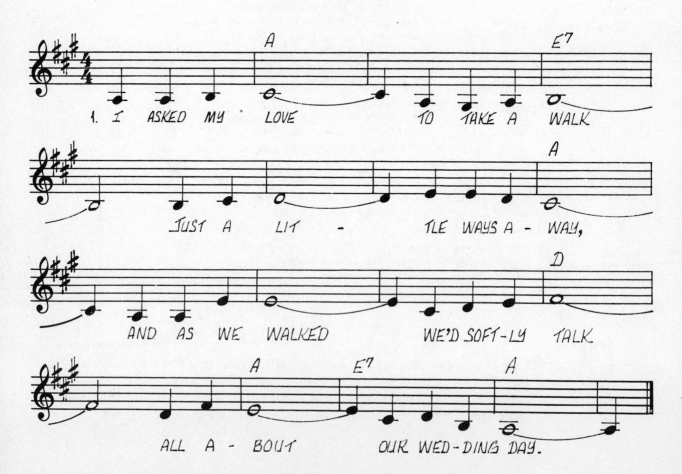

(*Chorus*) Darling, say, ___ that you'll be mine, ___
           In no oth ___ -er's arms entwine. ___
           Down beside ___ where the waters flow, ___
           Down beside, ___ the Ohio. ___

2. I asked your moth ___ -er for you, dear, ___
   And she said ___ you were too young; ___
   Only say ___ that you'll be mine, ___
   Happiness ___ together we'll find. ___
   (*Chorus*)

3. I pressed a knife ___ against her breast, ___
   As gently in ___ my arms she pressed, ___
   Crying, Willie, ___ don't murder me, ___
   I'm unprepared ___ for eternity. ___
   (*Chorus*)

4. I took her by ___ her lily white hand, ___
   And led her down ___ that bank of sand. ___
   I plunged her in, ___ where she would drown, ___
   And I watched her as ___ she floated down. ___
   (*Chorus*)

5. Returning home ___ 'tween twelve and one, ___
   Thinking, "Lord, ___ what a deed I done. ___
   I killed the girl ___ I love, you see, ___
   Because she would ___ not marry me." ___
   (*Chorus*)

6. The very next day ___ at half past four, ___
   The sheriff walked ___ up to my door. ___
   He said, "Young man, ___ don't try to run, ___
   You'll pay a lot, ___ for this crime you've done." ___
   (*Chorus*)

THE G CHORD

There are several acceptable ways to finger a G-major chord. Choose the one that works best with the other chords in the song you are playing. The last fret diagram has a silent fifth string. In this fingering the second finger presses the third fret of the sixth string and at the same time mutes the fifth string by barely touching it.

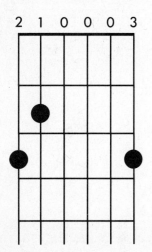 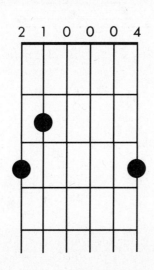 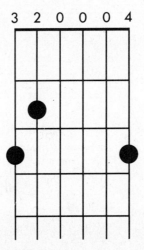 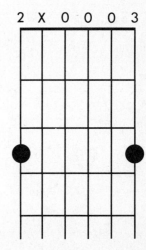

"Hush Little Baby" is a traditional lullaby and is slow enough to help you practice moving from G to D.

Song Performance Guide

CHORDS IN SONG: G D

SINGING PITCH:

PLAYER 1

PLAYER 2

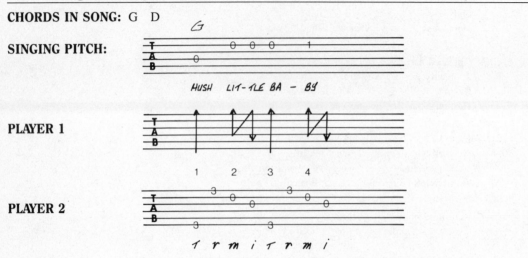

Hush Little Baby

2. If that mocking bird can't sing,
   Papa's gonna buy you a diamond ring.

3. And if that diamond ring is brass,
   Papa's gonna buy you a looking glass.

4. And if that looking glass gets broke,
   Papa's gonna buy you a billy goat.

5. And if that billy goat don't pull,
   Papa's gonna buy you a cart and bull.

6. And if that cart and bull turn over,
   Papa's gonna buy you a dog named Rover.

7. And if that dog named Rover don't bark,
   Papa's gonna buy you a horse and cart.

8. And if that horse and cart fall down,
   You'll still be the sweetest little baby in town.

"The Yellow Rose of Texas" has a tempo reminiscent of a polka. Notice the different playing techniques on the first and third beats for players 1 and 2. Try each, and play the one that is easiest or that sounds the best.

Song Performance Guide

CHORDS IN SONG: G D

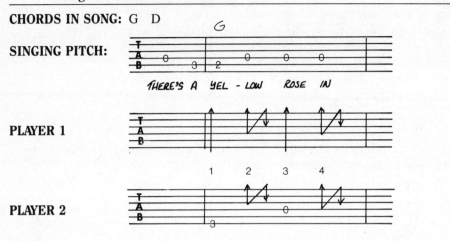

The Yellow Rose of Texas

2. She's the <u>sweet</u>est rose of <u>col</u>or this <u>sol</u>dier ever <u>knew</u>.
   Her <u>eyes</u> are bright as <u>dia</u>monds, they <u>spar</u>kle like the <u>dew</u>.
   You may <u>talk</u> about your <u>Dear</u>est May and <u>sing</u> of Rosa <u>Lee</u>,
   But the <u>yel</u>low rose of <u>Tex</u>as beats the <u>belles</u> of Ten<u>nes</u>see.

3. Where the <u>Rio</u> Grande is <u>flow</u>ing and the <u>star</u>ry skies are <u>bright</u>.
   She <u>walks</u> along the <u>ri</u>ver in the <u>qui</u>et summer <u>night</u>.
   She <u>thinks</u> if I re<u>mem</u>ber where we <u>part</u>ed long a<u>go</u>,
   I <u>prom</u>ised to come <u>back</u> again and <u>not</u> to leave her <u>so</u>.

4. Oh, <u>now</u> I'm going to <u>find</u> her for my <u>heart</u> is full of <u>woe</u>;
   And we'll <u>sing</u> the song to<u>geth</u>er that we <u>sung</u> so long a<u>go</u>.
   We'll <u>play</u> the banjo <u>gai</u>ly, and we'll <u>sing</u> the songs of <u>yore</u>,
   And the <u>yel</u>low rose of <u>Tex</u>as shall be <u>mine</u> forever <u>more</u>.

"Red River Valley" uses three chords in the key of D major. It is a good song to practice some fingerpicking techniques that will be learned in Chapter 6.

Song Performance Guide

CHORDS IN SONG: D   G   A7

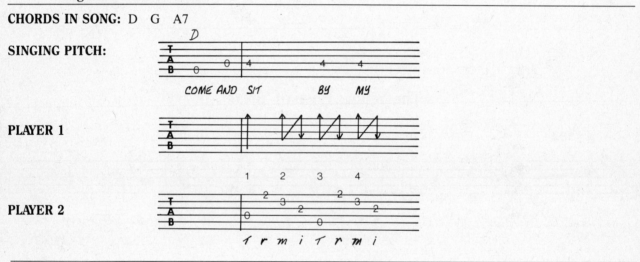

Red River Valley

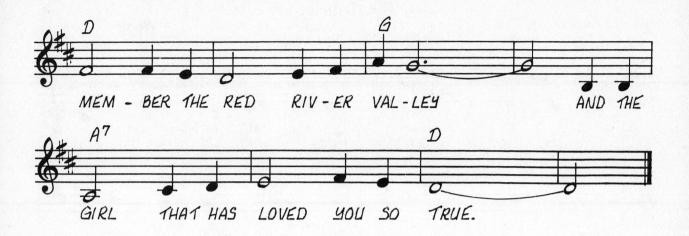

MEM - BER THE RED RIV - ER VAL - LEY   AND THE

GIRL THAT HAS LOVED YOU SO TRUE.

1. Won't you <u>think</u> of this <u>valley</u> you're <u>leaving</u>, ___
   Oh, how <u>lovely</u>, how <u>sad</u> it will <u>be</u>, ___
   Oh, <u>think</u> of the <u>fond</u> heart you're <u>breaking</u>, ___
   And the <u>grief</u> you are <u>causing</u> <u>me</u>. ___
   (*Chorus*)

2. From this <u>valley</u> they <u>say</u> you are <u>going</u>, ___
   When you <u>go</u> may your <u>darling</u> go, <u>too</u>? ___
   Would you <u>leave</u> her <u>behind</u> unprotected? ___
   When she <u>loves</u> no <u>other</u> but <u>you</u>? ___
   (*Chorus*)

The chord changes in "The Gambler" are faster than those in the preceding songs. This song can be played with many of the strums and fingerpicks described in Chapters 4 and 6.

Song Performance Guide

CHORDS IN SONG: D G A7

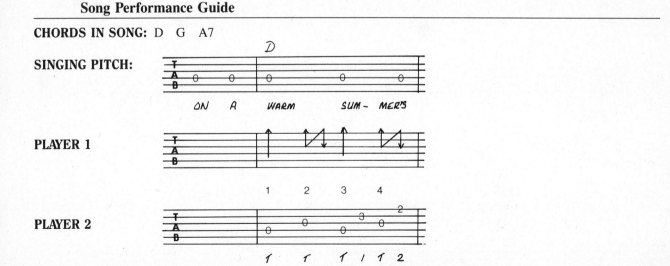

The Gambler

Moderate country

Words and music by
Don Schlitz

(Chorus) 1.   ON A   WARM   SUM - MER'S EV'N - IN'   ON A
YOU   GOT TO   KNOW   WHEN   TO   HOLD 'EM

TRAIN   BOUND   FOR   NO - WHERE   I   MET   UP   WITH   A
KNOW   WHEN   TO   FOLD 'EM   KNOW   WHEN   TO

GAM - BLER   WE WERE BOTH TOO   TIRED   TO   SLEEP   SO
WALK A - WAY   AND KNOW WHEN   TO   RUN   YOU NE-VER

WE   TOOK   TURNS   A   STAR - IN'   OUT THE WIN - DOW   AT   THE
COUNT   YOUR   MON - EY   WHEN YOU'RE SIT - TIN'   AT   THE

DARK - NESS   'TILL BORE-DOM O - VER - TOOK US   AND
TA - BLE   THERE'LL BE TIME E - NOUGH FOR   COUNT-IN'

HE   BE - GAN   TO   SPEAK.
WHEN   THE   DEAL - IN'   IS   DONE.

2. He said, "Son, I've made a life out of readin' people's faces,
And knowin' what their cards were by the way they held their eyes.
And if you don't mind my sayin', I can see you're out of aces.
For a taste of your whiskey I'll give you some advice."

3. So I handed him my bottle and he drank down my last swallow.
___ Then he bummed a cigarette and asked me for a light.
And the night got deathly quiet, And his face lost all expression.
Said, "If you're gonna play the game, boy, ya gotta learn to play it right.

(Chorus) You got to know when to hold 'em, know when to fold 'em,
___ know when to walk away And know when to run.
You never count your money when you're sittin' at the table,
There'll be time enough for countin' ___ when the dealin's done.

4.   ___   Ev'ry gambler <u>knows</u> that the <u>secret</u> to sur<u>vivin'</u>
Is <u>knowin'</u> what to <u>throw</u> away And <u>knowin'</u> what to <u>keep</u>.
'Cause <u>ev'ry</u> hand's a <u>winner</u> and <u>ev'ry</u> hand's a <u>loser</u>,
And the <u>best</u> that you can <u>hope</u> for is to <u>die</u> in your <u>sleep</u>."

5. And <u>when</u> he'd finished <u>speakin'</u>, he <u>turned</u> back towards the <u>window</u>,
   ___   Crushed out his <u>cigarette</u> and <u>faded</u> off to <u>sleep</u>.
And <u>somewhere</u> in the <u>darkness</u> the <u>gambler</u>, he broke <u>even</u>.
But <u>in</u> his final <u>words</u> I found an <u>ace</u> that I could <u>keep</u>.

(Chorus)

© 1978 by Writers Night Music (ASCAP)
3501 Belmont Blvd
Nashville, TN 37215

THE D7 CHORD

The previous two-chord songs that used D–A7 and A–E7 can also be played in the key of G with G–D7. Try shifting the index finger a little ahead of the others in this chord change to help reposition the rest of the fingers. Practice "Down in the Valley" in the key of G with G–D7.

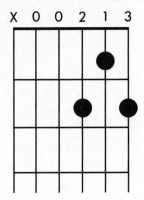

Song Performance Guide

CHORDS IN SONG: G   D7

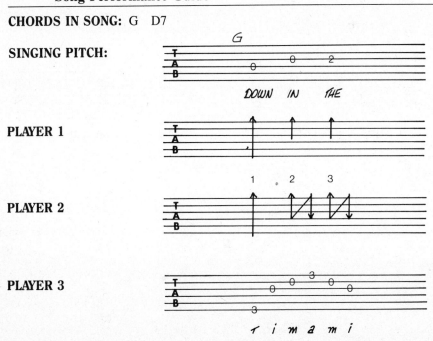

Down in the Valley

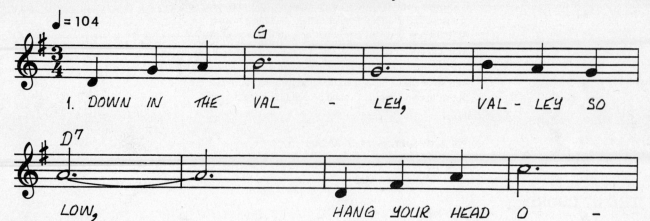

1. DOWN IN THE VAL - LEY,   VAL - LEY SO

LOW,   HANG YOUR HEAD O -

- VER   HEAR   THE   WIND   BLOW.

2. Hear the wind blow, dear, hear the wind blow, __
   Hang your head o ver, hear the wind blow. __

3. If you don't love me, love who you please, __
   Throw your arms 'round me, give my heart ease. __

4. Give my heart ease, love, give my heart ease, __
   Throw your arms 'round me, give my heart ease. __

5. Write me a let ter, send it by mail, __
   Send it in care of Birmingham Jail. __

6. Birmingham Jail, love, Birmingham Jail, __
   Send it in care of Birmingham Jail. __

7. Build me a cas tle, forty feet high, __
   So I can see her, as she rides by. __

8. As she rides by, love, as she rides by, __
   So I can see her, as she rides by. __

9. Roses love sun shine, violets love dew, __
   Angels in heav en know I love you. __

10. Know I love you, dear, know I love you. __
    Angels in heav en know I love you. __

Try playing this song in the key of D, using the D and A7 chords in place of G and D7. You will be singing in a lower key. See Chapter 12 for an explanation of transposing.

THE E-MINOR CHORD

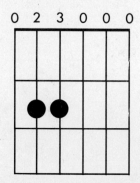

Finger the E-minor chord with the second and third fingers. Together with the major and seventh chords the minor chords make up the third fundamental chord type. There are many other kinds of chords, which will be discussed later, but these three types are the most important. Notice the different mood and flavor that the minor chord has. Take care not to strum the sixth string when playing the D chord in "Stewball."

Song Performance Guide

CHORDS IN SONG: D Em A7

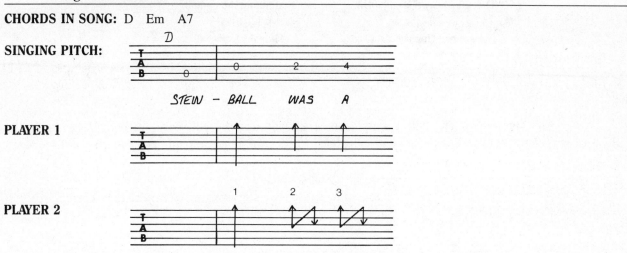

Try playing "Stewball" in Dropped-D tuning. See Chapter 6 for an explanation and fingering diagrams.

Stewball

Robert Yellin,
John Herald, Ralph Rinzler

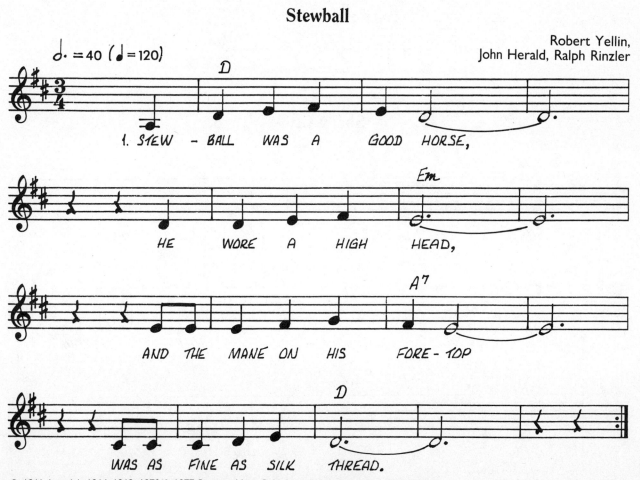

2. I <u>ro</u>de him in <u>Eng</u>land, __ __   I <u>ro</u>de him in <u>Spain</u>, __ __
   And I <u>nev</u>er did <u>lose</u>, boys, __ __   I <u>al</u>ways did <u>gain</u>. __ __

3. So <u>come</u> all you <u>gam</u>blers, __ __   Wher<u>ev</u>er you <u>are</u>, __ __
   And <u>don't</u> bet your <u>mon</u>ey, __ __   On that <u>lit</u>tle gray <u>mare</u>. __ __

4. Most <u>like</u>ly she'll <u>stum</u>ble, __ __   Most <u>like</u>ly she'll <u>fall</u>, __ __
   But you <u>nev</u>er will <u>lose</u>, boys, __ __   On my <u>no</u>ble <u>Stew</u>ball. __ __

5. As <u>they</u> were a-<u>rid</u>ing, __ __   'Bout <u>half</u>way '<u>round</u>. __ __
   That <u>gray</u> mare she <u>stum</u>bled, __ __   And <u>fell</u> on the <u>ground</u>. __ __

6. And <u>way</u> over <u>yon</u>der, __ __   A<u>head</u> of them <u>all</u>, __ __
   Came a-<u>pranc</u>ing and <u>danc</u>ing, __ __   My <u>no</u>ble <u>Stew</u>ball. __ __

Although shown here with a simple strum, "Shady Grove" will sound good with a wide variety of strums. Try several of those from Chapter 4 to see which accompaniment pattern you like best.

Song Performance Guide

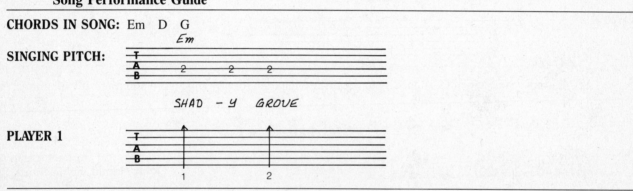

1. Have a guitar <u>made</u> of gold,
   Every string does <u>shine</u>.
   Only song that <u>it</u> can play,
   <u>Wish</u> that girl was <u>mine</u>.
   (*Chorus*)

2. I <u>went</u> to see my <u>Shady</u> Grove
   A-<u>standin'</u> in the <u>door</u>;
   <u>Shoes</u> and stockings <u>in</u> her hands,
   Little bare feet on the <u>floor</u>.
   (*Chorus*)

3. When I was a <u>little</u> boy,
   <u>All</u> I wanted was a <u>knife</u>;
   <u>Now</u> I am a <u>great</u> big boy,
   I'm <u>lookin'</u> for a <u>wife</u>.
   (*Chorus*)

4. <u>Shady</u> Grove, <u>you're</u> my love,
   <u>Shady</u> Grove, please <u>stay</u>;
   <u>Shady</u> Grove, <u>be</u> my love,
   <u>Do</u> not go <u>away</u>.
   (*Chorus*)

THE E-MAJOR AND A-MINOR CHORDS

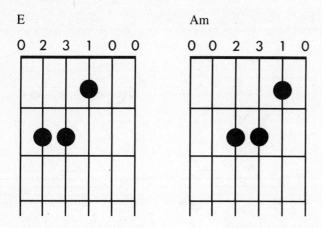

The E-major to A-minor change is easy since the two chords have the same physical shape. Practice this change in "Joshua Fit de Battle." Use a shuffle* rhythm.

Song Performance Guide

CHORDS IN SONG: Am   E

*See pp. 32 and 85.

Joshua Fit de Battle

♩ = 126

(Chorus) JOSH-UA FIT DE BAT-TLE OF JER-I-CHO   JER-I-CHO

JER-I-CHO,   JOSH-UA FIT DE BAT-TLE OF   JER-I-CHO,   AND THE

WALLS CAME TUM-BLIN' DOWN.   1. YOU MAY TALK A-BOUT YOUR KINGS OF

GID-E-ON,   YOU MAY TALK A-BOUT YOUR MEN OF   SAUL,   BUT THERE'S

NONE LIKE GOOD OLD JOSH-U-A,   AT DE BAT-TLE OF JER-I-CHO.

2. Well, the Lord done told old Joshua,
   You must do just what I say,
   March 'round that city seven times,
   An' de walls will tumble 'way.
   (Chorus)

3. Right up to de walls of Jericho,
   They marched with spear in hand,
   "Go blow them ram horns," Joshua cried,
   "'Cause de battle is in my hand."
   (Chorus)

4. Then de lamb, ram, sheep horns began to blow,
   And de trumpets began to sound,
   Joshua told de children to shout that mornin'
   And de walls came tumblin' down.
   (Chorus)

"Rye Whiskey" is in the key of E major. It is played in $\frac{3}{4}$ time and should be strummed with a heavy accent on the first beat of each measure.

Song Performance Guide

CHORDS IN SONG: E   A

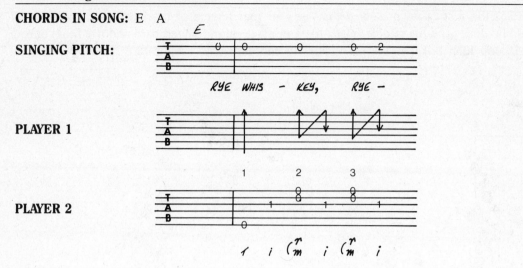

SINGING PITCH:

RYE WHIS - KEY,   RYE -

PLAYER 1

PLAYER 2

Rye Whiskey

♩ = 120

1. RYE   WHIS - KEY,   RYE   WHIS - KEY,   RYE

WHIS - KEY   I   CRY;   IF I   DON'T   GET   RYE

WHIS - KEY   I   SURE - LY   WILL   DIE.

2. I eat when I'm hungry, I drink when I'm dry,
   If I don't get Rye Whiskey, I surely will die.

3. Rye Whiskey, Rye Whiskey, Rye Whiskey I crave,
   If I don't get Rye Whiskey, then show me my grave.

4. I'll go to yonder holler, I'll build me a still,
   And I'll give you a gallon for a five dollar bill.

5. Rye Whiskey, Rye Whiskey, you're no friend to me,
   You killed my poor Pappy, now damn you try me.

THE B7 CHORD

The B7 chord is the first chord presented that uses all four fingers of the left hand. The E-to-B7 change should be done with the middle finger fixed in place on the fingerboard and not lifted during the change. "Sloop John B." uses the E, A, and B7 chords, which are the three primary chords in the key of E.

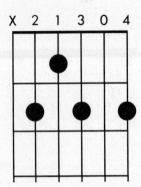

Song Performance Guide

CHORDS IN SONG: E   A   B7

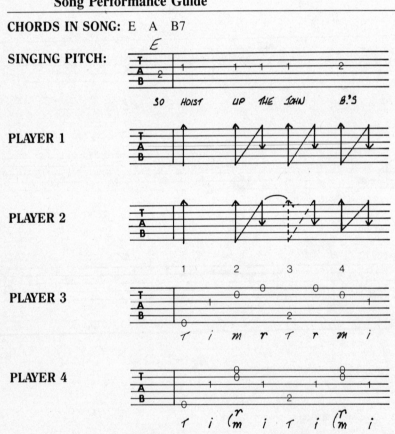

Sloop John B.

♩=104

(Chorus) SO HOIST UP THE JOHN B.'S SAILS, SEE HOW THE MAIN SAIL

SETS. CALL FOR THE CAP-TAIN A - SHORE, LET ME GO

HOME; LET ME GO HOME. I WAN-NA GO

HOME. I FEEL SO BROKE UP,

I WAN-NA GO HOME.

1. We come on the Sloop John B.
   My Grandfather and me
   Around Nassau town we did roam. ___
   Drinkin' all night, ___ got into a fight ___
   I feel so broke up, ___ I wanna go home. ___
   (Chorus)

2. The first mate he got drunk,
   And broke in the captain's trunk,
   The constable had to come take him away. ___
   Sheriff John Sloan, ___ you leave me alone, ___
   I feel so broke up, ___ I wanna go home. ___
   (Chorus)

3. The poor cook he got the fits,
   Threw away all my grits,
   And then he took and he ate up all of my corn. ___
   Let me go home, ___ why don't they let me go home? ___
   This is the worst trip ___ I've ever been on. ___
   (Chorus)

Some other songs that can be played in the key of E with the E, A, and B7 chords include "Careless Love," "Blue Eyes Crying in the Rain," "Going down the Road Feeling Bad," and "Red River Valley." The key of E is commonly used to play blues on guitar, and most blues songs use the E, A, B7, and sometimes the A7 chords. See the section on twelve-bar blues in Chapter 11.

THE C CHORD

There are three common fingerings of the C chord. The second fingering given here requires all four fingers, but it sounds less muddy than the first fingering. Many guitarists play an alternating bass (see Chapter 4 for an explanation of alternating bass) on the C chord by moving the third finger back and forth between the fifth and sixth strings. This is pictured in the third fingering diagram.

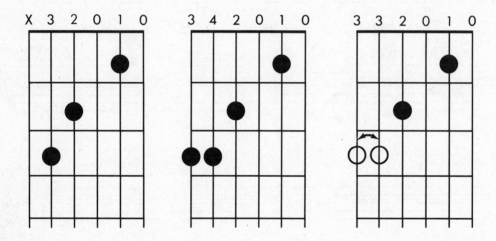

The old spiritual "Down by the Riverside" uses G and D7 for the verses. The C chord is added in the chorus.

Song Performance Guide

CHORDS IN SONG: G   D7   C

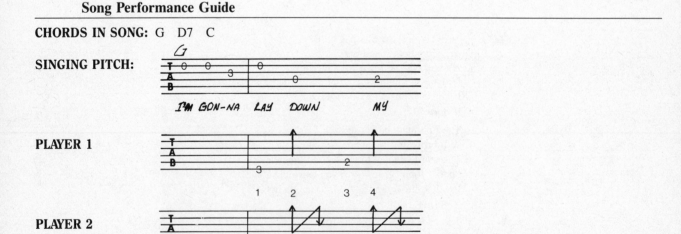

Down by the Riverside

2. I'm gonna <u>lay</u> down my <u>sword</u> and shield.

3. I'm gonna <u>put</u> on my <u>long</u> white robe.

4. I'm gonna <u>talk</u> with the <u>Prince</u> of Peace.

5. I'm gonna <u>join</u> hands with <u>everyone</u>.

Try playing some other songs in the key of G with the G, C, and D7 chords. "Jesse James," "Gold Watch and Chain," and "Roll in My Sweet Baby's Arms" will work fine. If the key of G is too difficult for you, then try the Half-Open A configuration fingering with the Third-Hand capo. See Chapter 7 for an explanation. You will have to sing one step higher with this device, but the left-hand skills required are easier.

Try the Carter-style instrumental solo in Chapter 8 as an introduction to and between the fourth and fifth verses in "John Hardy."

Song Performance Guide

CHORDS IN SONG: G   C   D   (Capo 4 = B, E, F#)

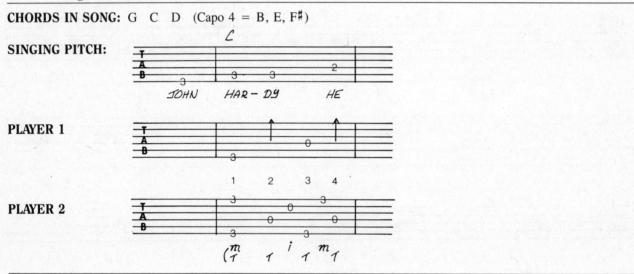

John Hardy

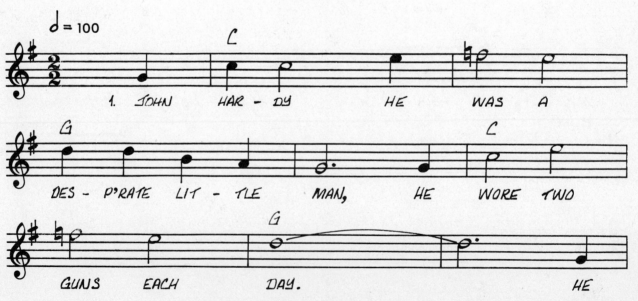

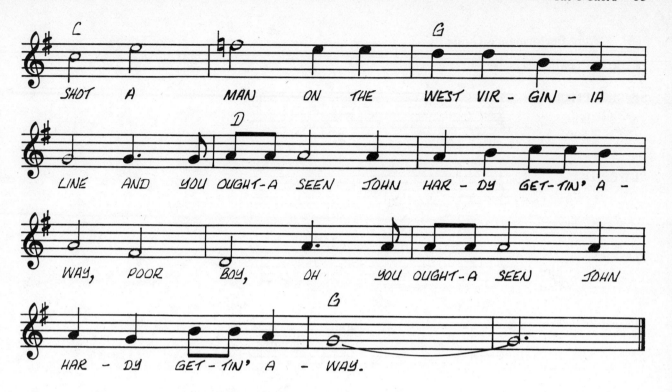

2. John Hardy had come for over twenty miles,
   And half of that he ran ___,
   He ran 'till he came to the moonlit river bank
   And he fell in the water and he swam, poor boy,
   And he fell in the water and he swam. ___

3. He swam 'till he came to his mother's house.
   She asked what he had done ___.
   "I've killed a man in West Vir-gin-i-a
   And they're out to see that I get hung, poor boy,
   And they're out to see that I get hung." ___

4. John Hardy he caught the midnight train,
   So dark he could not see ___.
   He rode it to a town far away
   And he went into the bar a-feelin' free, poor boy,
   And he went into the bar a-feelin' free. ___

5. John Hardy was by the barroom door,
   So drunk he could not see ___,
   Along came the sheriff and took him by the hand
   Saying, "John, you better come with me, poor boy,"
   Saying, "John, you better come with me." ___

6. They took John Hardy to the old hangin' tree,
   They hung him there to die ___.
   He said these words as his legs fell free,
   "Oh, I should have passed the whiskey by, poor boy,
   Oh, I should have passed the whiskey by." ___

"Greensleeves," a song that is centuries old, is also one of the most beautiful. As you practice the chord progression, try to bring out the descending bass line created by playing the chord roots (E, D, C, B). After you learn to play the chord progression without hesitating over chord changes, try to sing along with your accompaniment.

Song Performance Guide

CHORDS IN SONG: Em   D   C   B7   G

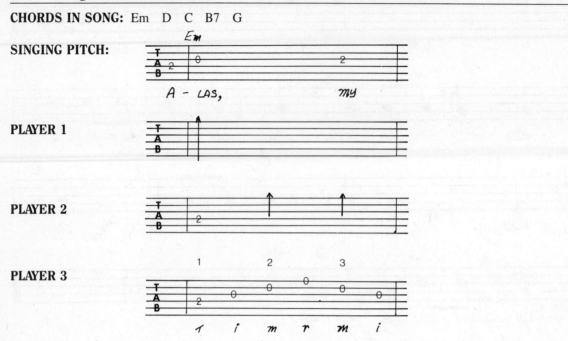

Greensleeves

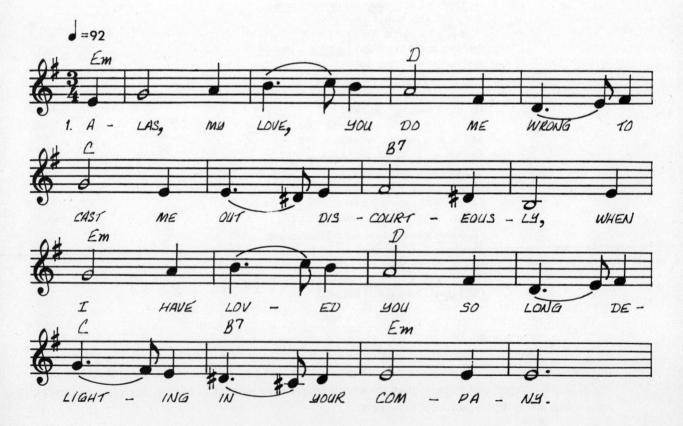

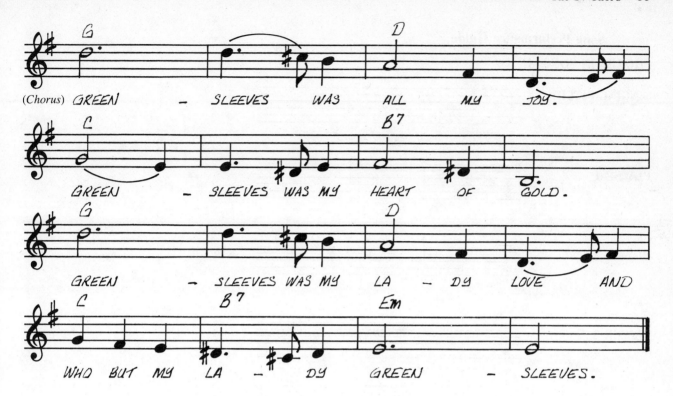

(Chorus) GREEN – SLEEVES WAS ALL MY JOY.

GREEN – SLEEVES WAS MY HEART OF GOLD.

GREEN – SLEEVES WAS MY LA – DY LOVE AND

WHO BUT MY LA – DY GREEN – SLEEVES.

2. I have been ready at your hand,
   To grant whatever you would crave;
   I have both wagered life and land,
   Your love and good will for to have.
   (*Chorus*)

3. Thou couldst desire no earthly thing,
   But still thou hadst it readily;
   Thy music still to play and sing,
   And yet thou wouldst not love me.
   (*Chorus*)

4. Well, I will pray to God on high,
   That thou my constancy mayst see;
   And that yet once before I die,
   Thou wilt vouchsafe to love me.
   (*Chorus*)

5. Oh, Green sleeves, now farewell, adieu,
   God I pray to prosper thee;
   For I am still thy lover true
   Come once again and love me.
   (*Chorus*)

THE G7 CHORD

There are hundreds of variations of "Barb'ra Allen." Here is a version that uses just the C–G7 change.

Some guitarists think the voicing of the normal fingering can be improved by muting the fifth string with the third finger, as was suggested in the G chord on page 35.

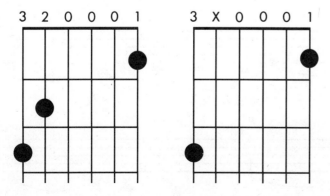

Song Performance Guide

CHORDS IN SONG: C G7

SINGING PITCH:

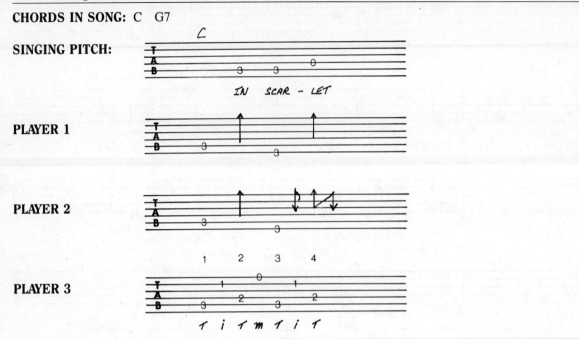

PLAYER 1

PLAYER 2

PLAYER 3

Barb'ra Allen

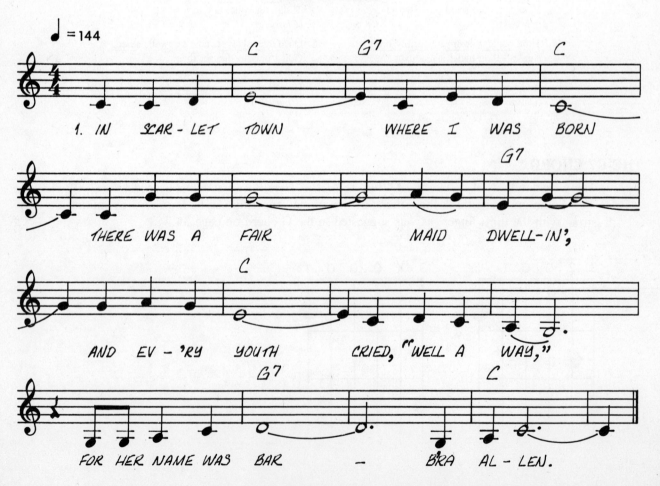

2. 'Twas in the <u>mer</u> ___ ry month of <u>May</u>, ___ the green buds <u>were</u> ___ a-<u>swell</u>ing, ___
   Sweet William <u>on</u> ___ his deathbed <u>lay</u> ___ for the love of <u>Barb</u> ___ 'ra <u>Allen</u>.

3. He sent his <u>serv</u> ___ ant unto <u>her</u> ___ to the <u>place</u> ___ she was <u>dwelling</u>,
   Saying, "You must <u>come</u> ___ to his bedside <u>now</u>, ___ if your name be <u>Barb</u> ___ 'ra <u>Allen</u>."

4. Slowly, <u>slow</u> ___ ly she got <u>up</u>, ___ slowly, <u>slow</u> ___ ly she came <u>nigh</u> him. ___
   And the only <u>words</u> ___ to him she <u>said</u>, ___ "Young man, I <u>think</u> ___ you're <u>dying</u>." ___

5. As she was <u>walk</u> ___ ing over the <u>fields</u> ___ she heard the <u>death</u> ___ bell knelling, ___
   And every <u>stroke</u> ___ it seemed to <u>say</u>, ___ "Hard-hearted <u>Barb</u> ___ 'ra <u>Allen</u>." ___

6. "Oh, Mother, <u>Moth</u> ___ er, make my <u>bed</u>, ___ make it <u>long</u> ___ and make it <u>narrow</u>. ___
   Sweet William <u>died</u> ___ for me to<u>day</u>; ___ I'll die for <u>him</u> ___ to<u>morrow</u>." ___

7. They buried <u>her</u> ___ in the old church<u>yard</u>, ___ they buried <u>him</u> ___ in the <u>choir</u>. ___
   And from his <u>grave</u> ___ grew a red, red <u>rose</u>, ___ from her <u>grave</u> ___ a green <u>briar</u>. ___

8. They grew and <u>grew</u> ___ to the steeple <u>top</u>, ___ till they could <u>grow</u> ___ no <u>higher</u>. ___
   And there they <u>twined</u> ___ in a true love's <u>knot</u>, ___ red rose a<u>round</u> ___ green <u>briar</u>. ___

THE D-MINOR CHORD

"Drunken Sailor" and "Sinner Man" are in the D Dorian mode and use only the D-minor and C chords. (See Chapter 11 for a discussion of modes.)

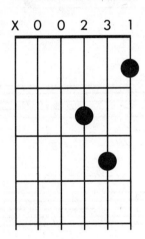

Song Performance Guide

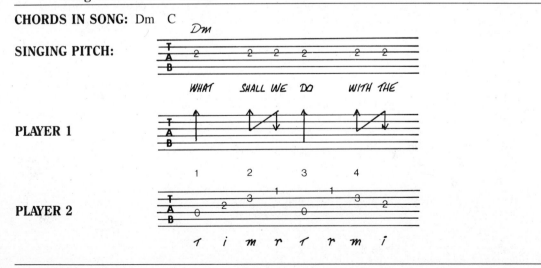

Drunken Sailor

♩ = 132

1. WHAT SHALL WE DO WITH THE DRUNK-EN SAIL-OR, WHAT SHALL WE DO WITH THE

DRUNK-EN SAIL-OR, WHAT SHALL WE DO   WITH THE DRUNK-EN SAIL-OR,

EAR-LY IN THE MORN-ING ? WAY HEY AND UP SHE RIS-ES,
(Chorus)

WAY   HEY   AND UP SHE RIS-ES, WAY HEY AND

UP SHE RIS-ES, EAR-LY IN THE MORN-ING.

2. Put him in a long boat till he's sober, (3 times)
   Early in the morning.
   (Chorus)

3. Pull out the plug and wet him all over, (3 times)
   Early in the morning.
   (Chorus)

4. Put him in the bilge and make him drink it, (3 times)
   Early in the morning.
   (Chorus)

5. Put him in a leaky boat and make him bale her, (3 times)
   Early in the morning.
   (Chorus)

6. Tie him to the scuppers with a hose pipe on him, (3 times)
   Early in the morning.
   (Chorus)

7. Shave his belly with a rusty razor, (3 times)
   Early in the morning.
   (Chorus)

8. <u>Make</u> him swab the deck with a <u>tiny</u> toothbrush, (3 times)
<u>Early</u> in the <u>morning</u>.
(*Chorus*)

9. <u>Make</u> him play guitar with <u>nothin'</u> but barre chords, (3 times)
<u>Early</u> in the <u>morning</u>.
(*Chorus*)

10. <u>Give</u> him a hair of the <u>dog</u> that bit him, (3 times)
<u>Early</u> in the <u>morning</u>.
(*Chorus*)

11. <u>That's</u> what we do with the <u>Drunken</u> Sailor, (3 times)
<u>Early</u> in the <u>morning</u>.
(*Chorus*)

Song Performance Guide

CHORDS IN SONG: Dm   C

SINGING PITCH:

EASY STRUM:

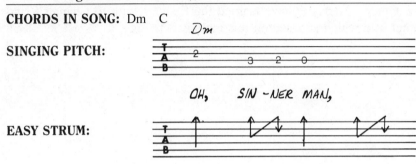

Sinner Man

2. <u>Run</u> to the rock, the <u>rock</u> was a-melting. (3 times) <u>All</u> on that <u>day</u>.

3. <u>Run</u> to the sea, the <u>sea</u> was a-boiling. (3 times) <u>All</u> on that <u>day</u>.

4. <u>Run</u> to the moon, the <u>moon</u> was a-bleeding. (3 times) <u>All</u> on that <u>day</u>.

5. <u>Run</u> to the devil, the <u>devil</u> was a-waiting. (3 times) <u>All</u> on that <u>day</u>.

6. <u>Oh</u>, sinner man, you <u>should</u> have been a-praying. (3 times) <u>All</u> on that <u>day</u>.

THE F CHORD

The F chord is often played with a full barre chord (see Chapter 9). However, it is also played with the following fingering in many songs. This fingering can be moved up the fretboard to create F♯ at the second fret and G at the third fret. Practice changing from the C to the F and then back to the C chord. "Can the Circle Be Unbroken" is an appropriate song on which to practice this chord because the song sounds good at a slow tempo. After you have learned the F chord, turn to Chapter 8 and learn the Carter-style instrumental solo which is based on this melody.

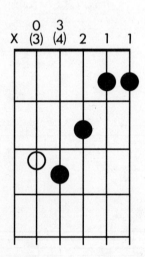

Song Performance Guide

CHORDS IN SONG: C F G7   (Capo 3 = E♭ A♭ B♭7)

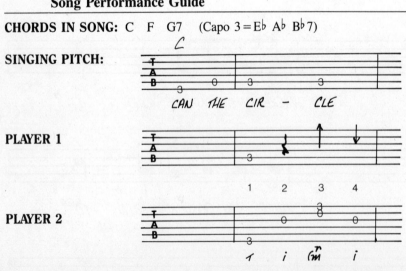

Can the Circle Be Unbroken

1. I was standing ___ by the window ___
   On one cold and dreary day; ___
   And I saw the ___ hearse come rolling ___
   For to carry my mother away. ___
   (*Chorus*)

2. Lord, I told the ___ undertaker, ___
   "Undertaker, please move slow; ___
   For the body ___ you are hauling, ___
   Lord, I hate to see her go." ___
   (*Chorus*)

3. Oh, I followed ___ close behind her, ___
   Tried to hold up and be brave; ___
   But I could not ___ hide my sorrow ___
   When they put her in the grave. ___
   (*Chorus*)

4. Went back home, Lord, ___ on, it was empty ___
   Since my mother has been gone; ___
   All my brothers, ___ sisters crying, ___
   What a home, without a song. ___
   (*Chorus*)

"Dust in the Wind" provides you with an opportunity to play some more advanced chord sounds such as the Dm7. See Chapter 11 for an explanation of the slash (C/C) symbol. Fingerings for these chords follow.

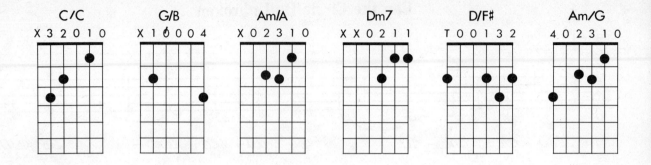

Song Performance Guide

CHORDS IN SONG: C/C G/B Am/A Am/G G Dm7 D/F#

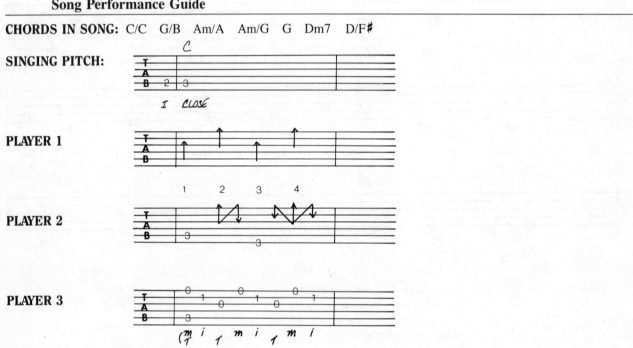

Dust in the Wind

Kerry Livgren

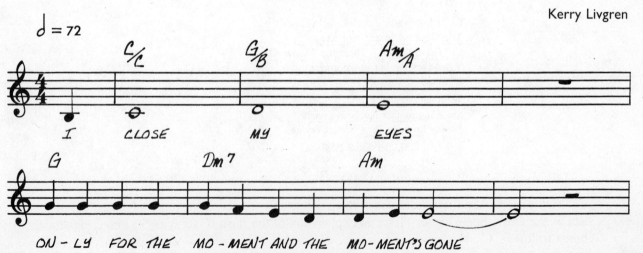

2. Same old song __
   Just a drop of water in an endless sea __
   All we do __
   Crumble to the ground though we refuse to see __
   __ Dust __ in the wind __
   All we are is dust in the wind.

3. Don't hang on __
   Nothing lasts forever but the earth and sky __
   It slips away __
   And all your money won't another minute buy __
   __ Dust __ in the wind __
   All we are is dust in the wind. __

Figure 3.1 shows the open-chord fingerings for the major, minor, and seventh chords, which are the most common types of chords. Most beginning guitar accompaniment programs work with these basic chords, and it is a good idea to learn them as soon as possible. For this reason the entire list has been included at the end of the chapter. The chords are presented here in the same order as they appear in the learning sequence around which the chapter is organized. Some of these chords have more than one acceptable fingering. What seems to be the most popular fingering is given in the figure; other ways are given throughout the chapter.

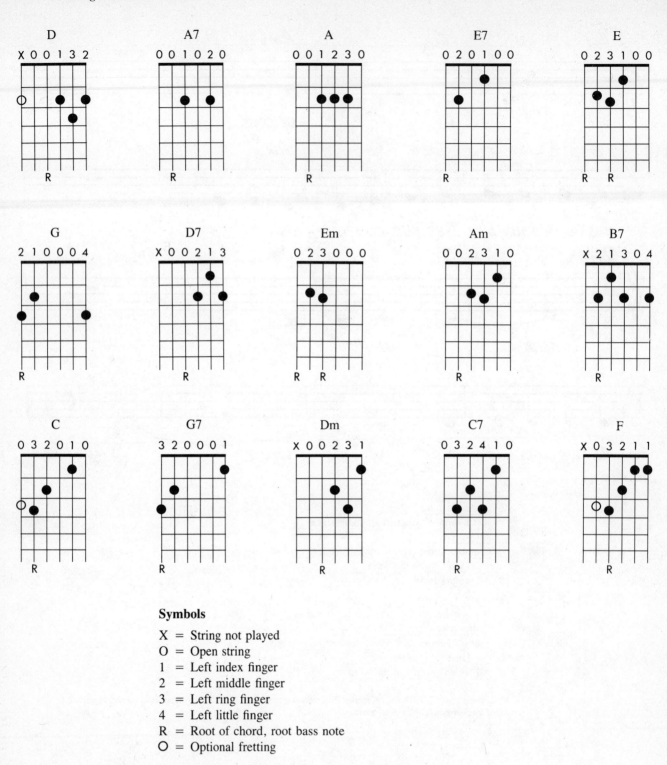

Symbols

X = String not played
O = Open string
1 = Left index finger
2 = Left middle finger
3 = Left ring finger
4 = Left little finger
R = Root of chord, root bass note
O = Optional fretting

FIGURE 3.1 Summary of Basic Open Chords Presented in Chapters 2 and 3

SONG SUGGESTIONS

Song (Artist/Author)	Key: Chords	Comments
The Blind Fiddler (Eric Andersen)	Dm: Dm, C	Play in Am: Am, G
Blowing in the Wind (Bob Dylan)	D: D, G, A7	Play in A: A, D, E7
Blue Eyes Crying in the Rain (Willie Nelson/Fred Rose)	D: D, G, A7	Church lick, Chapter 6
Bye Bye Love (Felice/Boudleaux Bryant)	D: D, G, A7	Alternating bass, Chapter 6
Help Me Make It through the Night (Kris Kristofferson)	D: D, G, A7, E7, Em	Syncopated strum, Chapter 6
The Gambler (Kenny Rogers/Don Schlitz)	D: D, G, A7	Play in E: E, A, B7
If I Were a Carpenter (Tim Hardin)	A: A, G, D	Play in E: E, D, A
Jambalaya (Hank Williams)	D: D, G, A7	Alternating bass, Chapter 6
King of the Road (Roger Miller)	A: A, D, E7	Travis picking, Chapter 7
Leaving on a Jet Plane (John Denver)	G: G, C, Em, D	Syncopated strum, Chapter 6
Me and Bobby McGee (Kris Kristofferson/Fred Foster)	D: D, G, A7	Travis picking, Chapter 7
Paradise (John Prine)	D: D, G, A7	Strumming waltzes, Chapter 6
Tennessee Waltz (Pee Wee King/Redd Stewart)	G: G, C, D7, B7	Strumming waltzes, Chapter 6
You Ain't Going Nowhere (Bob Dylan)	G: G, Am, C	Church lick, Chapter 6
You Are My Sunshine (Jimmie Davis/Charles Mitchell)	E: E, A, B7	Play in D: D, G, A7

chapter 4
Strumming
Accompaniments

There are hundreds of subtly different rhythms that are associated with various kinds of music, and any attempt to organize and catalog them would be fruitless. The underlying "swing" of a particular player's rhythm is a combination of the various styles that have taken their place in our musical culture. Shuffle rhythms and bebop figures appeared in the 1940s outside their normal domain of jazz and blues music, perhaps due to the war, which brought people of different backgrounds and from various parts of the nation together. Latin, calypso, mambo, samba, bossa nova, and rumba beats began to appear in pop music in the 1950s and 1960s, while the 1970s saw reggae and disco rhythms permeating even country music. Thus, the "natural" rhythm of a song or of a player is variable, and the process of selecting an appropriate strumming pattern for a song involves a combination of factors: the rhythmic ideas of the player, the basic-beat feeling of the song, the tempo, the natural rhythm of the words as they are sung, and the accenting of the beats in the measures.

The best way to get a good feel for the rhythms and dynamic characteristics of strumming is to listen to players and recordings, although there are some basic strumming concepts and skills that can be applied to many songs to create effective accompaniments.

The basic beat of the song determines whether you strum in patterns of two, three, or four, or in larger or mixed beat groupings. The first beat of such a grouping usually receives an accent, which should not conflict with the natural accents and rhythm of the song. This is considered primarily when the song is familiar, since the natural beat of a song may not first be apparent if the song is unfamiliar. The notation of the song should give clues. But there can be problems with this, since the rhythmic notation of a song may not be the best way to perform it. For example, "Row, Row, Row Your Boat," in the previous chapter, has a basic feeling of two beats to the measure but is notated with six beats per measure. "Mer-ri-ly, mer-ri-ly, mer-ri-ly, mer-ri-ly . . ." is written in $\frac{6}{8}$ time but is usually performed using a dotted quarter note as the beat rather than the eighth note that is written.

The beat groupings are determined in many cases by the tempo of the song. A certain strumming pattern will work well for a song only within a certain tempo range. The songs in this book that are given with a suggested strum appear with metronome figures to indicate the tempo and thus to ensure that the rhythm of the accompaniment is appropriate. A very fast song will most likely have an accompaniment that is not complicated and that will not require a strum on every beat simply because the right hand cannot move fast enough. Always use a strum that is comfortable. If the pace seems rushed, try strumming on every other beat; likewise, if the song is very slow, fill in the rhythm with more strumming to keep an even flow. The strumming suggestions that appear with each song in this text have been chosen to lie within a "natural" range and should not require regrouping. However, it is important to be able to develop the ability to feel the basic tempo and beat of a song and translate them into a guitar strum without relying on notation. The strumming patterns covered in this chapter will provide a way to accompany a very large body of songs and, we hope, will point to other ways of strumming that combine and extend the ideas presented here.

STRUMMING BASIC-BEAT GROUPINGS

In order to develop skill at keeping a basic strum pattern synchronized with the beat, we have developed a few exercises. The strumming motion consists of downstrokes and upstrokes, and it is important to develop a balanced relationship between them. In most straight strumming the accented beats occur on downstrokes and the unaccented beats or secondary accents occur on the upstrokes, but some of the more complex and useful strums give an accent to a beat that is strummed with an upstroke.

Use a flatpick to play the following counting and strumming exercises. Work for balance in the sounds produced.

Exercises: Strumming with a Flatpick

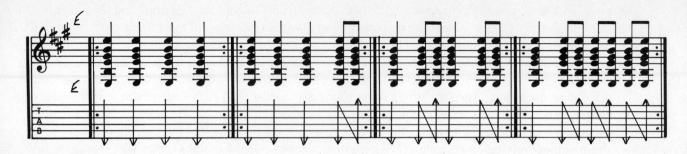

STRUMMING WALTZES

Songs in $\frac{3}{4}$ meter are generally strummed with a duple, eighth-note feel instead of the stiff, one-strum-per-beat accompaniment that might seem logical to use. There are several choices as to how to divide up the beats.

"Home on the Range" can be strummed in any of the different waltz groupings. Try strumming once per beat, then breaking the second and third beats up into eighth notes (see Chapter 5 for an explanation of rhythm counting).

Song Performance Guide

CHORDS IN SONG: D   G   E7   A7

SINGING PITCH:

Home on the Range

2. How often at night when the heavens are bright,
   From the light of the glittering stars;
   Have I stood there amazed, and asked as I gazed,
   If their glory exceeds that of ours.
   (*Chorus*)

3. Where the air is so pure and the zephyrs so free,
   And the breezes so balmy and light;
   Oh, I would not exchange my home on the range
   For the glittering cities so bright.
   (*Chorus*)

4. Oh, give me the land where the bright diamond sand
   Flows leisurely down with the stream,
   Where the graceful white swan glides slowly along
   Like a maid in a heavenly dream.
   (*Chorus*)

"Irene, Goodnight" was a big hit in the 1940s. It should be played with a waltz rhythm.

Song Performance Guide

CHORDS IN SONG: D A7 D7 G

SINGING PITCH:

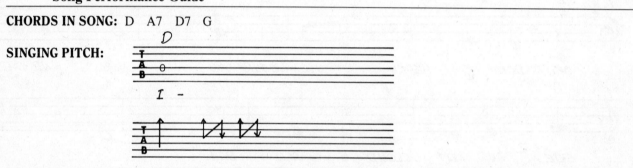

Irene, Goodnight

Huddie Ledbetter

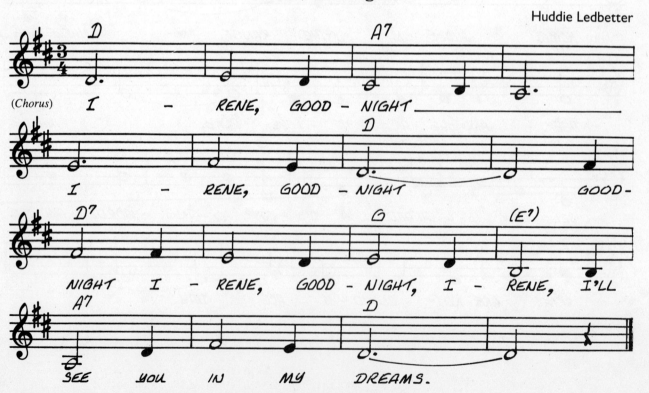

1. Sometimes I lives in the country. ___
   Sometimes I lives in town, ___
   Sometimes I haves a great notion, ___
   To jump in the river and drown. ___
   (*Chorus*)

2. Last Sat'dy night I got married, ___
   Me an' my wife settled down, ___
   Now me an' my wife have parted, ___
   Gonna take me a stroll uptown. ___
   (*Chorus*)

3. I loves Irene, God knows I do,
   I loves her till the sea runs dry. ___
   But if Irene turns her back on me,
   I'll take morphine an' die. ___
   (*Chorus*)

Chord progression:

D	/	A7	/
A7	/	D	/
D7	/	G	/
A7	/	D	/

4. Quit your ramblin', quit your gamblin',
   Quit your stayin' out late at night, ___
   Go home to your wife an' your family,
   Sit down by the fireside bright. ___
   (*Chorus*)

THE CHURCH LICK

For songs with a straight four-beat feel, the *church lick* is commonly employed. It is most effective for songs that are performed at a medium tempo, since with a fast song it would not be feasible to strum twice on each beat. A simple, strummed church lick looks like this:

"Jesse James" is a common outlaw ballad that normally moves at a good tempo for the church lick. Relax the right hand, and keep the down-up motion smooth.

Song Performance Guide

CHORDS IN SONG: G C D7

SINGING PITCH:

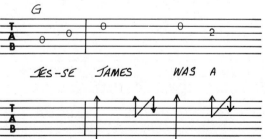

Jesse James

2. It was Robert Ford that dirty little coward.
   I wonder how he does feel.   ___
   For he ate of Jesse's bread and he slept in Jesse's bed
   And he laid poor Jesse in his grave.   ___
   (*Chorus*)

3. How the people held their breath when they heard of Jesse's death
   And wondered how he ever came to die.   ___
   It was one of the gang, called Little Robert Ford
   That shot poor Jesse on the sly.   ___
   (*Chorus*)

4. Jesse was a man, a friend to the poor,
   He never would see a man suffer pain.   ___
   And with his brother Frank he robbed the Chicago bank,
   And stopped the Glendale train.   ___
   (*Chorus*)

5. It was on a Wednesday night, the moon was shining bright,
   They stopped the Glendale train.   ___
   And the people they did say for many miles away,
   It was robbed by Frank and Jesse James.   ___
   (*Chorus*)

6. They went to a crossing not very far from there.
   And there they did the same.   ___
   With the agent on his knees, he delivered up the keys
   To the outlaws Frank and Jesse James.   ___
   (*Chorus*)

7. It was on a Saturday night Jesse was at home,
   Talking to his family brave.   ___
   Robert Ford came along like a thief in the night
   And laid poor Jesse in his grave.   ___
   (*Chorus*)

8. This song was made by Billy Gashade
   As soon as the news did arrive.   ___
   He said there was no man with the law in his hand
   Who could take Jesse James while alive.   ___
   (*Chorus*)

Another song that moves at a good tempo for the church lick is "Since I Laid My Burden Down."

Song Performance Guide

CHORDS IN SONG: G   C   D7

SINGING PITCH:

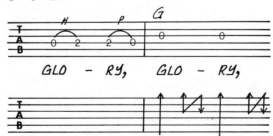

Since I Laid My Burden Down

2. No more sickness, ___ no more sorrow, ___
   Since I laid my ___ burden down. ___
   (*Chorus*)

3. I'm goin' home to ___ live with Jesus, ___
   Since I laid my ___ burden down. ___
   (*Chorus*)

4. Burden down, Lord, ___ Burden down, Lord, ___
   Since I laid my ___ burden down. ___
   (*Chorus*)

5. Glory, glory, ___ Halleluia, ___
   Since I laid my ___ burden down. ___
   (*Chorus*)

The church lick can also be used when you play "The Wreck of the Old Ninety-Seven."

Song Performance Guide

CHORDS IN SONG: A D E

SINGING PITCH:

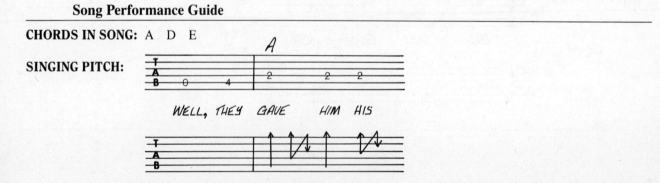

The Wreck of the Old Ninety-Seven

2. He turned and said to his black greasy fireman,
   "Just shovel on a little more coal, ___
   And when we cross the White Oak Mountain
   You can watch old 'ninety-seven' roll." ___

3. It's a mighty rough road from Lynchburg to Danville,
   On a line with a three-mile grade. ___
   It was on that grade that he lost his air brakes,
   You should have seen the jumps that he made. ___

4. He was going down the mountain makin' ninety miles an hour,
   When his whistle broke into a scream. ___
   They found him in the wreck with his hand on the throttle;
   He was scalded to death by the steam. ___

5. A telegram came into Washington station,
   And this is the way that it read: ___
   "A brave engineer tried to pull old 'ninety-seven,'
   Now he's lying near Danville dead." ___

6. Now you ladies listen and heed this warning,
   And this lesson you will learn, ___
   Never speak harsh words to your true loving husband,
   He may leave you and never return. ___

ROOT BASS

Although many songs can be played with only a strummed accompaniment, it is very common to find strumming patterns that have a bass note alternated with the strumming of the chord. For many country and folk songs this is the only way to capture effectively the natural rhythm of the song, and it is a very versatile method of accompaniment. In this style a single bass note alternates with a strummed chord. Chords are made up of three different tones: the root, third, and fifth. (See Chapter 11 for a complete discussion.) The root bass note, the principal bass note, has the same letter name as the chord. It is usually played on the first and third beats of a four-beat measure and alternates with the chord, which is strummed on the second and fourth beats. The bass note must be found on the low strings of the guitar. The root-bass strum pattern is shown for the D, A7, and G chords in both notation and tablature. Adding an upstroke turns this into a church lick.

Play "This Land Is Your Land" using the root-bass strum both with the upstroke and without it. Be sure that you are playing the correct string on the first and third beats of each measure as you change chords.

Song Performance Guide

CHORDS IN SONG: G   D   A7

SINGING PITCH:

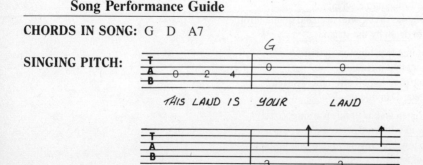

This Land Is Your Land

Words and music by
Woody Guthrie

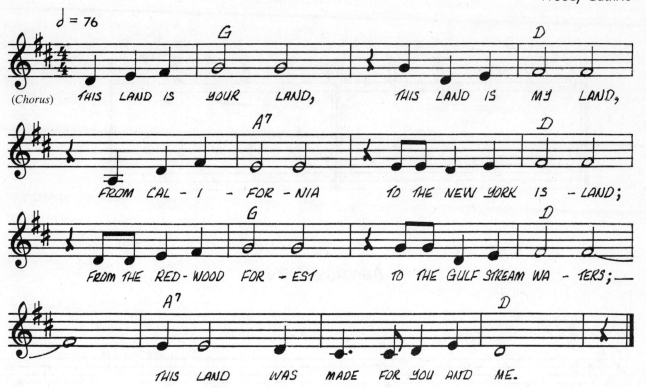

(Chorus) THIS LAND IS YOUR LAND, THIS LAND IS MY LAND, FROM CAL-I-FOR-NIA TO THE NEW YORK IS-LAND; FROM THE RED-WOOD FOR-EST TO THE GULF STREAM WA-TERS;— THIS LAND WAS MADE FOR YOU AND ME.

1. As I was walking, that ribbon of highway,
   I saw above me that endless skyway;
   I saw below me that golden valley;
   This land was made for you and me.
   (Chorus)

2. I've roamed and rambled and I followed my footsteps
   To the sparkling sands of her diamond deserts;
   And all around me a voice was sounding;
   This land was made for you and me.
   (Chorus)

3. One bright Sunday morning in the shadows of the steeple
   By the Relief Office I seen my people;
   As they stood there hungry, I stood there whistling;
   This land was made for you and me.
   (Chorus)

4. When the sun came shining, and I was strolling,
   And the wheat fields waving and the dust clouds rolling,
   As the fog was lifting a voice was chanting;
   This land was made for you and me.
   (Chorus)

5. Nobody living can ever stop me,
   As I go walking that freedom highway;
   Nobody living can make me turn back,
   This land was made for you and me.
   (Chorus)

6. As I went walking, I saw a sign there,
   And on the sign it said "No Trespassing,"
   But on the other side it didn't say nothing,
   That side was made for you and me.
   (Chorus)

The root-bass strum can be used in ¾ meter also. It can be played in a straightforward manner or with the upstroke added after the second and third beats. Try the following strums on "Amazing Grace."

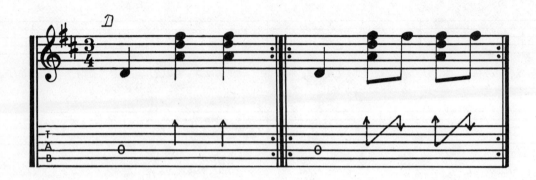

Amazing Grace

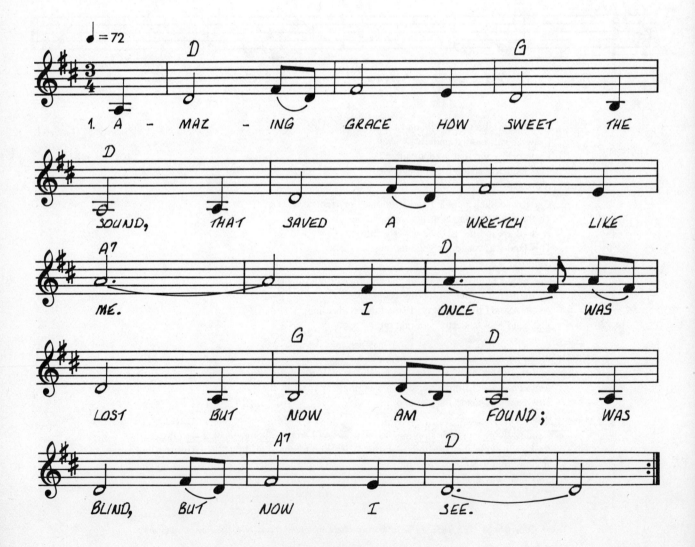

2. 'Twas <u>grace</u> that taught my <u>heart</u> to fear,
   And <u>grace</u> my fears re<u>lieved</u>.
   How <u>precious</u> did that <u>grace</u> appear;
   The <u>hour</u> I first be<u>lieved</u>.

3. Through <u>many</u> dangers, <u>toils</u> and snares,
   I <u>have</u> already <u>come</u>.
   'Tis <u>grace</u> hath brought me <u>safe</u> thus far,
   And <u>grace</u> will lead me <u>home</u>.

4. When <u>we've</u> been there ten <u>thousand</u> years,
   Bright <u>shining</u> as the <u>sun</u>.
   We've <u>no</u> less days to <u>sing</u> God's praise,
   Than <u>when</u> we first be<u>gun</u>.

ALTERNATING BASS

The effect of the root bass can become monotonous if played throughout a song. For that reason, most guitar players use an alternating bass in which the bass notes played between strums of the chord follow a sequence. In most cases the bass note will alternate between the principal bass note and an adjacent string. An alternating-bass strum pattern for a D chord is shown:

The root bass in the D chord was on the fourth string, and the alternating-bass note was on the fifth string. In the G chord the bass root G is on the sixth string, and an alternating-bass note can be found on the fifth string. A guitarist might use the following pattern:

If the chord is held for long periods of time, then a sequence of bass notes can be played that creates an interesting accompaniment:

Various alternating-bass patterns can be easily constructed to go with the other common chords according to the tastes of the player and the needs of the particular song.

"She'll Be Comin' 'round the Mountain" is a fast-paced song that works very well with an alternating bass. Just pluck a bass note on the first and third beats, and strum the chords on the others.

Song Performance Guide

CHORDS IN SONG: G   D7   C

SINGING PITCH:

She'll Be Comin' 'round the Mountain

2. She'll be driving six white horses . . . (Hey, hey)

3. We will all go out to meet her . . . (Hi, babe)

4. We will kill the old red rooster . . . (Oh, boy)

5. We will cook some chicken and dumplin's . . . (Yum, yum)

6. We will sleep in Grandma's soft bed . . . (Snore, snore)

The "oom-pah" effect of the alternating bass can be put to good effect in "Roll in My Sweet Baby's Arms."

Song Performance Guide

CHORDS IN SONG: A   E   D

SINGING PITCH:

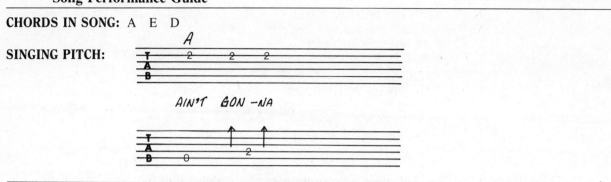

Roll in My Sweet Baby's Arms

2. Mama's a <u>gin</u>ger cake <u>bak</u>er, ___
   Sister can <u>weave</u> and can <u>spin</u>, ___
   Dad's got an <u>in</u>terest in that <u>old</u> cotton <u>mill</u>,
   Just to <u>watch</u> that old <u>mon</u>ey roll <u>in</u>. ___
   (*Chorus*)

3. They <u>tell</u> me your <u>par</u>ents do not <u>like</u> me, ___
   They have <u>drove</u> me a<u>way</u> from your <u>door</u>; ___
   If I <u>had</u> my <u>time</u> to do <u>over</u> a<u>gain</u>
   I would <u>never</u> go <u>there</u> any <u>more</u>. ___
   (*Chorus*)

4. Now <u>where</u> were <u>you</u> last <u>Fri</u>day <u>night</u>
   While I was <u>locked</u> up in <u>jail</u>? ___
   Walking the <u>streets</u> with an<u>other</u> <u>man</u>,
   Would<u>n't</u> even <u>go</u> my <u>bail</u>. ___
   (*Chorus*)

If you have found the alternating-bass strum easy, look ahead into bass runs and try to add some to "Long Journey Home" as you work on your right-hand technique.

Song Performance Guide

CHORDS IN SONG: G   C   D

SINGING PITCH:

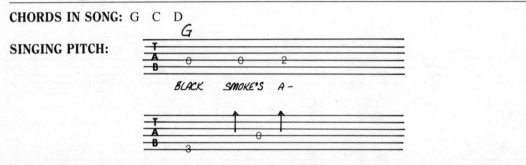

Long Journey Home

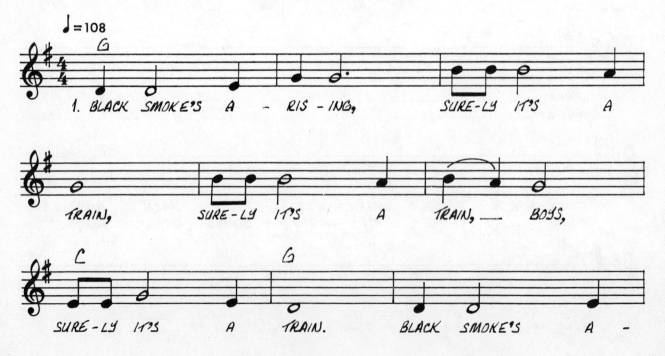

RIS - ING AND IT SURE - LY IS A TRAIN; I'M

D A

ON MY ___ LONG JOUR - NEY HOME. ___

2. Lost all my money but a two-dollar bill,
   Two-dollar bill, boys,
   Two-dollar bill.
   Lost all my money but a two-dollar bill,
   I'm on my long journey home.

3. Homesick and lonesome and feeling kinda blue,
   Feeling kinda blue, boys,
   Feeling kinda blue.
   Homesick and lonesome and feeling kinda blue,
   I'm on my long journey home.

4. Dark and a-rainin' and I got to go home,
   Got to go home, boys,
   Got to go home.
   Dark and a-rainin' and I got to go home,
   I'm on my long journey home.

Since virtually every song can be played with some form of alternating bass, it is one of the most widely used styles. For each chord it is necessary to know where the root bass note is and which bass notes will work as alternating notes. Go back and devise an alternating-bass accompaniment for each of the songs in Chapter 3. Because many of the songs have different rhythms, you will end up with many differently "flavored" accompaniments derived from one concept. Alternating bass is also very useful in the fingerpicking patterns that are discussed in Chapter 6.

Shuffle Rhythm

The *shuffle* is a common rhythmic device often associated with "bluesy" or "swinging" songs. It is written in straight $\frac{4}{4}$ time but is played with uneven beat divisions. The four beats of the measure are divided into *triplets*:

One   Two   Three   Four

It is often played by combining the first two eighth notes of each beat, giving the characteristic uneven quality to the beat divisions.

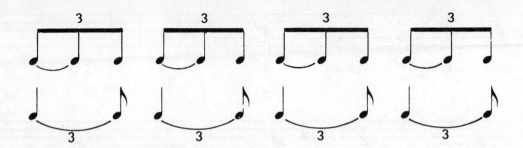

Performing musicians are familiar with this style and know when it is appropriate. This familiarity is important because songs that should be played in this style are often notated with even beat divisions

even though they should be performed in the shuffle rhythm.

The shuffle rhythm is used extensively in blues and rock music. It often features subtle variations characteristic of the styles of different players and further combinations of rhythms that arise when drummers and bass players work together with guitars to create complicated cross-rhythms. Practice the shuffle on "Frankie and Johnny," "Mama Don't 'Low," and "Down by the Riverside." "Midnight Special," a favorite of Leadbelly, works well with a shuffle-rhythm strum.

In "Midnight Special" you can combine elements of the alternating bass, church lick, and shuffle rhythm to produce the following strum. You can also damp strings with your right hand (see the next section in this chapter).

Song Performance Guide

CHORDS IN SONG: G   C   D7

SINGING PITCH:

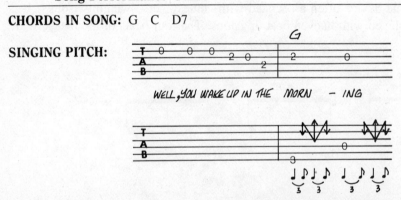

Midnight Special

2. If you ever go to <u>Houston</u>, you'd better walk <u>right</u>,
   And you better not <u>gamble</u> and you better not <u>fight</u>.
   'Cause the sheriff will <u>arrest</u> you and he'll carry you <u>down</u>,
   And you can bet your bottom <u>dollar</u> you're penitentiary <u>bound</u>.
   (*Chorus*)

3. Yonder comes Miss <u>Rosie</u>, tell me how do you <u>know</u>?
   I know her by her <u>apron</u> and the dress she <u>wore</u>.
   Umbrella on her <u>shoulder</u>, piece of paper in her <u>hand</u>,
   Well, I heard her tell the <u>captain</u>, "I want my <u>man</u>."
   (*Chorus*)

Strumming with Right-Hand Damping

Interesting rhythms and variations of strumming skills already presented can be created with the use of right-hand *damping*. Chords can be "chopped" off or cut short and a staccato sound obtained. In addition, a different, muted tone can be achieved on the bass strings that is very common in rock and blues music.

To damp the strings simply drop the fleshy heel of the right hand onto the strings immediately after strumming them. This will mute their vibration. The timing of the damp is crucial; it can be done instantly or delayed by a beat or half a beat for different effects. To achieve the muted but not completely deadened sound, put the heel of the hand close to the bridge. Experiment with strumming chords while leaving the heel of the hand on the strings. If your hand is too far from the bridge, the strings won't sound at all; if it is directly on the bridge, the strings may not be damped. With just the right positioning of the heel of the hand, a "funky," muted sound can be obtained (see Figure 1.2).

Two Robert Johnson blues songs in this book can be played effectively with the damped shuffle (in fact, these songs were important in defining the style): "Sweet Home Chicago" in Chapter 7 and "Ramblin' on My Mind" in Chapter 11. It is hard to play these songs properly without using this technique.

SYNCOPATED STRUM

What is often called a syncopated strum is actually related to a number of Caribbean rhythms but has found its way into modern "folk" guitar music. Its characteristic rhythm is obtained by placing an accent on the upstroke in the second half of the second beat and resting on the first half of the third beat.

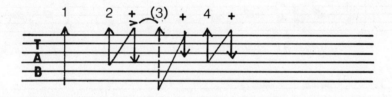

"Gold Watch and Chain" is a song that can be played with a syncopated strum. Be sure you can perform the pattern before singing the melody.

Song Performance Guide

CHORDS IN SONG: A   E   B7

SINGING PITCH:

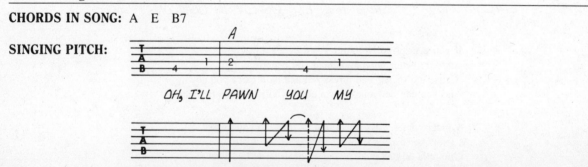

OH, I'LL PAWN YOU MY

Gold Watch and Chain

(Chorus) OH, I'LL PAWN YOU MY GOLD WATCH AND CHAIN, LOVE,

AND I'LL PAWN YOU MY GOLD WED-DING RING.

OH, I'LL PAWN YOU THIS HEART IN MY BOS-OM,

IF YOU'LL SAY THAT YOU LOVE ME A - GAIN.

1. Darling, how can I stay here without you? ___
   I'll have nothing to cheer my poor heart. ___
   This old world will seem sad here without you; ___
   Tell me now that we never more will part. ___
   (Chorus)

2. Take back all of the gifts that you gave me, ___
   A gold ring and a lock of your hair; ___
   And a card with your picture upon it, ___
   It's a face that is false, but it's fair. ___
   (Chorus)

3. Oh, the wild rose that blooms in the garden, ___
   It grows with the love of my heart, ___
   It grew through on the day that I met you, ___
   It will die on the day that we part. ___
   (Chorus)

"Mama Don't 'Low" is often used as a showpiece for many different bands—from jazz and blues to bluegrass and country. It can be played successfully with a church lick, alternating bass, or several fingerpicking patterns. Try it here with the syncopated strum.

Song Performance Guide

CHORDS IN SONG: G   D7   C

SINGING PITCH:

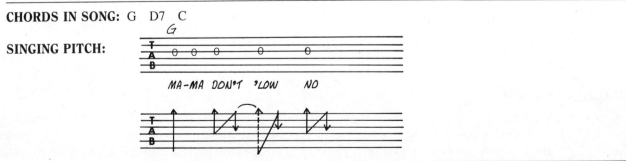

Mama Don't 'Low

2. Mama don't 'low no banjo playin' 'round here __ . . .
3. Mama don't 'low no cigar smokin' 'round here __ . . .
4. Mama don't 'low no midnight ramblin' 'round here __ . . .
5. Mama don't 'low no bad guitar playin' 'round here __ . . .
6. Mama don't 'low no flunking exams 'round here __ . . .
7. Mama don't 'low no hand clappin' 'round here __ . . .*

*This song can have as many verses as you like; they are easily invented.

CALYPSO STRUM

There are many subtle and intricate rhythms from the West Indies that have found their way into the folk and popular music of the United States. "Pay Me My Money Down" has such a rhythm, called a "calypso." When it is strummed on a guitar, it is most easily played with downstrokes on accented parts of beats. Be sure you feel a normal four beats against the syncopated rhythm.

Song Performance Guide

CHORDS IN SONG: C   G7

SINGING PITCH:

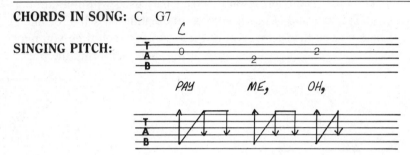

Pay Me My Money Down

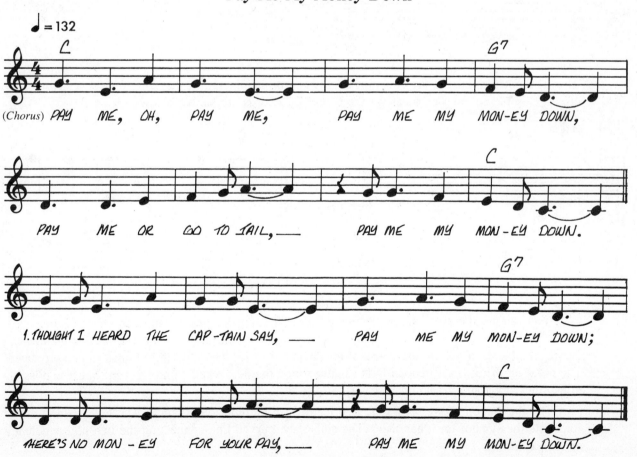

2. Bills to pay, no food to eat, Pay me my money down;
    Got no shoes for my feet, Pay me my money down.
    (*Chorus*)

3. Worked five weeks, but still no pay, Pay me my money down;
    Can't go on a-livin' this way, Pay me my money down.
    (*Chorus*)

THE HAMMER-ON

The *hammer-on* is a simple effect used extensively by most guitar players. Physically, a hammer-on is two notes sounded on the same string while plucking the string just one time. The most common hammer-on is to pluck an open string and then quickly bring the fretting finger down to sound another note, usually one or two frets above the open string. It takes a bit of practice to get the "hammered" note to sound as loud as the first, plucked note. Hammering-on is most easily used within a familiar chord to add rhythmic interest. Hold a G chord, and strum it with an alternating-bass figure, interchanging the G bass root with the B bass note at the second fret of the A string. Each time you play the B alternating-bass note, lift up the first finger, pluck the open A string, and then bring the finger back down to "hammer" the B:

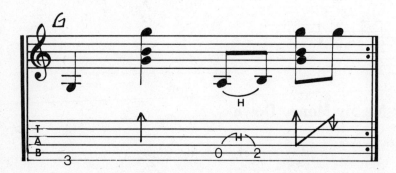

The notes of any of the common chords can be hammered in the same fashion to create new effects. Simple hammer-on ideas for the C and D7 chords are shown below:

You can use these examples of hammering-on in any song accompaniment. "Jesse James" and "She'll Be Comin' 'round the Mountain" work very well with the G, C, and D7 chords. Try hammering the fingered notes in each of the chords from Chapter 3 to see what different sounds can be produced. The notes on the first and second frets usually sound the best when hammered-on, but it is possible to hammer any note over an open string.

The illustration above shows the two features of hammer-on notation. The letter *H* and a slur constitute the symbol for a hammer. (The slur is the curved line connecting the two notes included in the hammer-on.)

PULL-OFF

In the *pull-off*, two notes are also sounded with only one right-hand motion, but this time the fretted note is played first, and then the fretting finger plucks the string while releasing pressure so that the open string sounds as the second note. Pulling-off is harder to do than hammering-on since it requires plucking with the left hand, but simple applications of the pull-off can be easily learned. The notation for the pull-off is a slur and the letter *P*. Hold a D chord, and then pull off the F♯ on the high E string onto the open E string:

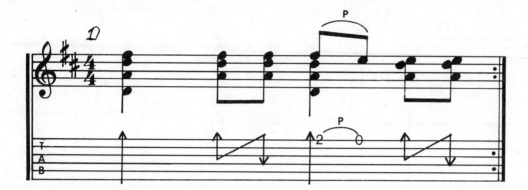

A hammer-on and a pull-off can be combined. This can be done either by first playing an open string, hammering on to a fretted note, and then pulling off onto the original open string again, or by starting with the fretted note. An example of each is given below.

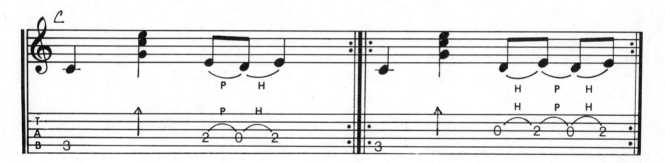

The hammer-on and pull-off are noted as eighth notes but are usually not played with equal durations. The first note is most often played on the beat but very quickly. The remainder of the beat is taken up by the second note. The second note is the more melodically important one of the two.

BASS RUNS

Bass runs—the various ways of using a progression or series of bass notes to connect chord changes in a song—can be simple or complex. There are some basic, easily learned bass runs that can be used to good advantage by a beginner to connect the chord changes in any accompaniment. The most frequently used bass runs move stepwise up or down the scale between the root bass notes of two chords. For example, to move from A to D in the key of D major a bass run would include A–B–C♯–D:

Bass runs are usually played on the beat of the music and start a number of beats ahead of the chord change so that the final note of the bass run, which is the root bass note of the new chord, coincides with the first beat of the sounding of the new chord. Sometimes bass runs can be fingered with the chord still held down, but usually you have to release the chord, play the run, and then form the next chord in time for the rhythm to remain steady. It takes practice, and the fingerings of many of the runs will depend on personal taste. Here are some common bass runs connecting familiar chords.

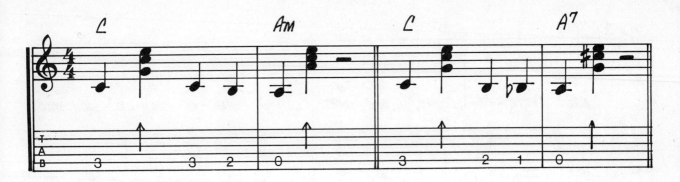

BASS-RUN ARRANGEMENTS

The following songs have been arranged to help you learn to play bass runs. Play these arrangements slowly and evenly, making sure not to lose the beat of the song when playing the bass runs or when changing chords.

The Wreck of the Old Ninety-Seven*

*See page 75 for the remaining verses.

NOT "THIR-TY EIGHT," BUT IT'S OLD "NINE-TY-SEV-EN," YOU MUST

PUT HER IN-TO DAN-VILLE ON TIME."

Red River Valley*

(Chorus) COME AND SIT BY MY SIDE IF YOU LOVE ME, DO NOT

*See page 38 for the verses.

HAS - TEN TO BID ME A - DIEU,   BUT RE-

MEM - BER THE RED RIV - ER VAL-LEY,   AND THE

GIRL THAT HAS LOVED YOU SO TRUE.

On Top of Old Smoky

2. Oh, <u>court</u>in's a <u>pleas</u>ure, __ and <u>part</u>ing is <u>grief</u>, __ __
   But a <u>false</u>-hearted <u>lov</u>er __ is <u>worse</u> than a <u>thief</u>. __ __

3. A <u>thief</u> will just <u>rob</u> you, __ of <u>all</u> that you <u>save</u>, __ __
   But a <u>false</u>-hearted <u>lov</u>er __ will <u>lead</u> you to the <u>grave</u>. __ __

4. The <u>grave</u> will decay <u>you</u> __ and <u>turn</u> you to <u>dust</u>, __ __
   Not a <u>boy</u> in a <u>mil</u>lion __ a <u>poor</u> girl can <u>trust</u>. __ __

5. They'll <u>hug</u> you and <u>kiss</u> you, __ and <u>tell</u> you more <u>lies</u>, __ __
   Than <u>cross</u> ties on <u>rail</u>roads, __ or <u>stars</u> in the <u>skies</u>. __ __

6. They'll <u>tell</u> you they <u>love</u> you, __ to <u>give</u> your heart ease, __ __
   But <u>soon</u> as your <u>back's</u> turned, __ they'll <u>love</u> who they <u>please</u>. __ __

7. I'll <u>climb</u> up Old <u>Smok</u>y, __ the <u>mountain</u> so <u>high</u>, __ __
   Where the <u>wild</u> geese and <u>turtle</u> <u>doves</u> __ can <u>hear</u> my sad <u>cry</u>. __ __

Salty Dog Blues

(*CHORUS*) If I can't be your salty dog.
            I won't be your man at all.
            Honey, let me be your salty dog. ___

2. Standin' at the corner with the low-down blues,
   Gotta big hole in the bottom of my shoes.
   Honey, let me be your salty dog. ___
   (*Chorus*)

3. I came home to my surprise,
   Another man there was twice my size.
   Honey, let me be your salty dog. ___
   (*Chorus*)

4. I had a bad day in my life,
   When my friend caught me kissin' his wife.
   Honey, let me be your salty dog. ___
   (*Chorus*)

5. Two old maids, sittin' in the sand,
   Each one wishin' that the other was a man.
   Honey, let me be your salty dog. ___
   (*Chorus*)

"Salty Dog Blues" is a popular bluegrass song that has many verses, some clean and some funny.

Marines' Hymn

Exercise: Bass Runs

"All the Good Times Are Past and Gone" is usually played in a moderately slow tempo and has several bass runs occurring in the measures preceding chord changes. Learn this song, inserting bass runs where they seem appropriate.

All the Good Times Are Past and Gone

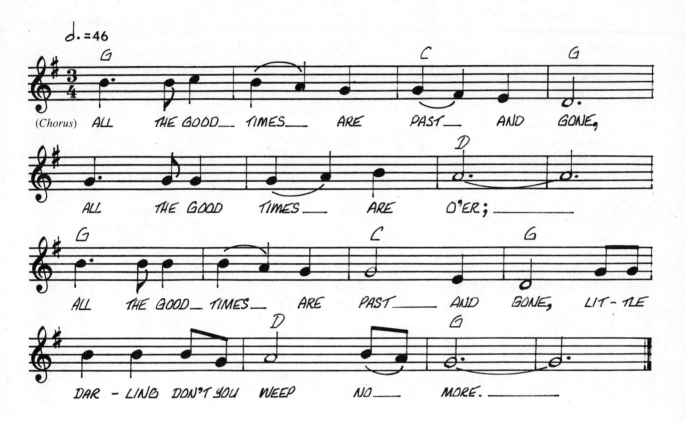

(Chorus) ALL THE GOOD TIMES ARE PAST AND GONE,
ALL THE GOOD TIMES ARE O'ER;
ALL THE GOOD TIMES ARE PAST AND GONE, LIT-TLE
DAR - LING DON'T YOU WEEP NO MORE.

1. I wish to the Lord I'd never been born,
   Or died when I was young. __
   I'd never have seen your sparkling blue eyes
   Or heard your lying tongue. __
   (*Chorus*)

2. Oh don't you see that passenger train
   A-coming around the bend? __
   It's taking me away from this lonesome old town
   To never return again. __
   (*Chorus*)

3. Oh don't you see that lonesome dove
   A-flying from pine to pine? __
   He's mourning for his own true love
   Just like I mourn for mine. __
   (*Chorus*)

SONG SUGGESTIONS

Song (Artist/Author)	Key: Chords	Comments
Blue Eyes Crying in the Rain (Willie Nelson/Fred Rose)	D: D, G, A7	Alternating-bass strum Bass runs in D
Flag Decal (John Prine)	D: D, G, A7	Alternating-bass strum Bass runs in D
Glendale Train (New Riders of the Purple Sage)	G: G, C, D	Church-lick strum Bass runs in G
Good Hearted Woman (Waylon Jennings)	D: D, G, A7	Alternating-bass strum
Green Green Grass of Home (Curley Putnam)	E: E, A, E7, B7	Alternating-bass strum Bass runs in E
I Walk the Line (Johnny Cash)	D: D, G, A7	Bass runs in D
If I Were a Carpenter (Tim Hardin)	A: A, G, D	Syncopated strum
If I Were Free (Travis Edmonson)	E: E, A, B7	Syncopated strum
Jamaica Farewell (Harry Belafonte)	A: A, D, E	Calypso rhythm
Long Black Veil (Danny Dill)	D: D, G, D7, A7	Syncopated strum
Lucille (Kenny Rogers/Bowling-Bynum)	A: A, D, E7	Alternating-bass strum Bass runs in A $\frac{3}{4}$ time
Margaritaville (Jimmy Buffett)	D: D, G, A7	Syncopated strum or calypso strum
Norwegian Wood (John Lennon/Paul McCartney)	D: D, C, Dm, G, A7	Fast waltz strum
Paradise (John Prine)	D: D, G, A7	Alternating bass with $\frac{3}{4}$ time bass runs in D
There's a Place in the World for a Gambler (Dan Fogelberg)	A: A, D, E	Waltz strum

chapter 5
Playing Melody from Standard Notation and Tablature

Most folk guitar players learn their technique by listening to recordings and live performances, and then attempting to imitate those performances. Nevertheless, many people who want to learn to play guitar either can't hear well enough, can't remember tunes and chord progressions with enough accuracy, or do not have the dedication to learn everything by rote. In addition, there are many times when learning by rote isn't efficient or when sound models are not available. Self-instruction and class-instruction situations often require a way for learners to follow a specific set of directions. Standard notation, too, has its drawbacks. It can be argued that learning by listening and imitating is the only way to get a comprehensive command of the rhythmic subtleties and melodic nuances in music. Standard notation, as good as it is, simply does not convey those subtleties and nuances. Nevertheless, it is the most common and effective notational system.

This chapter, following as it does those on chording and strumming, is intended to introduce the aspiring guitarist to melody playing. Learning to read music is a necessary part of this activity. Music notation for the first four frets (open position) is presented in both standard notation and tablature. As you learn to play melodies, you will learn the fingerboard placement of each note on the staff.

NOTATING MUSICAL PITCHES

Musical notation has been evolving for several centuries and in many ways is similar to a language in that it has its irregularities and peculiarities as well as its shortcomings. Reading pitch notation on the guitar is complicated by the fact that the same pitch can be played on several different strings. On the piano there is only one key that is middle C; but on a guitar this note can be found on at least three strings, and extra notation is needed to indicate a particular one. Nevertheless, standard notation is superior in important respects to the other systems of guitar-based notation. Musical notation can portray the four characteristics of single musical tones: pitch, rhythm, timbre, and loudness or dynamics. It can also portray the simultaneous sounding of two or more tones. Because of the importance of standard notation, all musicians should understand it.

The Staff and the Clef Sign

The staff with notes placed on it is probably the easiest and most straightforward part of reading music because it is just a graph of pitch against time, with the pitch being represented on the vertical axis, up and down, and time being represented on the horizontal axis from left to right. The staff is an arrangement of five lines and four spaces on which notes are placed. Vertical lines that touch all five staff lines are called *bar lines*. These bar lines create *measures*, which represent rhythmic groups of beats. A double bar marks the end of a section of music.

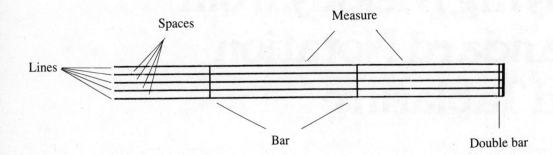

On the staff is another symbol, the *clef*, which assigns a letter name to one of the lines or spaces and thereby provides names for the other lines and spaces. The clef most widely used today is the *G* or *treble clef*; it is the only one used for guitar notation. The *F* or *bass clef* is used extensively in piano music and many song books. The treble or G clef indicates that the second line from the bottom is G above middle C.

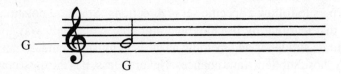

The bass or F clef indicates that the fourth line from the bottom is F below middle C.

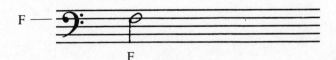

Once the clef has named one of the lines on the staff, the other lines and spaces are fixed. The rule is that each line and space of the staff is assigned a letter name from A through G, just like the white keys on the piano, with sharps and flats being added as needed. The names for the notes on the treble clef are probably familiar, with the spaces being F–A–C–E from the bottom up and the lines being E–G–B–D–F. Notes placed on each line and space of the *grand staff*, the juxtaposition of an F clef (bass clef) and a G clef using two staffs, are shown in Figure 5.1.

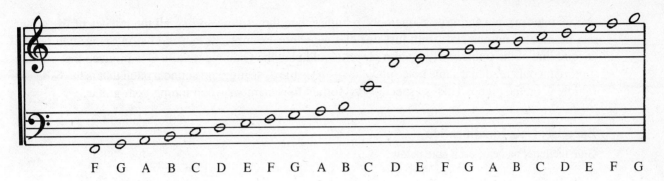

F G A B C D E F G A B C D E F G A B C D E F G

FIGURE 5.1 Notes on the Grand Staff

The treble clef marks the second line as a G, but which G? There are four different Gs on the guitar and many more on the piano, so a convention is required to indicate which one it is. In guitar notation the second line of the treble clef is read as the open G string on the guitar.

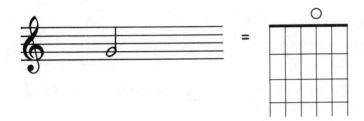

If you look at where each of the other open strings lie on the staff, you will find that a way to extend the staff both up and down is needed, since the nine pitches represented by the five lines and four spaces are hardly enough to encompass the pitch range of the guitar. *Ledger lines* are short lines added when necessary above and below the staff to increase the range of the staff. The letter names that correspond to the ledger lines are found just by continuing alphabetically up and down from the highest and the lowest notes on the staff (see Figure 5.2).

E F G A B C D E F G A B C D E F G A B C D E

FIGURE 5.2 Extending the Treble Staff with Ledger Lines

The open strings of the guitar and the twelfth fret E on the first (E) string are shown in Figure 5.3 as they are notated on the treble-clef staff.

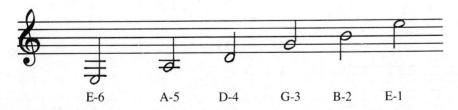

E-6   A-5   D-4   G-3   B-2   E-1

FIGURE 5.3 Open Strings of the Guitar

Guitar pitches are written one octave higher than they sound so that all the pitches of the guitar can be notated on one staff with just one clef sign. For example, the open G string is written on the second line of the treble staff; a piano player would play the G above middle C to produce that pitch; a guitarist would read that same note, play the open G (third) string, and sound a pitch that is the G below middle C on the piano. This is especially important to remember when tuning your guitar.

Exercise: Note Identification

Give the letter name of each note below:

Guitar Tablature

The idea of guitar tablature is not a new one. Several forms of tablature very similar to those used today were developed in the sixteenth century. Because a great deal of today's guitar music, especially folk, country, and blues music, is being written in tablature, it is important to understand how tablature works. Tablature is a good way of indicating where pitches are to be played on the fretboard; however, it is not a good way to indicate rhythmic intricacies. For this reason much guitar music is written in both standard notation and tablature.

Tablature consists of six lines, each representing one of the guitar's six strings, with the treble on top and the bass on the bottom, as shown below:

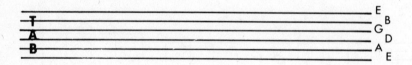

Rather than showing notes, as does standard notation, tablature shows the fret number and string on which the note is played. Shown below in both standard and tablature notation are the third fret G on the high E string, followed by the open G string and the third fret G on the bass E string:

Accidentals

The lines and spaces on the staff represent the white keys of the piano. Three special symbols, called *accidentals*, are used to indicate chromatic (that is, raised or lowered) pitches. The *sharp* (♯) and *flat* (♭) symbol placed just before a note respectively raise or lower the pitch of the note one half step:

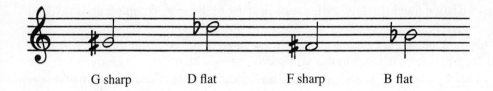

    G sharp   D flat   F sharp   B flat

A *natural* (♮) cancels the effect of a sharp or a flat. *The effect of all accidentals is canceled by a bar line*. This is a convention. Some examples are shown:

   C   C♯   C   C♯   B♭   B♭   B   C♯

Exercises: Note Identification with Accidentals

1. Give the letter names for the following notes:

2. Turn to "Ramblin' on My Mind" (p. 253), and name the notes in the song.

3. Write the following notes on the treble staff:

  G   C   D♭   E   A♯   A   B♭   F♯

READING GUITAR MUSIC

The following section is a systematic introduction to the reading of guitar music. Each string is covered individually so that the pitches on that string can be learned, and exercises and songs for practice are given in both standard notation and tablature. It is important to note that tablature alone does not effectively portray the elements of rhythm. Although familiarity with tablature is essential for those who work with the many folk and ethnic music instruction materials that rely heavily on it, every effort should be made to learn to read the guitar music in standard notation because of the more complete and universal nature of the system.

The words, chords, and melody are presented together in most of the songs in this book, but the songs appearing as melody-reading exercises in this section are given with only the melody notes. The first song, "Boil That Cabbage Down," is shown in full lead-sheet form to illustrate the differences between songs as they are sung and melody-playing arrangements, and because it is the only song in this chapter that does not occur elsewhere in the book. The other songs used as exercises can be located in the song index for access to their words and chords. The songs in this section may appear in a different key than elsewhere, and a capo may be needed for multiple-player arrangements where one player is playing the melody and another the chords. (See Chapter 12 for a discussion of transposition and capos.) The intent of this chapter is to focus the attention of the student on reading the melody from staff and playing the notes on the guitar.

Most students should use a flatpick for playing the melody arrangements in this chapter, although the right-hand thumb or fingers can also be used. Most of the easier examples can be played all in downstrokes (toward the floor). (The more detailed issues of upstrokes and pick direction will not enter the discussion at this point.) If the melody is to be played finger style, then the first and second fingers will be used and will alternate to accommodate the more rapid melodic passages.

The songs and exercises in this chapter should provide a workable introduction to the sight-reading of guitar music, with the skills increasing in difficulty and focusing on the playing of actual songs. Many practice hours are necessary to master the reading of music, and the student is encouraged to play the other songs in this book and to look elsewhere for additional practice material.

Notes on the E string

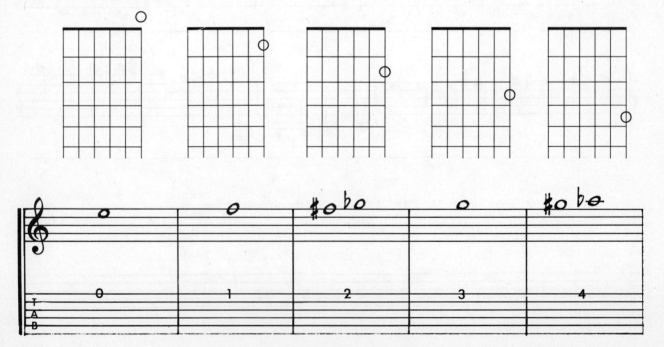

First-Position Pitches on the Guitar

The notes occupying the first four frets (first position) of the guitar neck are shown as they appear on the fretboard, on the staff, and in TAB. The placement of notes on the staff and fretboard must be memorized for each note of each string.

Notes on the B string

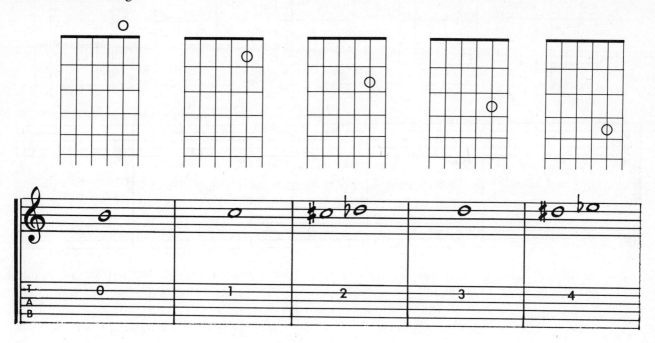

Notes on the G string

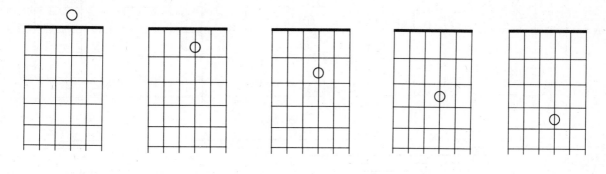

Notes on the D string

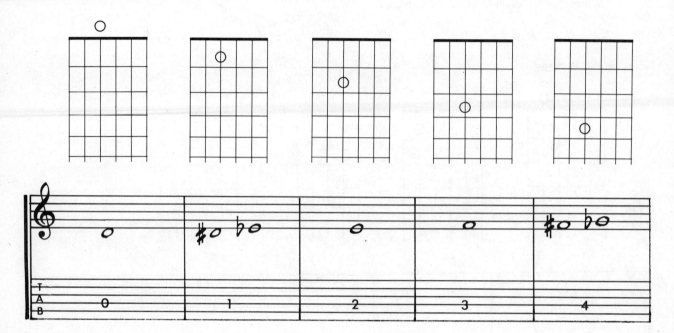

Notes on the A string

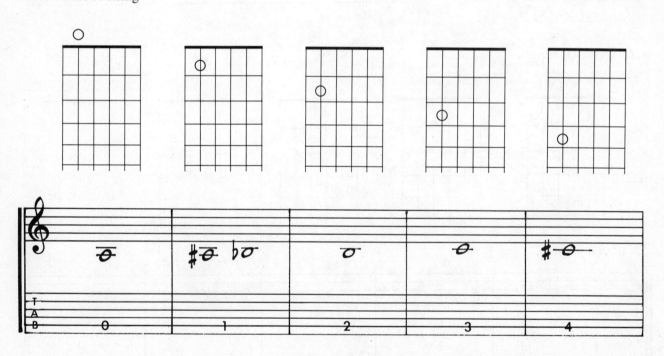

Notes on the bass E string

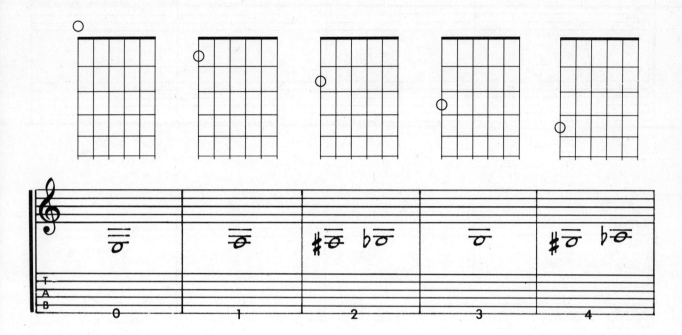

Exercises: Tablature

1. Write the tablature version of the following notes:

2. Write the notes on the staff for the following tablature indications:

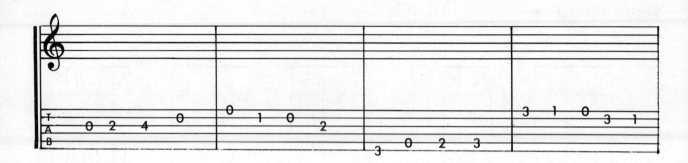

3. Play the notes in Exercises 1 and 2 on your guitar.

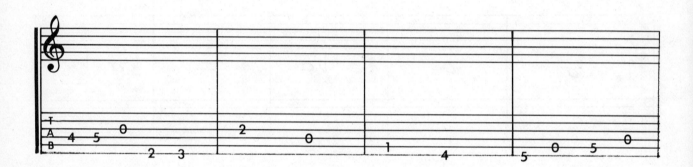

NOTATING RHYTHM

The notation system for rhythm is designed to portray rhythm's basic qualities. The *tempo* is the speed of the steady, underlying *beat* of the music, as represented by a metronome or the tapping of a foot. The *meter* refers to the grouping of beats into *measures*, which most commonly contain two, three, four, or six beats each. The first beat of each metric grouping is usually accented. The *melodic rhythm*, as the name implies, derives from characteristics of the melody much in the same way that poetry derives a "word rhythm" from the syllabic content of the text.

Tempo Notation

The notation of tempo can be either precise or suggestive. Metronome numbers are sometimes given on the top left-hand side of a piece of music to indicate the precise number of beats per minute (for example, ♩ = 100). In other pieces the tempo is suggested by words such as "very fast" or "moderately slow" appearing at the top of the page. The songs in this book use a metronome marking.

Notes and Rests

Each beat, or portion of a beat, is depicted by either a note or a rest. Notes on a staff represent specific pitches and durations of sounds, and rests indicate durations of silences. There are seven commonly used note and rest symbols which you should be able to recognize and name. These are pictured in Figure 5.4.

Name	Note	Rest
Whole	𝅝	𝄻
Half	𝅗𝅥	𝄼
Quarter	♩	𝄽
Eighth	♪	𝄾
Sixteenth	𝅘𝅥𝅯	𝄿
Dotted Half	𝅗𝅥.	𝄼:
Dotted Quarter	♩.	𝄽.

FIGURE 5.4 Note and Rest Names

The note (and rest) durational equivalencies given in Figure 5.5 are universally true: one whole note is always equal in duration to two half notes; one half note is always equal in duration to two quarter notes; and so on. A dot added to a note or to a rest increases the note's (or rest's) duration one-half of its normal value. Therefore, a dotted half note is equal in duration to three quarter notes.

FIGURE 5.5 Note Durational Equivalencies

Beams and *flags* attached to note stems are equivalent ways to indicate eighth and sixteenth notes. Two eighth notes notated with a beam are the same as two eighth notes written with flags.

The absolute duration of any given note or rest depends on the tempo of the piece and on the note value indicated in the lower part of the time signature. For example, a quarter note in one song could actually be longer than a half note in another song. What really matters—and what notation shows—is the relative duration of notes and rests within a song.

Exercise: Note and Rest Durational Equivalencies

Write one note or rest which shows the durational equivalency of the symbols added together.

Meter

Meter is created by accenting the first of regularly recurring groups of beats. Often-heard meters group two, three, four, or six beats per measure. A measure is the distance between two bar lines. The basic symbol in meter notation is the *time signature*. This signature consists of two numbers written at the beginning of the first staff.

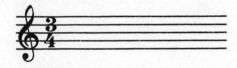

The top number represents the number of beats in each measure. The bottom number indicates the kind of note that receives one beat. Therefore, one measure of ¾ time always contains three beats, as specified by the upper number, and a quarter note receives one beat.

Compare the two measures of $\frac{3}{4}$ time, shown above, with the two measures of $\frac{4}{4}$ time, below.

Likewise, a meter of $\frac{6}{8}$ contains six beats per measure with an eighth note receiving one beat.

Exercises: Meter

1. Locate the following songs in this book, and identify the number of beats per measure and the note value that receives one beat for each song.

"Amazing Grace" (p. 78)

"Deep in the Heart of Texas" (p. 139)

"The Gambler" (p. 40)

"Michael Row the Boat Ashore" (p. 211)

"Row, Row, Row Your Boat" (p. 30)

"Sloop John B." (p. 49)

"Stewball" (p. 43)

Counting Melodic Rhythm Notation

In reading the rhythmic notation of a song's melody, you must begin each note at the precise moment indicated by its duration. Notes can begin on the beat or in between the beats. This rhythmic structure of the melody can be perceived more easily at first if the melodic rhythm is juxtaposed against the beat. In the following examples, the beat is represented by the notes with stems pointing down, and the melodic rhythm is represented by notes with stems pointing up:

Several rhythmic counting systems have been devised to assist in the interpretation of melodic rhythm. This book employs spoken syllables, which represent the different rhythmic durations of melodic tones. Each beat is spoken as a number (1,   2,   3,   4 .   .   .); the first beat division is called "and" and is notated with a plus sign (+):

For note durations that include more than one beat, a dash symbol is used:

A dotted half note is counted as shown below:

A tie combines the note durations of two notes of the same pitch so that they appear on the page as two notes but are only sounded once:

A tie can also combine portions of beats, although the same rhythm may appear written without the ties:

In the example below a dotted quarter note is counted so that the impulse of the beat is felt before the pronunciation of the word "and":

When the eighth note precedes the dotted quarter note, the dotted quarter note is sounded on the "and" and held through the next beat:

Rests can be counted in the same manner as notes and may be underlined to indicate their silence:

Many songs begin with an incomplete measure; these songs must end with an incomplete measure, the combination equaling one complete measure. The initial incomplete measure has a note or notes called an anacrusis or pickup. These notes are counted as though they are the last note(s) in a full measure:

Exercises: Counting Melodic Rhythm

1. Complete the following measures with just one note:

2. Complete the following measures with just one rest:

3. Insert the bar lines in the following:

4. Give the appropriate meter signatures for the following:

5. Indicate the counting syllables for the following melodic rhythms:

ORGANIZATIONAL SYMBOLS

In order to indicate repetition of certain sections of music and to fit the music on a smaller number of pages, special organizational symbols are used:

‖: :‖ *Repeat signs*: repeat once whatever is contained between the symbols.

D.C. *Da capo*: repeat from the beginning.

D.S. *Dal segno*: repeat from the 𝄋 sign.

al fine Usually accompanies D.S. or D.C. to indicate that the piece is to end at the occurrence of the printed word *Fine*.

⊕ *Coda*: a special section that is used to end a piece. Its beginning is marked with the symbol, and you will be referred to "coda" when necessary.

⌐1. ⌐2. Used to indicate different endings. Often used with repeat signs to show that something slightly different is done the second time or to indicate endings for different verses.

Fine End of the piece.

‖ *Double bar*: indicates the end of a piece or a major structural division.

⁒ Repeat the measure before this one.

Exercise: Notational Symbols

Write out the entire chord progression for the following song as it would appear if repeat signs and other organizational symbols had not been used.

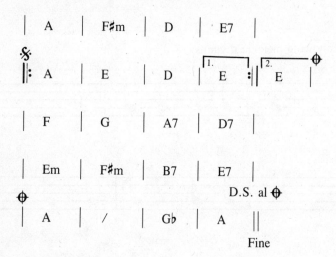

Melody-Playing Arrangements

The following arrangements are intended to provide practice in reading guitar melodies. Each song contains certain elements of pitch or rhythm reading that differ from the others, and the first pieces emphasize treble strings and following pieces emphasize bass strings. You may find that some songs or skills are easier to master than others, but on the whole the progression of skills to be learned and the difficulty of the songs should be manageable.

All the melody notes in the following song "Boil That Cabbage Down" occur on the first two strings of the guitar. The first two staffs contain the chorus and the last two a verse. Watch out for the rests in measures 4, 8, 12, and 16.

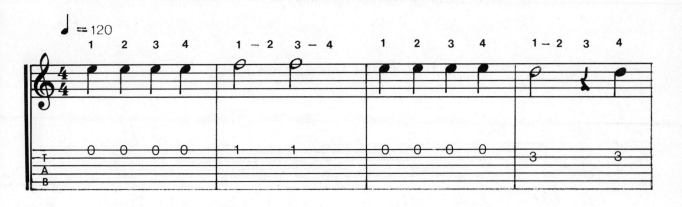

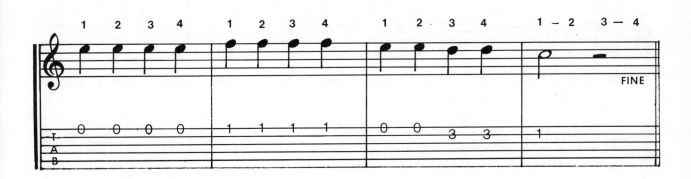

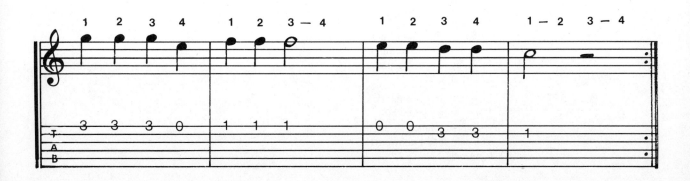

The lead sheet for "Boil That Cabbage Down" is included here not only to give you the words and chords to the song, but to provide you with comparison between the melody as it is played and as it is sung. Notice how the different words in the verses create different word rhythms in the melody. Also notice that the melody in the lead sheet is written an octave lower than the melody version.

Boil That Cabbage Down

2. I eat my cabbage cold, boys,
   And I like it steamin' hot,
   Served up ev'ry mornin'
   In Pappy's great big pot.
   (Chorus)

3. I play my four-string fiddle,
   With my two-string bow,
   I scrape out tunes by the light of the moon,
   The only tune I know (is) . . .
   (Chorus)

Play "London Bridge" at a slow tempo until you have complete control over the melody. Then gradually increase the tempo until you feel only two beats per measure (on the first and third beats) rather than four beats per measure.

London Bridge

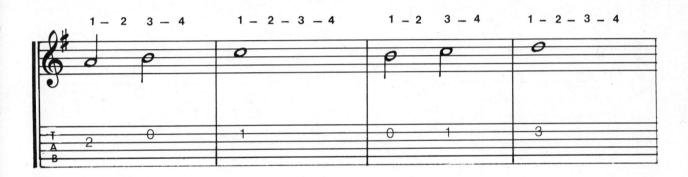

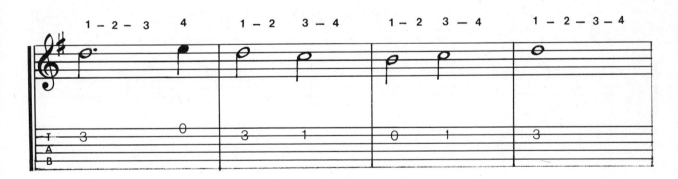

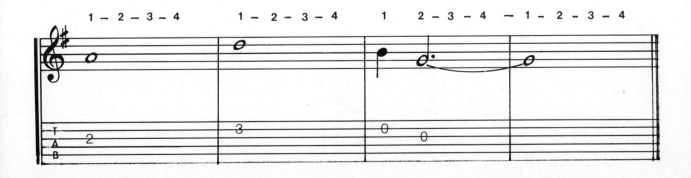

"Go Tell Aunt Rhody" is presented here in two forms, first with all the notes played on the B string and then with the notes played on both the B and E strings. The first is given as an example of awkward fingering; it is not a sensible way to arrange or play the tune. The fingerings in all other tunes in this chapter have been designed properly. Count out the beats carefully, and assign the proper time value to the half notes.

Go Tell Aunt Rhody
(Version 1)

Watch for the dotted half note in measure 11 of "Freight Train." This accompaniment is often played in a fingerpicking style, while the melody notes are played by various players with different nuances in timing. Try performing this melody with an accompanying guitar that is playing a strummed or Travis-style fingerpicking rhythm.

Freight Train

"Gold Watch and Chain" can be played with the strummed accompaniment for the song given in Chapter 4. Notice that all the notes lie on open strings or on the second and fourth frets, and be sure to watch for the sharped notes. The sharps have all been inserted at the beginning of each staff, as is usually the custom, rather than written before every appropriate note. All the F, C, G, and D notes written on the staff are to be read as F♯, C♯, G♯, and D♯, respectively. (Chapter 11 contains an explanation of key signatures.) This song begins with an anacrusis, or two pickup notes, on the third and fourth beats of the first incomplete measure. Balance is provided in that the last measure of the song also contains only two beats.

Gold Watch and Chain

"Old Joe Clark" introduces the G string for two of the melody notes. Most of the rhythm is quarter notes and half notes, although there are dotted quarter notes in the chorus in measures 9, 11, and 13.

Old Joe Clark

"Hush, Little Baby" is a lullaby that introduces the open D string. It should be easy to play. Maintain an evenness of timbre between open and fretted strings.

Hush, Little Baby

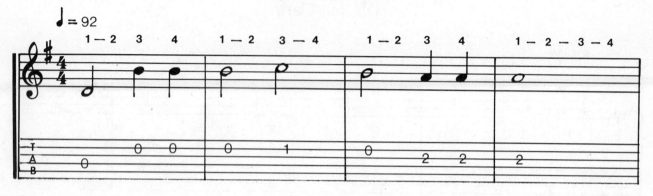

Note that although the key signature has an F♯ in it, there are no F notes in this song. Even though a song is based on a particular scale—in this case the G-major scale—all the tones of the scale do not necessarily have to be used in the melody.

Frère Jacques

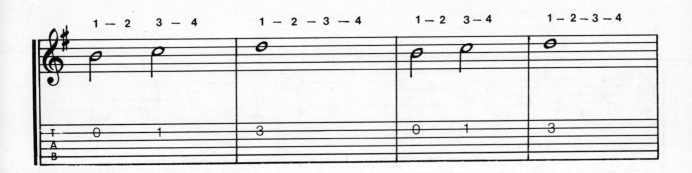

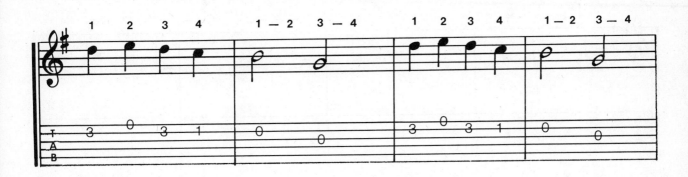

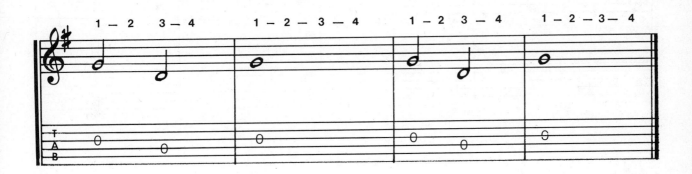

Try reading the melody lines of "Down in the Valley" in Chapter 3 and "Five Hundred Miles" in Chapter 6.

"Red River Valley" introduces the A string. It is a slow-moving song and should not be difficult to count properly. Be careful with the ties, and remember to extend the duration of the first note in the tie to include the duration of the note to which it is tied.

Red River Valley

Try playing "Amazing Grace," "Home on the Range," and "Drunken Sailor," all of which are found in Chapter 4. They also feature melody notes on the A string.

"Tom Dooley" is included here because it lies entirely on the D and A strings and because it is interesting rhythmically. Count the beats carefully. Notice how placing a half note on the second beat in the first measure causes an accent. This accented note creates a *syncopation* because it displaces the usual accent on beat 1 to beat 2 of the measure.

Tom Dooley

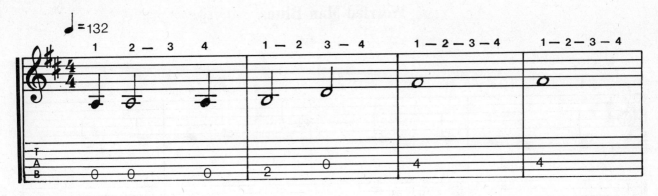

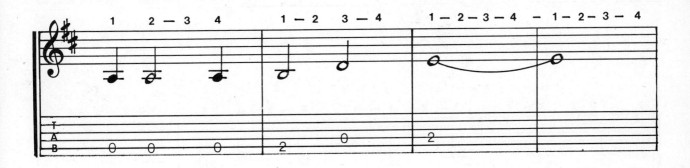

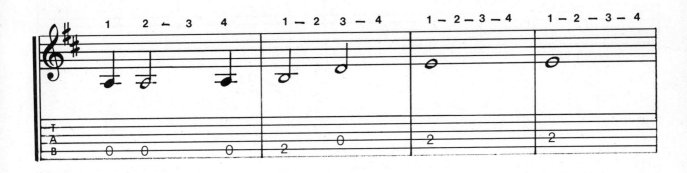

After you learn to play this melody you might look at the Carter-style arrangement of the "Worried Man Blues" that is given in Chapter 8. The melody played on the bass strings of the guitar is a distinctive sound of the Carter Family style.

Worried Man Blues

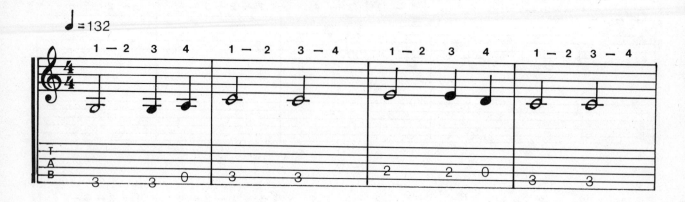

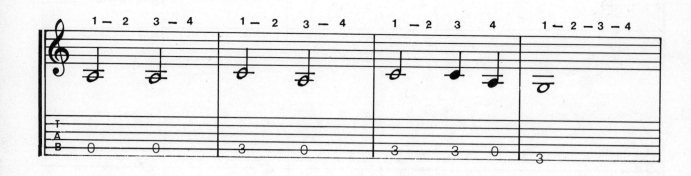

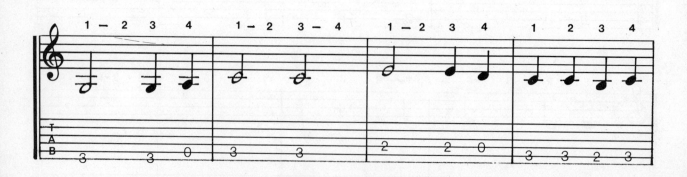

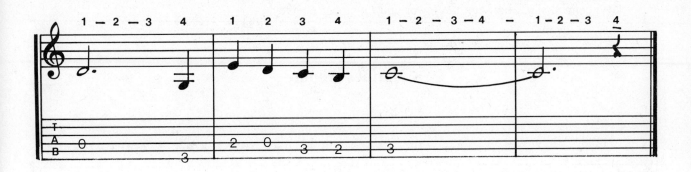

"Michael Row the Boat Ashore" lies entirely on the A and bass E strings. This song can be played along with the accompaniment given in Chapter 2, since they are both in the key of E. Be sure to play the sharped notes in the melody.

Michael Row the Boat Ashore

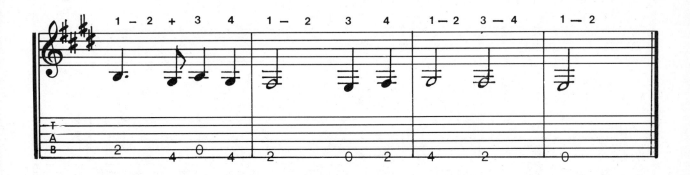

Play the melody notes in "Wayfaring Stranger" in Chapter 9. It features a low G note on the bass E string.

"Marines' Hymn" will teach you to move over all six strings of the guitar. The melody in this arrangement shifts between the lower and the upper octaves.

Marines' Hymn

Alternate Interpretations of Time Signatures

Sometimes when a song is notated in $\frac{4}{4}$ time, it will be performed at a fast tempo that makes it seem more natural to feel only two pulses in each measure rather than four. Astute arrangers may use $\frac{2}{2}$ as the meter signature for such songs. However, it is most often up to the performer to decide whether to feel four or two beats per measure. In the instance in which two beats are felt, the performer would place beats only on the first and third quarter notes in $\frac{4}{4}$ time. See "This Land Is Your Land" on page 77 for an example.

The $\frac{6}{8}$ time signature presents a similar interpretative problem. Should the piece be played with six beats in each measure, each eighth note receiving one beat, or should it be played with two beats in each measure, an accent on the first and fourth eighth notes? The performer must decide, and the type of strum or fingerpick used should reflect this decision. An example of this is "Row, Row, Row Your Boat" on page 30.

Many songs are notated in $\frac{3}{4}$ time but may move too fast to be performed with three beats per measure. These songs, like "Irene Goodnight" on page 70, are often played with one pulse per measure instead of the three suggested by the time signature.

The problem of how to interpret the beat from notated music can arise in yet another way. While some styles are notated in $\frac{4}{4}$ time,

they actually call for strums or fingerpicking that are more accurately represented as triplets (three equal divisions per beat):

The words *shuffle*, *blues*, and *swing* normally require you to play uneven beat divisions in $\frac{4}{4}$ meter.

Exercises: Alternative Interpretations of Meter Signatures

1. Play the following songs, and decide if you *feel* the beat and meter the way it is given in the meter signature or if an alternative interpretation is required.

"Down in the Valley" (p. 26)

"John Hardy" (p. 52)

"Oh, Susanna" (p. 309)

"Red River Valley" (p. 38)

"Shady Grove" (p. 74)

"Streets of Laredo" (p. 307)

2. Can you describe another way to notate those songs in Exercise 1 that seemed to require an alternative interpretation?

3. Did the tempo at which the songs in Exercise 1 were played affect your decision?

All the songs in this book have been written in keys that are comfortable for the guitar, and most of them make good sight-reading exercises. Every song has its own rhythmic feel and melodic range. Practicing each song will offer you a way to develop and test your reading skills. Good reading ability comes only through long and steady practice but is an invaluable aid in the learning and communicating of music of all kinds. Because this book is intended for the beginning guitar player, the arrangements presented for the teaching of melody-playing skills in this chapter have been restricted to the first position (first four frets) of the guitar neck. Chapter 10 provides some insight into how scales and melodies are fingered in the higher positions of the neck, although sight-reading in that style is much more difficult and is beyond the scope of this text.

chapter 6
Fingerpicking Accompaniments

In normal usage, the word *fingerpicking* has a more specific meaning than simply playing the guitar with the fingers. Classical guitarists are not generally referred to as "fingerpickers" even though their techniques include highly developed right-hand skills that utilize the fingers. The American fingerpicking style is characterized by a steady, rhythmic bass line provided by the thumb that is offset by either rolling patterns or syncopated melody lines played by the rest of the fingers. It is used both as an accompaniment style to songs and as a solo instrumental style, and found its way into the native music of the United States through the early blues players, who developed the sound to a sophisticated degree in the early part of this century. In this chapter, the word *fingerpicking* is used to describe any of several ways to provide accompaniment to songs by playing repeating patterns over chord changes.

In the 1930s and 1940s the fingerpicking, or finger-style, guitar found its way to a larger audience through the playing of Sam McGee and Merle Travis, popular country performers who learned from black guitarists. The style of playing a syncopated melody against a steady bass is now referred to as *Travis picking*, even when it involves only pattern playing. What most folk guitarists call Travis picking is more reminiscent of the sound of Mississippi John Hurt or Elizabeth Cotten, since Travis himself usually played an electric guitar and employed a trademark bass-string muting technique not conventional in Travis picking. The widespread adoption of the style in the 1960s seems to be much more a result of the influence of Hurt, Cotten, and to some extent Reverend Gary Davis, who were more visible to the new urban guitar players. Modern fingerpickers are adapting the style to everything from hymns to ragtime piano pieces, Indian ragas, and old Broadway hits, and developing the techniques to great levels of sophistication.

Steel-string fingerpickers often use a thumbpick and sometimes metal or plastic fingerpicks to pluck the strings since the steel strings and the occasionally forceful style are rough on fingernails (see the photographs in Chapter 1). An increasingly popular hybrid style, mostly associated with electric guitarists, involves holding a flatpick between the thumb and first finger and using the remaining fingers in conjunction with the flatpick to play a fingerpicking style in which the pick acts as the thumb.

PLUCKING CHORDS

A good way to develop right-hand position and to accompany very fast songs that need a bouncy rhythm is to pluck chords with the thumb and three fingers simultaneously or to use the thumb alternately with the fingers much in the manner of alternating-bass chord strumming (discussed in the previous chapter). With a bare-finger, right-hand technique that does not require fingerpicks, plucking chords can be combined with brushing chords with the backs of the fingers to create interesting rhythms. "Camptown Races" normally moves fast, has an almost polkalike flavor, and works very well with the alternating bass played by the thumb and the chords plucked with the fingers.

Song Performance Guide

CHORDS IN SONG: D A7 G

SINGING PITCH:

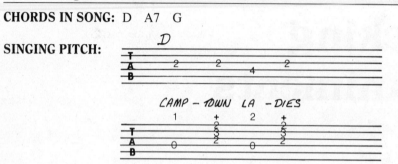

Camptown Races

Stephen Foster

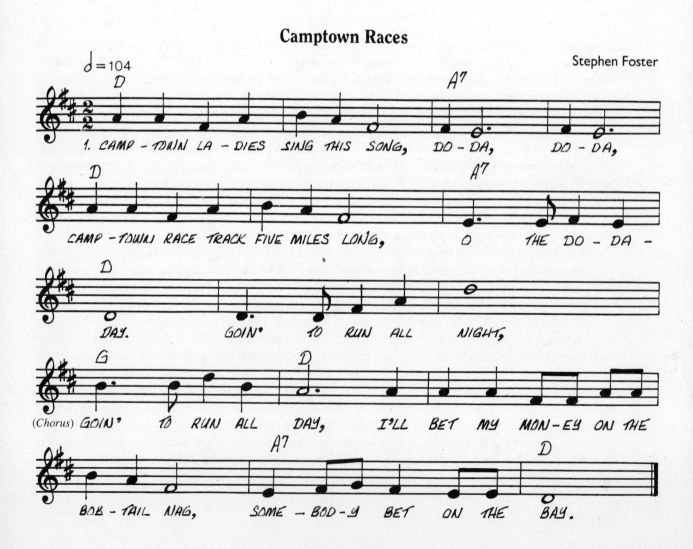

2. See those horses 'round the bend, do-da, do-da,
   Guess that race will never end, O the do-da-day.
   (Chorus)

3. The long-tail filly with the big black horse, do-da, do-da,
   They flew the track and both cut across, O the do-da-day.
   (Chorus)

4. Blind horse sticking in a big mud hole, do-da, do-da,
   Couldn't touch bottom with a ten-foot pole, O the do-da-day.
   (Chorus)

5. See them fly on a ten-mile heat, do-da, do-da,
   Around the track and then repeat, O the do-da-day.
   (Chorus)

6. I win my money on the bobtail nag, do-da, do-da,
   I keep my money in an old tote bag, O the do-da-day.
   (Chorus)

Song Performance Guide

CHORDS IN SONG: D   A7

SINGING PITCH:

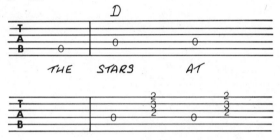

Deep in the Heart of Texas

Don Swander and
June Hershey

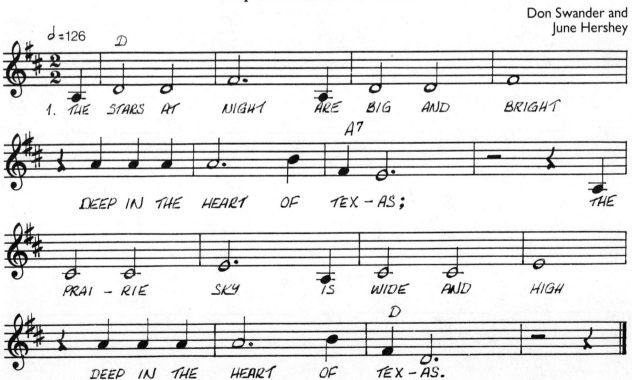

2. The <u>sage</u> in <u>bloom</u> is <u>like</u> per<u>fume</u>, ___ deep in the <u>heart</u> of Texas; ___
   Re<u>minds</u> me <u>of</u> the <u>one</u> I <u>love</u>, ___ deep in the <u>heart</u> of Texas.

3. The <u>coyotes</u> <u>wail</u> along the <u>trail</u>, ___ deep in the <u>heart</u> of Texas; ___
   The <u>rabbits</u> <u>rush</u> around the <u>brush</u>, ___ deep in the <u>heart</u> of Texas.

4. The <u>cowboys</u> <u>cry</u> ki-<u>yip</u>-ee-yi, ___ deep in the <u>heart</u> of Texas; ___
   The <u>doggies</u> <u>bawl</u> and bawl and <u>bawl</u>, ___ deep in the <u>heart</u> of Texas. ___

"Hava Nagila" is a favorite Israeli dance tune that is sometimes played incredibly fast. Plucking the chords gives it a good, crisp rhythm. The chords and the alternating bass lines are simple enough for the song to be played at a quick tempo, even for practice.

Song Performance Guide

CHORDS IN SONG: E   Am   Dm6

SINGING PITCH:

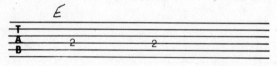

Hava Nagila

Israeli Folk Song

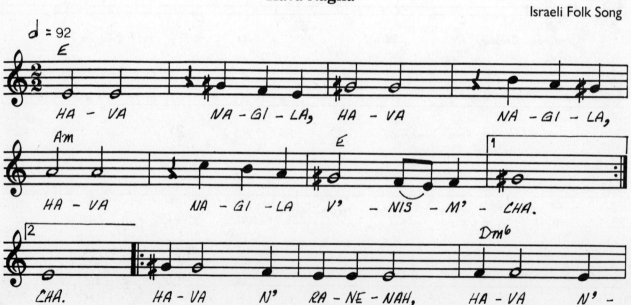

Translation
Let us rejoice and be happy.
Let us sing and be happy.
Stir yourselves, brethren, with a happy heart.

Pronunciation Guide
v' = vay, cha = ha, m' = muh, n' = nuh, ra = ra, na = nah, uru = ŏo -rŏo, achim = áh-hēem, b'lev = bē-lāv,
sameyach = säw-mā-ach.

ARPEGGIO FINGERPICKING
Learning to Fingerpick Arpeggio Patterns

A great deal of the fundamental nature of fingerpicking is derived from the driving rhythm provided by the constant bass notes played by the thumb. Much of the effort involved in learning to fingerpick is merely mastering the necessary motor skills to coordinate the fingers and the thumb. The rhythmic patterns must be played and practiced many times until the necessary smoothness is obtained. It seems that practicing a right-hand pattern until it requires a minimum of active concentration before increasing its complexity is the best way to learn, rather than starting with complex arrangements that combine several skills. For example, it is very hard to combine a fingerpicking pattern with an alternating-bass part unless you have first mastered fingerpicking without the alternating bass. The mind seems capable of concentrating on only one thing at a time, and in order for the fingerpicking to retain its essential elements of smoothness, evenness, and rhythm, the learning process must be set up this way. *What takes up a few pages in this text will actually require many weeks of hard practice that cannot be hurried.* It is worth noting, though, that fingerpicking skills are probably the most popular attained by students, who find that the sounds add a pleasant dimension to their playing. Many right-hand patterns have a habit of appearing more complex than they really are, a fact that seems to contribute greatly to their popularity.

Structurally, the simplest kinds of fingerpicking are the arpeggios, in which the left hand holds a chord, and the right hand plays a sequence of notes in the chord. Arpeggio patterns provide good training for the fingers and work very well as accompaniments to many types of songs, although they do not generate the sound associated with Travis picking. Figure 6.1 illustrates common arpeggio patterns.

Arpeggios with Root and Alternating Bass

The concepts of root bass and alternating bass that were encountered in the previous chapter lend themselves very well to arpeggio fingerpicking. This technique is accomplished by leaving the fingers in

FIGURE 6.1 Arpeggio Fingerpicking Patterns

position over the first three strings and playing the appropriate bass notes with the thumb. Even a simple, repeated arpeggio pattern played over chords with the correct bass notes will sound very complete and very musical. It takes a great deal of practice to develop the right-hand accuracy necessary to find the various bass notes that go with the chords, and maintaining a good right-hand position can be very helpful. Try some of the examples given in Figure 6.2 before playing the songs in this section.

FIGURE 6.2 Alternating-Bass Arpeggio Fingerpicking Patterns

Fingerpicking Song Accompaniments

The songs in this section are good starting examples of fingerpicking but by no means provide sufficient practice for mastery of the techniques. It is essential to develop fingerpicking to the point where the chords can be changed without disturbing the flow of the pattern. It is also important to practice slowly and carefully and to increase the tempo gradually. Arpeggio picking is especially suited to slow, melodious songs, and for further practice there are a number of appropriate songs in other chapters in this book that can be played in the arpeggio style. It may take several weeks to develop finger dexterity, even with constant practice. "Hush, Little Baby" has only two chords. It is a perfect place to start learning fingerpicking technique. Keep the hand relaxed, and count the beats carefully.

Song Performance Guide

CHORDS IN SONG: G   D7

SINGING PITCH:

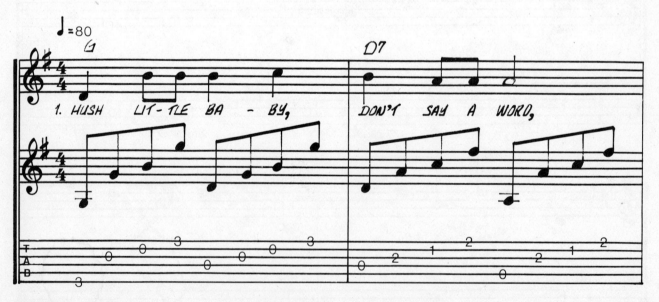

Hush, Little Baby*

*See page 36 for the remaining verses.

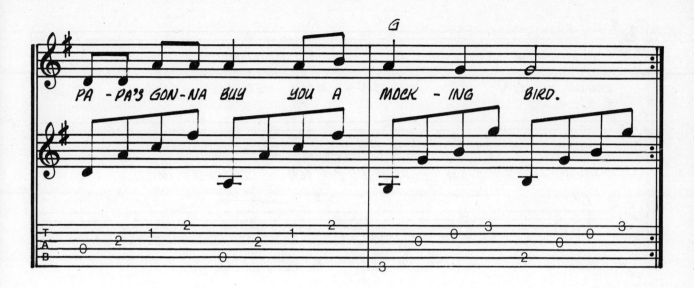

"Silent Night," a song performed in slow waltz time, lends itself very well to fingerpicked arpeggios. In fact, the song was originally written for guitar.

Song Performance Guide

CHORDS IN SONG: A   E7   D

SINGING PITCH:

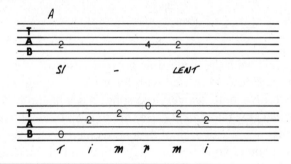

Silent Night

Joseph Mohr and
Franz Gruber

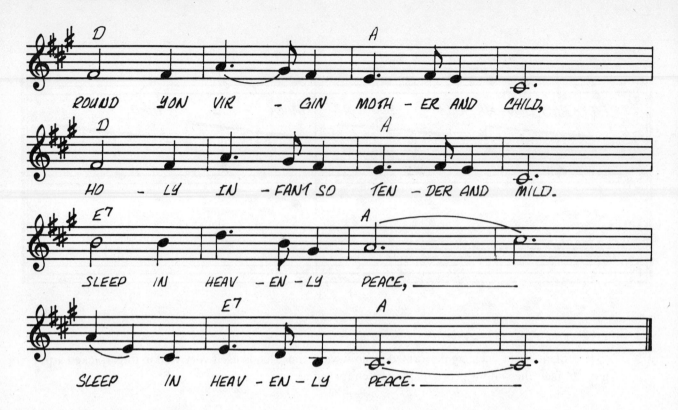

ROUND YON VIR - GIN MOTH - ER AND CHILD,

HO - LY IN - FANT SO TEN - DER AND MILD.

SLEEP IN HEAV - EN - LY PEACE, _____

SLEEP IN HEAV - EN - LY PEACE. _____

2. Silent night, holy night, shepherds quake at the sight,
Glories stream from heaven afar,
Heavenly hosts sing "Alleluia."
Christ, the Savior is born, Christ, the Savior is born. __

3. Silent night, holy night, Son of God, love's pure light,
Radiant beams from Thy holy face,
With the dawn of redeeming grace,
Jesus, Lord at Thy birth, Jesus, Lord at Thy birth. __

Try playing "Down in the Valley" with the waltz-time arpeggio used in "Silent Night." "Streets of Laredo" and "On Top of Old Smoky" also work well with fingerpicked arpeggios.

"Five Hundred Miles," a modern version of a very old song, has a haunting melody and moves slowly enough so that you can practice arpeggio picking. Be sure to keep track of the bass notes and to play the root bass and alternating bass notes with each of the chord changes. It takes some practice but is worth the effort. Other songs that sound good with fingerpicking pattern include "Greensleeves," "Amazing Grace," "Michael Row the Boat Ashore," "Tom Dooley," and "Red River Valley."

Song Performance Guide

CHORDS IN SONG: G Em Am C D7

SINGING PITCH:

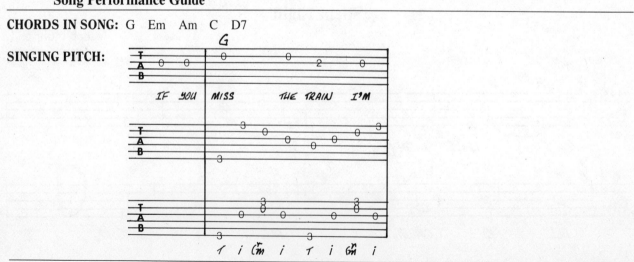

Five Hundred Miles

Hedy West

1. IF YOU MISS THE TRAIN I'M ON, YOU WILL KNOW THAT I AM GONE, YOU CAN HEAR THE WHIS-TLE BLOW A HUN-DRED MILES, A HUN-DRED MILES, A HUN-DRED MILES, A HUN-DRED MILES, A HUN-DRED MILES, YOU CAN HEAR THE WHIS-TLE BLOW A HUN-DRED MILES.

2. Lord I'm <u>one</u>, Lord I'm <u>two</u>, Lord I'm <u>three</u>, Lord I'm <u>four</u>
   Lord I'm <u>five</u> hundred <u>miles</u> away from <u>home</u>. ___
   Away from <u>home</u>, away from <u>home</u>, away from <u>home</u>, away from <u>home</u>,
   Lord I'm <u>five</u> hundred <u>miles</u> away from <u>home</u>. ___

3. Not a <u>shirt</u> on my <u>back</u>, Not a <u>penny</u> to my <u>name</u>,
   Lord I <u>can't</u> go back <u>home</u> this <u>away</u>. ___
   This a<u>way</u>, this a<u>way</u>, this a<u>way</u>, this a<u>way</u>,
   Lord I <u>can't</u> go back <u>home</u> this <u>away</u>. ___

THE PINCH

A *pinch* is used in a fingerpicking pattern for emphasis and to add interest to patterns that by themselves can become overly repetitive. The pinch consists of plucking two strings simultaneously with the thumb and a finger. Two common pinch patterns are given below. Try these pinch patterns on "Five Hundred Miles."

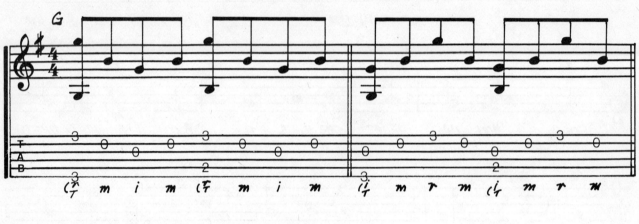

TRAVIS PICKING

Travis picking is similar to arpeggio picking in that the fingers of the right hand produce rhythmic patterns while the fingers of the left hand form a chord. Travis picking is the name ascribed to the familiar style of playing fingerpicked melodies against a steady bass line. The unique sound of the Travis style is due to the steady four-beat bass being played against the syncopation of the melody notes in such a way that the melody notes appear directly on the beat at some points and off the beat elsewhere, which is what gives the style its rhythmic "swing." This swing can be incorporated into an effective fingerpicking pattern that is not difficult to play. In this rhythmic pattern, groups of four steady bass notes played by the thumb are juxtaposed against the fingers pinching and plucking the higher strings. Several popular versions of this style of pattern picking are shown in Figure 6.3.

Try some of these Travis fingerpicking patterns while singing "Worried Man Blues." Work on each pattern until you feel comfortable with it and no longer have to concentrate to produce it. To test your control over a fingerpicking pattern, try to carry on a conversation while playing the pattern without dropping any notes. Also, try to sing the words and melody of the song without thinking about the finger movements.

FIGURE 6.3 Travis Fingerpicking Patterns

Song Performance Guide

CHORDS IN SONG: D G A7

SINGING PITCH:

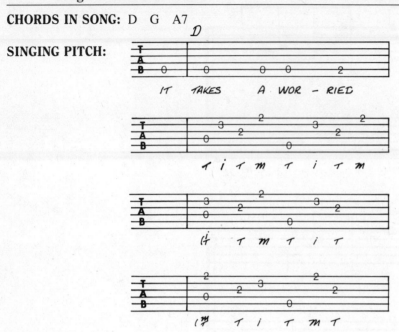

Worried Man Blues

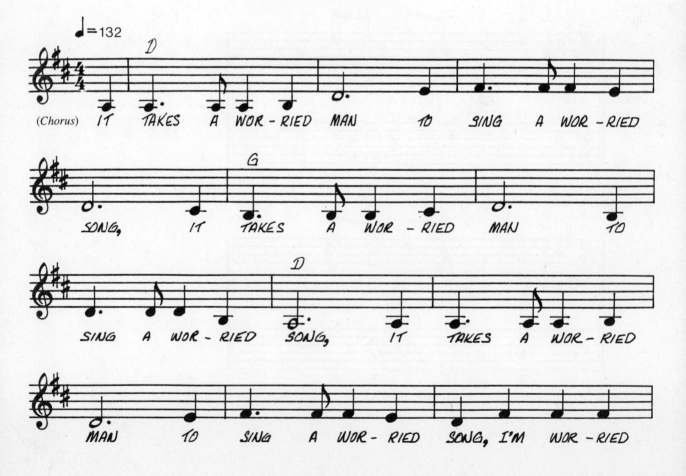

(Chorus) IT TAKES A WOR-RIED MAN TO SING A WOR-RIED

SONG, IT TAKES A WOR-RIED MAN TO

SING A WOR-RIED SONG, IT TAKES A WOR-RIED

MAN TO SING A WOR-RIED SONG, I'M WOR-RIED

NOW BUT I WON'T BE WOR - RIED LONG. _____

1. I <u>went</u> across the <u>river</u>, and I <u>lay</u> down to <u>sleep</u>, (3 times)
When I <u>awoke</u>, there were <u>shackles</u> on my <u>feet</u>. __
(*Chorus*)

2. <u>Twenty</u>-nine links of <u>chain</u>, <u>around</u> my <u>leg</u>, (3 times)
And on each <u>link</u>, an <u>initial</u> of my <u>name</u>. __
(*Chorus*)

3. I <u>asked</u> that <u>judge</u>, now <u>what</u> might be my <u>fine</u>? (3 times)
Twenty-one <u>years</u>, but I <u>still</u> got ninety-<u>nine</u>. __
(*Chorus*)

4. The <u>train</u> arrived, eighteen coaches <u>long</u>, (3 times)
The <u>girl</u> I <u>love</u>, is <u>on</u> that train and <u>gone</u>. __
(*Chorus*)

5. I <u>look</u> down the <u>track</u>, as <u>far</u> as I could <u>see</u>, (3 times)
Little bitty <u>hand</u>, was <u>wavin'</u> after <u>me</u>. __
(*Chorus*)

6. If <u>anyone</u> should ask <u>you</u>, who <u>wrote</u> this here <u>song</u>, (3 times)
Tell him 'twas <u>I</u>, and I <u>sing</u> it all day <u>long</u>. __
(*Chorus*)

"Wildwood Flower" has a flowing melody which complements the syncopated character of the Travis picking patterns. After you learn the song and can accompany it without faltering over either the left-hand chords or the right-hand strumming or fingerpicking, turn to the Carter-style instrumental solo in chapter 8 which is based on this melody.

Song Performance Guide

CHORDS IN SONG: G D7 C

SINGING PITCH:

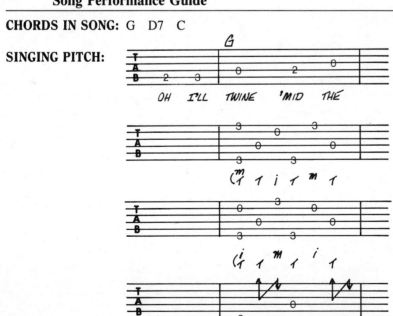

OH I'LL TWINE 'MID THE

Wildwood Flower

Maud Irving and
J. D. Webster

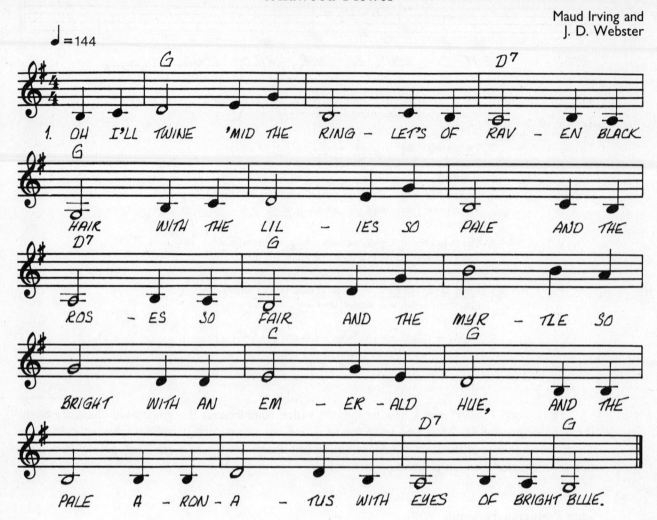

$\quad \bullet = 144$

G

D⁷

1. OH I'LL TWINE 'MID THE RING — LET'S OF RAV — EN BLACK

G

HAIR WITH THE LIL — IES SO PALE AND THE

D⁷   G

ROS — ES SO FAIR AND THE MYR — TLE SO

C   G

BRIGHT WITH AN EM — ER-ALD HUE, AND THE

D⁷   G

PALE A - RON - A — TUS WITH EYES OF BRIGHT BLUE.

2. I will <u>sing</u> and I'll <u>dance</u>, and my <u>laugh</u> shall be <u>gay</u>
I will <u>cease</u> this wild <u>weeping</u>, drive <u>sorrow</u> <u>away</u>.
Though my <u>heart</u> now is <u>breaking</u>, he <u>never</u> shall <u>know</u>
That his <u>name</u> made me <u>tremble</u>, my <u>pale</u> cheeks to <u>glow</u>.

3. I will <u>think</u> of him <u>never</u>, I'll <u>be</u> wildly <u>gay</u>
I will <u>charm</u> every <u>heart</u> and the <u>crowd</u> I will <u>sway</u>.
I'll <u>live</u> yet to <u>see</u> him <u>regret</u> the dark <u>hour</u>
When he <u>won</u>, then neglected the <u>frail</u> wildwood <u>flower</u>.

4. He <u>told</u> me he <u>loved</u> me and <u>promised</u> to <u>love</u>
Through <u>ill</u> and mis<u>for</u>tune all <u>others</u> <u>above</u>.
Another has <u>won</u> him, ah <u>misery</u> to <u>tell</u>
He <u>left</u> me in <u>silence</u>, no <u>word</u> of <u>farewell</u>.

5. He <u>taught</u> me to <u>love</u> him, he <u>called</u> me his <u>flower</u>
That <u>blossomed</u> for <u>him</u> all the <u>brighter</u> each <u>hour</u>.
But I <u>woke</u> from my <u>dreaming</u>, my idol was <u>clay</u>
My <u>visions</u> of <u>love</u> have all <u>faded</u> <u>away</u>.

FOLK FINGERPICK

The folk-style fingerpicking pattern incorporates the rhythm of the calypso strum given in Chapter 4 and some of the basic movements of Travis picking given in this chapter. These two ideas are melded into a rhythmically sophisticated sound that works well with modern folk-oriented songs in $\frac{4}{4}$ meter. The notation and tablature for the folk fingerpick are given below.

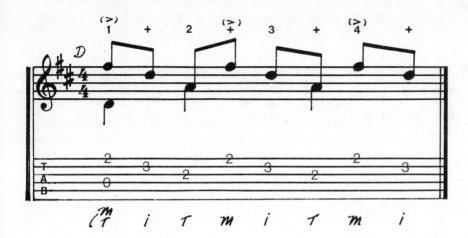

The second finger (m) creates a subtle accent pattern similar to the calypso strum,

which is felt within the context of $\frac{4}{4}$.

The example given is "Rock-a My Soul," but this fingerpicking pattern can also be used on such songs as "Blowin' in the Wind," "Dust in the Wind," "Early Mornin' Rain," "The Rose," and "Where Have All the Flowers Gone?"

Song Performance Guide

CHORDS IN SONG: D   A7

SINGING PITCH:

Rock-a My Soul

SONG SUGGESTIONS

Song (Artist/Author)	Key: Chords	Comments
As Tears Go By (Rolling Stones)	G: G, A, C, D, Em	$\frac{4}{4}$ arpeggio pick
Cobwebs and Dust (Gordon Lightfoot)	A: A, D, E7	$\frac{3}{4}$ time arpeggio
Deep in the Heart of Texas (Hershey/Swander)	D: D, G, A7	Plucked chord strum
Don't Think Twice (Bob Dylan)	G: G, C, D7, A7, Em	Travis pick
Dust in the Wind (Kansas)	Am: Am, C, G, Dm7, D/F♯	Travis pick
Early Mornin' Rain (Gordon Lightfoot)	D: D, G, A7, Em	Travis pick
Five Hundred Miles (Hedy West)	G: G, Em, Am, C, D7	Pinch pick

The Gambler (Kenny Rogers/Don Schlitz)	D: D, G, A7	Travis pick
Hello Stranger (A. P. Carter)	D: D, G, A7	Travis pick
If I Needed You (Townes van Zandt)	A: A, D, E7	Travis pick
The Last Thing on My Mind (Tom Paxton)	G: G, C, D7	Travis pick
Snowbird (Gene MacLellan)	C: C, Em, Dm, G7	Travis pick

chapter 7
Open and Simulated Tunings

The guitar has a standard tuning: E–A–D–G–B–E. But there is an increasingly large body of music that is being played in which the strings are tuned to different open pitches. These nonstandard, or "open," tunings are found to a great extent in American blues, folk, rock, ragtime, and popular music, and are used by folk players and many professional performers and arrangers. With the guitar tuned to an open chord, as is done in many of these tunings, a new resonance and flavor is obtained from the instrument reminiscent of the drone instruments such as the banjo and the dulcimer. While a certain amount of the versatility of standard tuning is lost when the guitar is retuned, the subsequent gain in the range of new sounds available more than makes up for it. When the guitar is retuned, chords and scales have to be relearned, and in many of the tunings there seems to be a more limited selection of chords available. Most players use a particular tuning to play a song in a particular key and will not, as in the case of standard tuning, use the same tuning to play in many different keys.

Using the information in Chapter 11, the student should be able to derive fingerings for chords and scales in the various open tunings given here, although many of the common chord fingerings will be provided in this chapter. Exploring open tunings is a considerable task and an interesting option for any guitarist. There is nothing inherently easy or hard about it; a beginner could start out very effectively with open tunings, while another player could play for a lifetime and never use anything but standard tuning.

DROPPED-D TUNING

The most common altered or open tuning is the Dropped-D tuning, where the bass E string is lowered one whole step (2 frets) to D. This tuning, used by many guitarists, injects new life into the key of D by offering a rich tonic bass note. The chord fingerings are altered slightly from standard, some useful ones being shown in Figure 7.1.

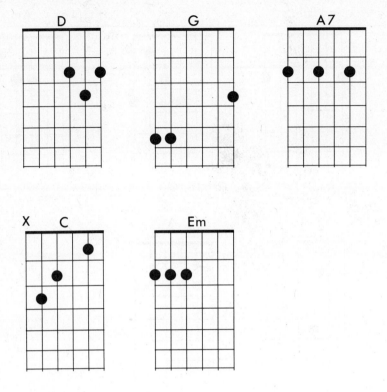

FIGURE 7.1 Chords in Dropped-D Tuning

Dropped-D tuning can be used to good advantage in almost any song performed in the key of D, and a wide variety of music ranging from classical pieces to blues and pop songs has been effectively arranged in this tuning. Many well-known songwriters such as Gordon Lightfoot and John Denver have made extensive use of the Dropped-D tuning.

Exercises: Dropped-D Tuning

1. Retune your guitar using the Dropped-D tuning. Then go back through the book and play all the songs that are in the key of D.

2. What happens to songs in the key of Dm when Dropped-D tuning is used? Is it feasible to play C, F, or Gm chords in this key?

OPEN G TUNING

Open G tuning (D–G–D–G–B–D) and Open A tuning (E–A–E–A–C♯–E) are structurally the same, with A tuning being pitched one whole step above G tuning. G tuning is more commonly used by acoustic-guitar players since it is achieved by loosening strings. Open A tuning may be used by players who use very light-gauge strings that are not in danger of breaking when tightened above standard tuning pitches. Oddly enough, the G tuning is often called "Spanish tuning" by country players, probably because a song called "Spanish Fandango" (p. 203) uses this tuning. This is a confusing name for the tuning, since standard tuning is the one associated with the music of Spain.

Open G and A tunings have been used for many years by blues players and have recently been adopted extensively by folk, rock, and instrumental players such as Joni Mitchell, Leo Kottke, and Keith Richard.

Common chord fingerings are shown in Figure 7.2 for Open G tuning only, since the same fingerings can be used for Open A tuning but will simply sound a whole step higher.

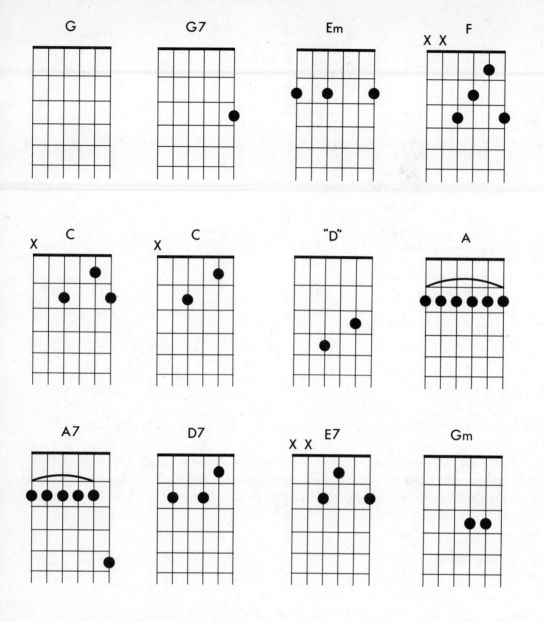

FIGURE 7.2 Chords in Open G Tuning

Exercises: Open G Tuning

1. Using Open G tuning, play "Gold Watch and Chain" from Chapter 4. Play the chords as written, using the fingerings given in Figure 7.2.

2. Using Open G tuning, try playing "Silent Night," "Tomorrow Is a Long Time" (Bob Dylan), "Amanda" (Bob McDill), and other traditional and popular songs.

3. Use a barre with your index finger across all six strings to play the C and D chords. At which fret is the barre for the C chord placed? The D chord? (See Chapter 9.)

4. Play "C. C. Rider," below, in Open G tuning, using a shuffle rhythm. In Open G tuning the seventh can be added to an open or to a barred chord by pressing the little finger on the first string three frets above the nut or the barre.

C. C. Rider

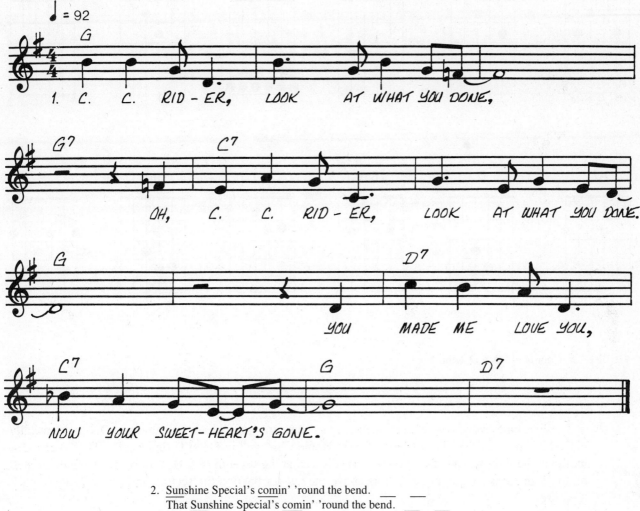

1. C. C. RID-ER, LOOK AT WHAT YOU DONE,

OH, C. C. RID-ER, LOOK AT WHAT YOU DONE.

YOU MADE ME LOVE YOU,

NOW YOUR SWEET-HEART'S GONE.

2. Sunshine Special's comin' 'round the bend. __ __
   That Sunshine Special's comin' 'round the bend. __ __
   It's got your woman, now our love must end. __ __

3. C. C. Rider, you sure made me cry, __ __
   Yes, C. C. Rider, you sure made me cry. __ __
   You make me feel, like I want to die. __ __

OPEN D TUNING

Open D and Open E tunings have the same relationship to each other as G and A tunings have in that they are structurally identical, with E tuning pitched a whole step higher than D tuning. Open D (D–A–D–F♯–A–D) is the more common since it is achieved by loosening strings. It gives the guitar a very deep, rich, and resonant sound and is fuller sounding than G tuning because it features two root bass strings.

In the chords shown in Figure 7.3 notice that some have no names and that major chords can be formed at any fret with a simple barre. This is true of any tuning in which the guitar is tuned to a chord. If the guitar were tuned to a minor chord, then the barre would make a minor chord at each fret.

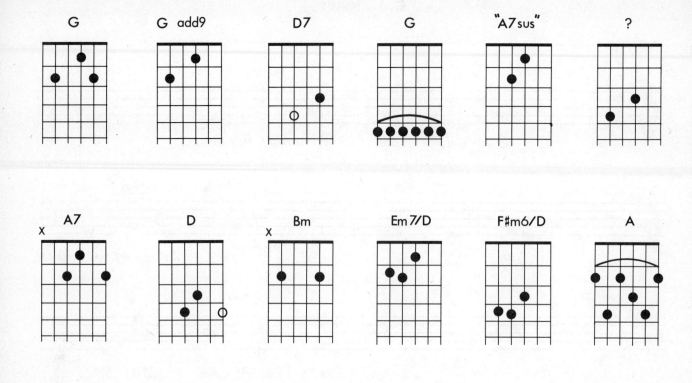

FIGURE 7.3 Chords in Open D Tuning

Blues tunes work very well in open tunings. Instruments such as the banjo and Dobro are usually played in open tunings. Try playing "Sweet Home Chicago" in Open D tuning. The IV (G) chord is barred at the fifth fret, and the V (A) chord is barred at the seventh fret. Bass movement can be created on the fifth string by playing two frets above the nut (or bar) on the second and fourth beats of each measure.

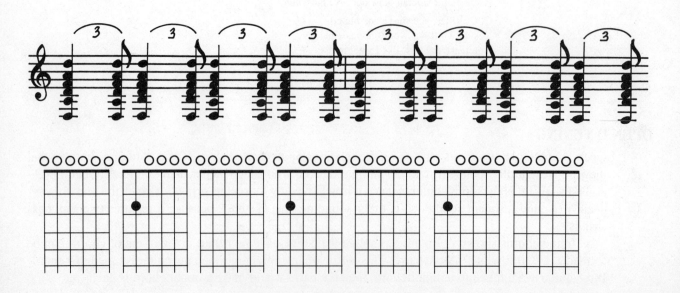

Use this shuffle accompaniment to play "Sweet Home Chicago," by Robert Johnson. Try this turnaround in measures 11 and 12:

Sweet Home Chicago

Robert Johnson

2. Now <u>one</u> and one is two <u>two</u> and two is four
   Oh, <u>b</u>aby don't you want to <u>go</u> no more?
   Oh, come on <u>b</u>aby don't you want to <u>go</u> __
   Back to the <u>land</u> of California, To my <u>sweet</u> home Chicago. __ __

3. <u>Four</u> and two is six and <u>six</u> and two is eight
   <u>I'm</u> in a hurry baby and I <u>don't</u> want to be late
   <u>Oh</u>, come on <u>b</u>aby, don't you want to <u>go</u> __
   Back to that <u>bright</u> light city mama <u>Sweet</u> home Chicago. __ __

4. <u>Six</u> and two is eight and <u>eight</u> and two is ten
   Friends <u>once</u> she trick you one time she <u>sure</u> going to do it again
   I'm crying <u>hey</u>, baby don't you want to <u>go</u> __
   Back to the <u>land</u> of California, To my <u>sweet</u> home Chicago. __ __ *

*Two of the verses in Robert Johnson's recording of this song are unintelligible, and the chorus does not make sense (Chicago in California?). The "two plus two" addition verses are typical of blues lyrics, and two verses have been added here. No two singers perform this song alike, even though it is a standard in the field. The first verse is sung two times. The melody of the first four measures changes on verses 2 through 4. Johnson tends to chant the lyrics very quickly on the note D for the first four measures of those verses.

While singing the melody, play the chords for "Shenandoah" in Open D tuning. Then try strumming it in dulcimer style, brushing across several strings in addition to the melody tone. Emphasize the melody note as you strum. You can also use a basic strumming pattern such as a church lick (↑ ↕↕) as your right-hand rhythmic motion in playing the melody. Play the melody alone several times in order to learn where the melody tones are located with respect to the chords on the fingerboard.

Shenandoah

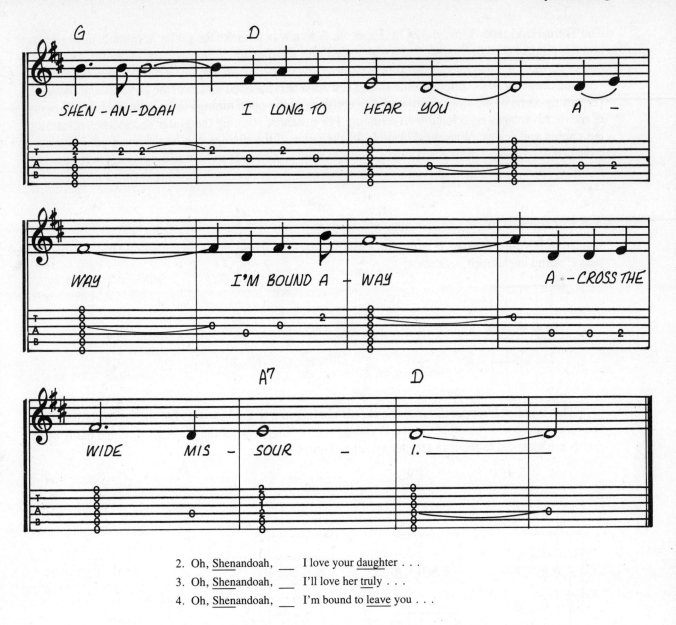

2. Oh, <u>Shenandoah</u>, ___ I love your <u>daughter</u> . . .
3. Oh, <u>Shenandoah</u>, ___ I'll love her <u>truly</u> . . .
4. Oh, <u>Shenandoah</u>, ___ I'm bound to <u>leave</u> you . . .

Figure 7.4 summarizes the open tunings presented in this chapter. The pitch of each string and the fretted-string tuning method for standard tuning and each open tuning is indicated.

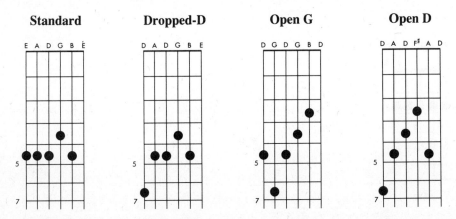

FIGURE 7.4 Fretted-String Tuning Method for Standard and Common Open Tunings

The Third-Hand capo is introduced in Appendix A as a way to make the guitar accessible to beginners and it is reintroduced in Chapter 8 as a way to facilitate the playing of fingerpicked melodies. However, one of its most immediately useful functions is as a way to capture the flavor of open tunings without retuning the guitar. By clamping some strings and not others the open strings of the guitar can be changed, permitting some of the open chord and drone effects of the open tunings to be imitated without many of the disadvantages associated with retuning. For instance, retuning the guitar necessitates relearning the chords and scales. With the Third-Hand, the color of the tunings can be achieved while keeping most of the advantages of standard tuning. Some examples of how it can be used are given in the remainder of this chapter.

Dropped-E Configuration

Instead of lowering the bass E string to D, simply place the Third-Hand on the second fret, leaving the bass E string unclamped, as shown:

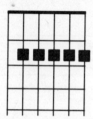

This is called Dropped-E since the chords are fingered in the key of D but the guitar sounds in E. The tonic bass note is obtained for the D chord, but the fingerings of the G, F, C, Em, and many other chords are identical to those in standard tuning (Figure 7.5):

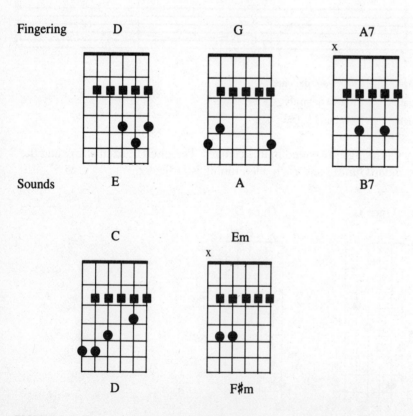

FIGURE 7.5 Chords in Dropped-E Configuration

Almost any song with chords fingered in the key of D can be played in this configuration with good results since it differs from normal tuning only in the bass string. However, the nature of the configuration is such that chords like the C chord can be played as in standard tuning (this is because the guitar still is in standard tuning), thus allowing a song with D–C chord change to have a root bass on the sixth string with the D chord. This voicing is not possible in real Dropped-D tuning. Play "Drunken Sailor" (p. 58) using Dropped-E configuration. It will come out pitched a whole step higher, but the Dm chord can be played without muting the bass string. Many other songs in the key of Dm can be effectively arranged this way.

OPEN A CONFIGURATION

The Open A configuration can be used to make the guitar sound as if it is in Open A tuning. Yet many of the chord fingerings from standard tuning can also be used to make it more versatile (in addition to being more convenient) than the real open tuning. Some chord ideas are shown in Figure 7.6 to illustrate how the tuning works.

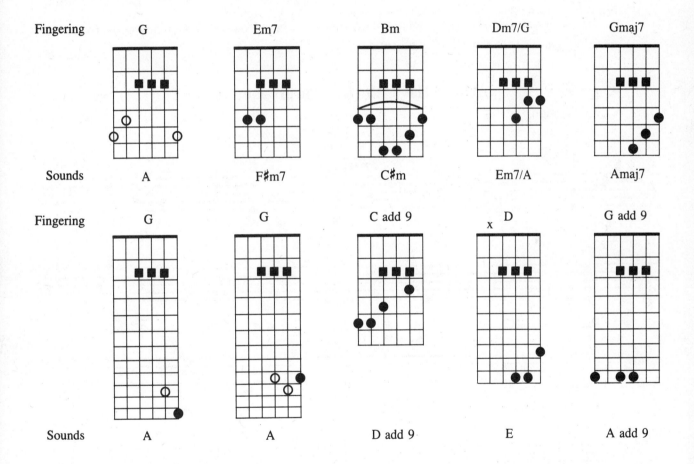

FIGURE 7.6 Chords in Open A Configuration

Open A configuration can be used to play simple songs with full-sounding chords. An A-major chord is formed by the capo itself, and satisfactory D, E7, and F♯m chords can be played with one and two fingers (see Figure 7.7).

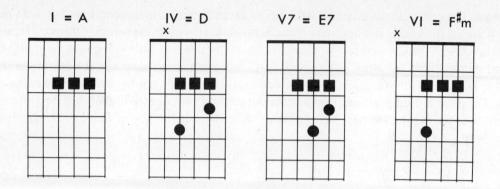

FIGURE 7.7 Simulated Open A Fingerings

The chords in this configuration, like some of the chords in Appendix A, have added tones and are not suitable for all purposes. However, many songs can be arranged effectively in this configuration so that beginners can get a full sound with easy fingerings, and more advanced players can achieve the sound of an open tuning and can arrange accompanied melodies.

Pete Seeger's "Where Have All the Flowers Gone?" can be played in open tuning. It also sounds good in Open A with the Third-Hand capo.

Where Have All the Flowers Gone?

Open A Configuration

Pete Seeger

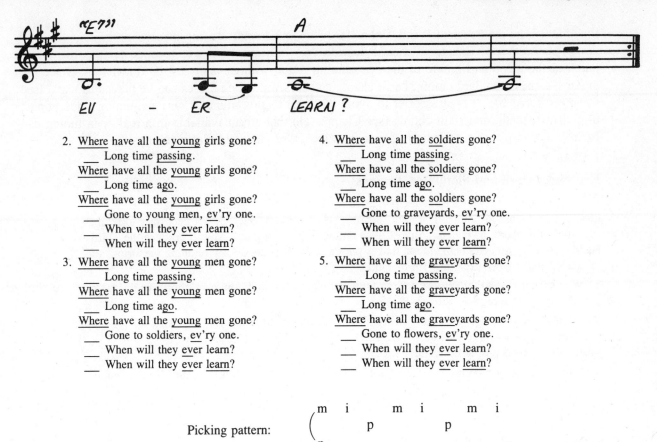

2. Where have all the <u>young</u> girls gone?
   ___ Long time <u>pass</u>ing.
   Where have all the <u>young</u> girls gone?
   ___ Long time a<u>go</u>.
   Where have all the <u>young</u> girls gone?
   ___ Gone to young men, <u>ev</u>'ry one.
   ___ When will they <u>ev</u>er learn?
   ___ When will they <u>ev</u>er <u>learn</u>?

3. Where have all the <u>young</u> men gone?
   ___ Long time <u>pass</u>ing.
   Where have all the <u>young</u> men gone?
   ___ Long time ago.
   Where have all the <u>young</u> men gone?
   ___ Gone to soldiers, <u>ev</u>'ry one.
   ___ When will they <u>ev</u>er learn?
   ___ When will they <u>ev</u>er <u>learn</u>?

4. Where have all the <u>soldiers</u> gone?
   ___ Long time <u>pass</u>ing.
   Where have all the <u>soldiers</u> gone?
   ___ Long time a<u>go</u>.
   Where have all the <u>soldiers</u> gone?
   ___ Gone to graveyards, <u>ev</u>'ry one.
   ___ When will they <u>ev</u>er learn?
   ___ When will they <u>ev</u>er <u>learn</u>?

5. Where have all the <u>graveyards</u> gone?
   ___ Long time <u>pass</u>ing.
   Where have all the <u>graveyards</u> gone?
   ___ Long time a<u>go</u>.
   Where have all the <u>graveyards</u> gone?
   ___ Gone to flowers, <u>ev</u>'ry one.
   ___ When will they <u>ev</u>er learn?
   ___ When will they <u>ev</u>er <u>learn</u>?

Picking pattern:
```
      m   i      m   i      m   i
(         p          p
  p
```

The following songs can be played with a Third-Hand capo in Open A configuration: "Amanda" (Bob McDill), "Billy Boy," "Blowin' in the Wind" (Bob Dylan), "Cotton Jenny" (Gordon Lightfoot), "Houston" (Lee Hazelwood), "Silent Night," and "There's a Place in the World for a Gambler" (Dan Fogelberg).

HALF-OPEN A CONFIGURATION

Half-Open A configuration is introduced in Chapter 8 as an easy way to play fingerpicked melodies. It is one of the most useful configurations of the Third-Hand capo since it allows fingerings from the key of G and open-string bass notes as in the key of A. The treble strings are played normally, and the root and alternating bass notes for many of the common chords are open strings. This leaves the left hand relatively free to find the melody notes. Some basic chord fingerings are shown in Figure 7.8.

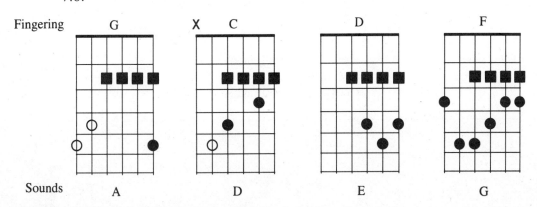

FIGURE 7.8 Chords in Half-Open A Configuration

Play "Down by the Riverside" and "John Hardy" from Chapter 3 using these fingerings.

This section of Chapter 7 should provide you with an alternative to open tunings that gives much of the mood and timbre of the open-tuning sound without many of the drawbacks. Since the guitar is kept in standard tuning, barre chords and closed-position scales can be played as usual (see Chapters 9 and 10). It is also easier to avoid the monotonous sound of an open tuning since minor, diminished, ninth, and sixth chords (see Chapter 11) that are unavailable in a real open tuning can be fingered normally in their barre forms with the Third-Hand simulated tunings.

Exercises: Open and Simulated Tunings

1. In Appendix A easy fingerings are presented to enable budding guitarists to play in a nonstandard simulated tuning. The term *simulated* is used because it was not necessary to retune the guitar to a chord, as is done in most open tunings. Can you find a way to produce the Third-Hand capo E suspended configuration that is presented in Appendix A by retuning the strings of the guitar and without using the Third-Hand capo?

2. What fingerings would you use for the tonic, subdominant, and dominant chords in the tuning you created for Exercise 1, above?

3. What aspects of playing are now easier or more difficult with your new open tuning? Does your tuning enable you to play scales with more or less difficulty? Do you have to relearn placement of notes on the fretboard?

4. Can all scale tones be produced with your nonstandard tuning? With the Third-Hand version?

SONG SUGGESTIONS

Song (Artist/Author)	Key	Tuning
Amanda (Bob McDill)	G or A	Open G or Third-Hand A
Back Home Again (John Denver)	D	Open D
Blowin' in the Wind (Bob Dylan)	D	Open D
Circle Game (Joni Mitchell)	G or A	Open G or Third-Hand A
Honky Tonk Woman (Rolling Stones)	G	Open G
Silent Night (Traditional)	G or A	Open G or Third-Hand A
Sloop John B. (P.D.)	D	Open D
Suzanne (Leonard Cohen)	G or A	Open G or Third-Hand A
Tomorrow Is a Long Time (Bob Dylan)	G or A	Open G or Third-Hand A
Yankee Lady (Jesse Winchester)	G or A	Open G or Third-Hand A

chapter 8
Playing Traditional Melody Styles

The melody-playing styles presented here consist of more than just the playing of the melody notes. They also provide the accompaniment to the melody. Playing only a melody line on the guitar does not provide a full sound and is associated more with ensemble playing. The melodic styles that give the complete sound are the more popular ones among solo guitarists. There are many ways to accompany a given melody, but only a few of them can also provide a rhythmic drive. This completeness of sound is what characterizes the Carter and Travis styles that are presented in this chapter.

THE CARTER MELODY STYLE

Named after Maybelle Carter who in the 1920s popularized the sound through her guitar playing with the original Carter Family, this melody style features the melody played on the bass strings, which is interwoven with a strummed accompaniment. Although most players use a flatpick in the Carter style, Maybelle used a thumbpick and brushed the chords between the melody notes with her fingers. Maybelle played everything in either C or G, and used a capo or tuned the strings down in order to sing in the other keys. Some of the Carter Family's recordings feature arrangements of traditional tunes that are usually done in $\frac{3}{4}$ meter but that are performed on the recordings in $\frac{4}{4}$ meter. The basic accompanying strum is the church lick (see page 71) in the Carter style, which can be applied to a large number of songs. "Frère Jacques," "Tom Dooley," "Go Tell Aunt Rhody," "Marines' Hymn," and several traditional songs are written out in notation and in tablature in basic Carter melody style.

    The melody notes have their stems pointing down in these arrangements. Try to leave your left-hand fingers on the chords whenever possible, moving them only to play melody notes on adjacent strings. After you have mastered these songs, you may wish to try "Since I Laid My Burden Down" (page 74) and "This Land Is Your Land" (page 77) in Carter style in the key of C. "This Land Is Your Land" can be played in the key of G, too. If these keys are too low for your vocal range, then use a capo to raise the pitch level of the song (see page 261).

The last few arrangements in this section use the hammering-on and pulling-off techniques. See pages 90–91 for an explanation.

Arrangements such as these can be used as an introduction to the performance of a song as well as an instrumental break between verses or instead of the singing of a chorus.

ARRANGEMENTS IN THE CARTER STYLE

Frère Jacques
Carter Melody Style

Tom Dooley

Carter Melody Style

Go Tell Aunt Rhody

Carter Melody Style

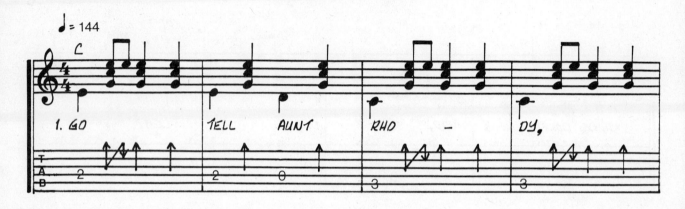

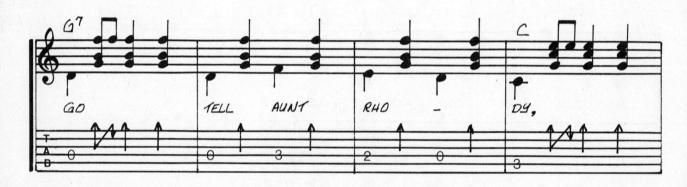

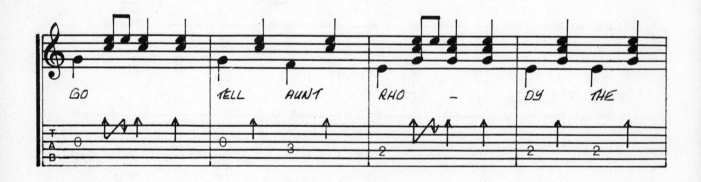

2. The <u>one</u> she was <u>sav</u>ing, (3 times)
   To <u>make</u> a feather <u>bed</u>.

3. She <u>died</u> in the <u>mill</u>pond, (3 times)
   A-<u>stand</u>ing on her <u>head</u>.

4. The <u>gos</u>lings are <u>cry</u>ing, (3 times)
   Be<u>cause</u> their mother's <u>dead</u>.

5. The <u>gan</u>der is <u>weep</u>ing, (3 times)
   Be<u>cause</u> his wife is <u>dead</u>.

Marines' Hymn*
Carter Melody Style
Instrumental

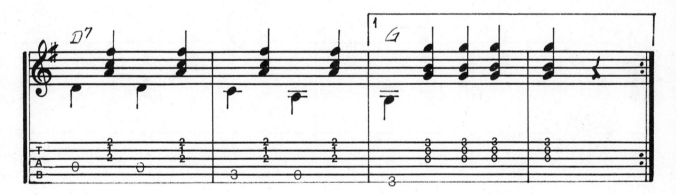

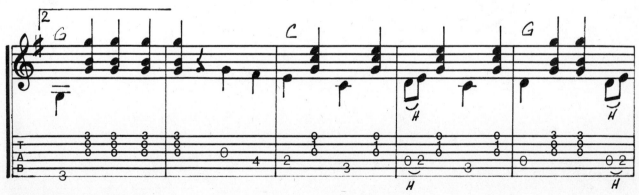

*See page 99 for the words to this song.

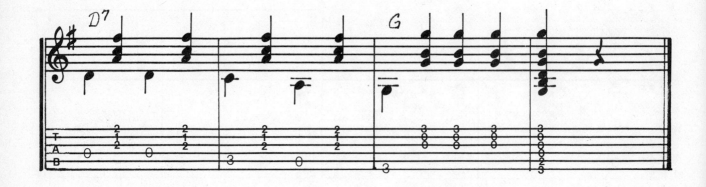

East Virginia*

Carter Melody Style
Instrumental

*See page 255 for the words to this song.

Wildwood Flower*

Carter Melody Style
Instrumental

*See page 152 for the words to this song.

Can the Circle Be Unbroken*

Carter Melody Style
Instrumental

*See page 61 for the words to this song.

Practice this instrumental version of "Worried Man Blues" until it seems easy. Then turn to page 150, and play and sing the entire song. Use this instrumental version as an introduction and in lieu of the chorus after the fifth verse.

Worried Man Blues

Carter Melody Style
Instrumental

John Hardy*

Carter Melody Style
Instrumental

*See page 52 for the words to this song.

THE TRAVIS MELODY STYLE

The Travis style is somewhat inappropriately named after Merle Travis, who was probably the first player to gain widespread attention as a finger-style melody player. Travis did not invent the style, nor was he as influential as others in propagating it, but the name has stuck and is universally used.

The unique sound of the Travis melody style is the result of the playing of a syncopated melody against a steady, four-count bass line. The first and third bass notes are usually the root bass and alternating bass notes that would be used in a strummed accompaniment, and the second and fourth bass notes are performed with less accent and are usually played on whatever bass string is in the chord that is not used for the root bass or alternating bass. (For simplicity, the arrangements that follow use a root bass. As these arrangements are learned, the player can use an alternating bass.) To do this, one must play chords that have at least three bass strings available. Two or three melody notes are usually played for each four bass notes, with the first melody note in each measure falling directly on the first beat and the other(s) coming slightly ahead of the fourth and/or third beat(s). Therefore, melody notes can occur on these parts of beats: $\underline{1} + 2 \underline{+} 3 \underline{+} 4 +$. If the melody notes were all played on the beat, the arrangement would still "work" but would sound stilted. If they were all played off the beat, the song would lose its melodic continuity. The syncopation of the melody notes that fall in the middle of the measure does not interfere with the "naturalness" of the melody and allows almost any song in which the melody notes do not move too rapidly to be arranged in this style. Since in Travis style there are more bass notes than melody notes, "Flight of the Bumblebee" would not be a good tune to arrange in this style.

EASY ARRANGEMENTS IN UNSYNCOPATED "PRE-TRAVIS" STYLE

The following four songs—"Frère Jacques," "Tom Dooley," "Go Tell Aunt Rhody," and "London Bridge"—have steady, four-count bass lines and unsyncopated melodies. In true Travis-style arrangements the melody would be syncopated, but these four arrangements are used since they sound good and assist in developing the motor skills required in playing in this style. The songs have been selected also because they contain a minimum number of left-hand movements and can be played with very basic chord positions. As each chord change occurs, try to hold down as much of the chord as possible while moving fingers to play the melody notes. You may have to do a bit of hand stretching. Play the arrangements very slowly at first, concentrating on keeping the bass notes moving steadily. Compare this melody style to the Carter-style arrangements of the same tunes. In playing melodies the first left-hand finger will normally play notes on the first fret, the second finger will play notes on the second fret, and the third finger will play notes on the third fret.

If the following arrangements seem too difficult for your present left-hand technique, then you might skip to the section of this chapter entitled "Melody-Style Arrangements with the Third-Hand Capo" (page 191). Be sure to read "Syncopated Travis-Style Arrangements" (page 185) before playing the Third-Hand arrangements of "Go Tell Aunt Rhody" and "Marines' Hymn."

Frère Jacques
Unsyncopated Travis Melody Style

Tom Dooley

Unsyncopated Travis Melody Style

Go Tell Aunt Rhody

Unsyncopated Travis Melody Style

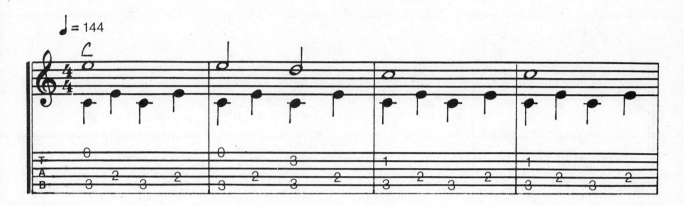

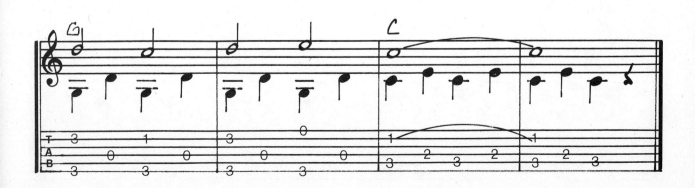

London Bridge

Unsyncopated Travis Melody Style

SYNCOPATED TRAVIS-STYLE ARRANGEMENTS

The arrangements in this section combine many of the skills presented elsewhere in the text, and although they are not easy, they are as simplified as arrangements in this style can be. The tunes have been selected for their suitability to this melody style and for the simplicity and convenience of the left-hand fingerings. They all depend on the Travis picking technique that was first introduced in Chapter 6:

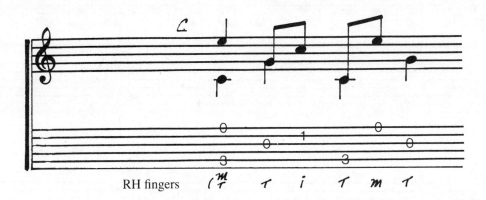

RH fingers

Before you attempt to play the songs in this section, you should be able to perform this pattern at a normal tempo (at least ♩ = 144), using the alternating bass for all the basic chords. Ideally, playing in the Travis style should be a subconscious activity; you should be able to sing, talk, or read while maintaining the steady fingerpicking pattern. Otherwise melody playing will be extremely difficult. The arrangements in the Third-Hand-capo section, which follows, are easier and more accessible than those in this section. Try them first if your left hand isn't agile enough to make the chord changes at tempo.

The first two arrangements in this section, "London Bridge" and "Go Tell Aunt Rhody," are syncopated versions of the arrangements of those tunes presented in the previous section. Notice that the second melody note in each measure is played slightly later than normal. It is that delay which creates the syncopated rhythmic feeling. The bass notes keep the same steady beat as before.

"Marines' Hymn" is presented here in a typical Travis-style arrangement that sounds good and works easily. No special or difficult left-hand positions are required for this song, and the melody notes can be reached relatively easily while still holding down the basic chord positions. "Freight Train" is a favorite Travis-style song of many guitarists. This arrangement works quite well when the melody notes are emphasized. The opening measures are often played without the syncopated feeling in the melody; however, the song works either way. There are many other songs that can be arranged in this melody style and that make good exercises. "Worried Man Blues," "Banks of the Ohio," and "Barb'ra Allen" work well in C, and "I'm Goin' Down That Road Feeling Bad" and "Blowin' in the Wind" can be played in G.

London Bridge
Syncopated Travis Melody Style

Go Tell Aunt Rhody
Syncopated Travis Melody Style

Marines' Hymn
Syncopated Travis Melody Style

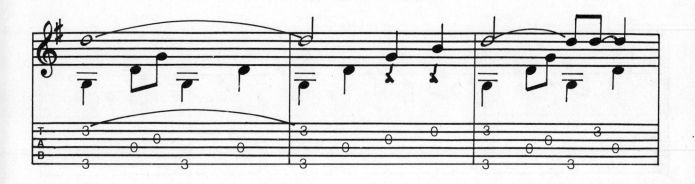

Freight Train
Syncopated Travis Melody Style

Basic pattern:

*A full barre chord is needed here. See page 205 for an explanation.

The Travis melody style has become very popular. There are many recording artists that make extensive use of it both as accompaniment to songs and as instrumental solos. Listen to Mississippi John Hurt and Elizabeth Cotten for clean, basic fingerpicking, since they were perhaps more responsible for the style than Merle Travis himself. Bob Dylan, Eric Andersen, Gordon Lightfoot, Paul Simon, John Denver, Tom Paxton, John Prine, Utah Phillips, and Doc Watson have all recorded many songs featuring Travis-style accompaniments, and there is instrumental fingerpicking available by John Fahey, William Ackerman, Robbie Basho, Doc Watson, Leo Kottke, and many other artists. Most players seem to learn the style by ear. It is essential to have a clear idea of the rhythmic feel of this style, something that is probably only obtainable by listening to players or recordings.

MELODY-STYLE ARRANGEMENTS WITH THE THIRD-HAND CAPO

One of the biggest problems in fingerpicking melody is that of left-hand position. Keeping a steady bass line going means that some fingers have to be left on the guitar at all times, and playing a melody line means that fingers are going to have to move around. Even for the arrangements in the previous section, which were selected to minimize left-hand complexity, undoubtedly there were times when there were not enough fingers to go around. It is difficult enough to concentrate on the right hand and to keep the bass notes moving steadily and the melody notes plucked on the correct string. But when you add to this a left hand that is constantly busy, it can make the whole process of fingerpicking melodies prohibitively difficult even for players of intermediate ability. C and G are the most commonly used keys since the melody notes lie within reach of the fingers when the basic chords are being held down. But the fact that the normal open bass strings of the guitar are not important notes in those keys means that part of the left hand is tied up almost at all times just holding bass notes. The key of A lends itself much more to bass-note playing, for example, since the root bass note of each primary chord is an open string.

For this reason it is not uncommon to find guitar players retuning the strings of the guitar, especially the bass strings, to make them more useful in the keys of G and C. Unfortunately, retuning the strings changes the fingering of the chords. A solution to the problem is offered by the Third-Hand capo, which can hold down an A chord and thus let you play and think as if you were in the key of G. Such fingering sounds in the key of A.

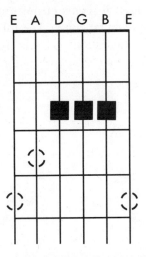

Use of this configuration of the Third-Hand capo liberates the left hand from having to hold bass notes down for every chord and allows you to concentrate on playing the melody. The following group of arrangements are done with this device and are easier to play than Travis arrangements in normal guitar fingering. All the arrangements are written in Half-Open A configuration (see Figure 8.1).

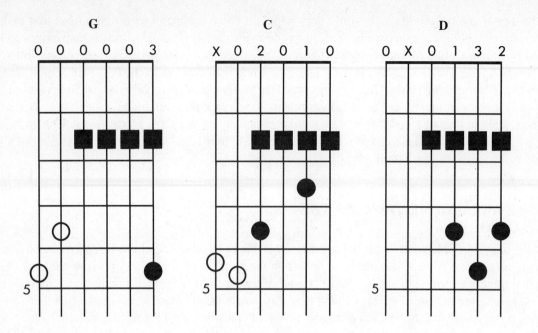

FIGURE 8.1 Chord Fingerings for G, C, and D in Half-Open A Configuration

NOTATION OF ARRANGEMENTS WITH THE THIRD-HAND CAPO

Whenever nonstandard tunings are used, a problem arises in notation, and the same problem is caused by the Third-Hand capo. If the capo is placed on the second fret to form a normal A chord, then songs played in G position will sound in A. This is no different than normal capo use, except that there are notes that now sound below the capo. Guitar tablature solves the problem since a note to be played three frets above the capo is notated with a 3, and an open string, even though it may lie below the capo, is still notated as a 0. The standard notation is trickier, since if it is written in the key it sounds in, the effect of playing in G position is lost. Nevertheless, it seems clearest to write the notes on the staff as they sound and to convey the fingering technique on tablature. The following arrangements require the use of a Third-Hand capo in Half-Open A configuration. A TAB signature is followed by the configuration used for each arrangement; the number above the capo configuration indicates the fret at which the capo is placed.

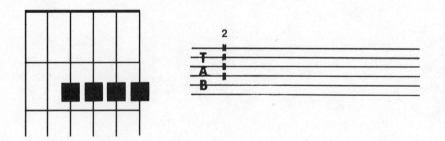

Numbers written on the tablature indicate where the fingers are placed above the Third-Hand capo and not above the nut. This method appears to be an effective way to reconcile the notation problems, and presumably the arrangements can be deciphered without confusion.

Frère Jacques
Third-Hand Melody Style

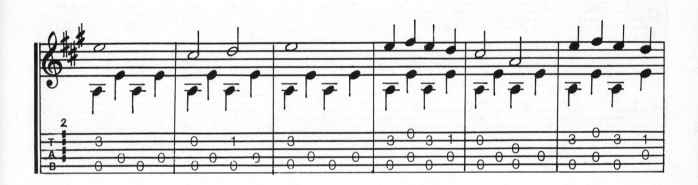

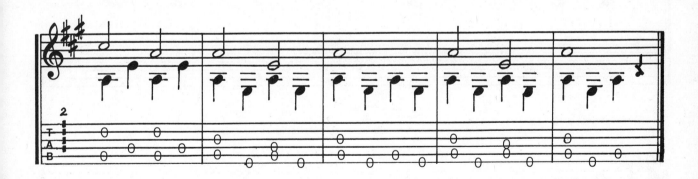

London Bridge

Third-Hand Melody Style

Since I Laid My Burden Down

Third-Hand Melody Style

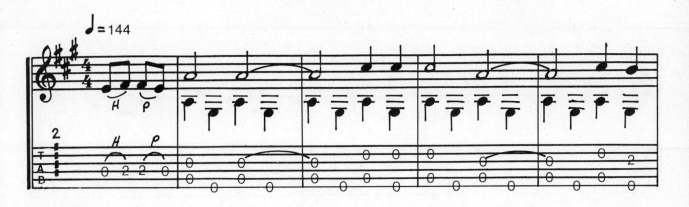

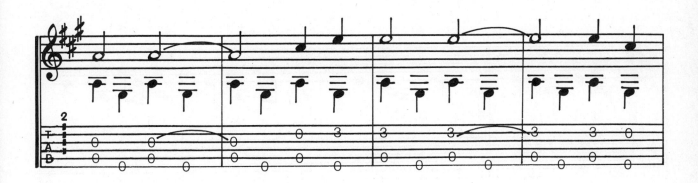

Tom Dooley
Third-Hand Melody Style

Go Tell Aunt Rhody
Third-Hand Melody Style

Marines' Hymn

Third-Hand Melody Style

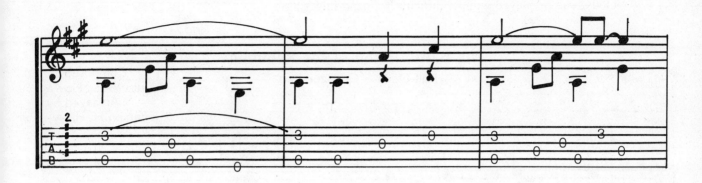

"The Battle Hymn of the Republic," a good example of a full-sounding arrangement of a familiar melody, can be played without difficult left-hand fingerings.

The Battle Hymn of the Republic
Half-Open A Configuration

Composed by
Julia Ward Howe
Arranged by
Jefferson H. Hickey

"Frère Jacques" is arranged in Half-Open A configuration as a two-part round for a solo player: The two parts are played in different octaves.

Frère Jacques

Arranged by Rex Holmes

The "E-Modal Boogie" is an example of how an "E-Modal" configuration can be used to play a boogie-woogie walking bass through all three chords of a twelve-bar blues progression (see page 250) with all of the chords fingered in nut position. This is probably the easiest way to play a walking bass in E. The "E-Modal" configuration is very useful since it provides a strong drone sound, yet allows normal fingering of barre chords.

E-Modal Boogie*

Rex Holmes

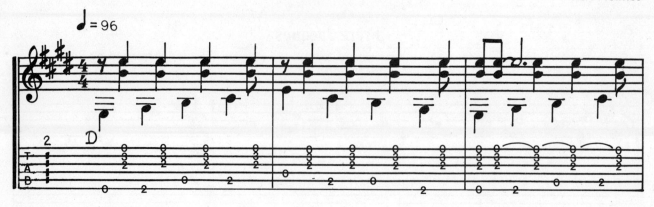

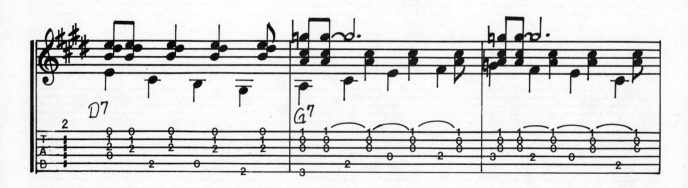

*Fingerings:

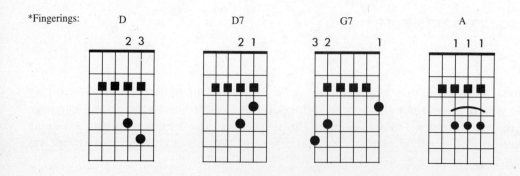

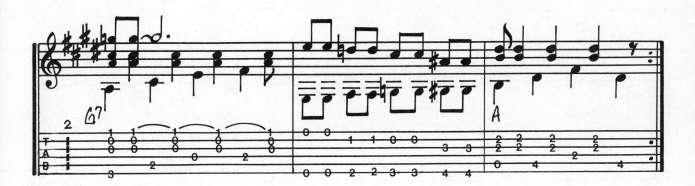

"Spanish Fandango" probably exists in as many versions as there are guitarists who play it. Such a charming piece in "classical" style is worth learning. Using Open G tuning, work out the technique for this song. Review the section on Open G tuning in Chapter 7 and combine those left-hand chord fingerings with the basic right-hand fingerpicking pattern $\frac{r}{T}$ m i to get started.

Spanish Fandango*

Open G Tuning

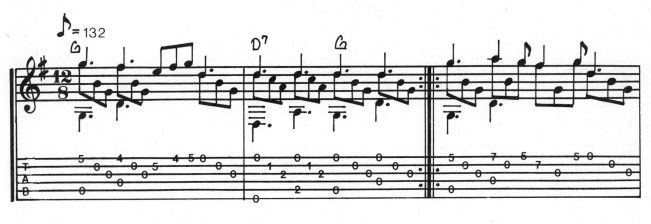

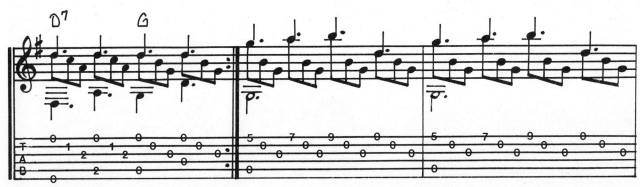

*As played by Daniel Jacoubovitch.

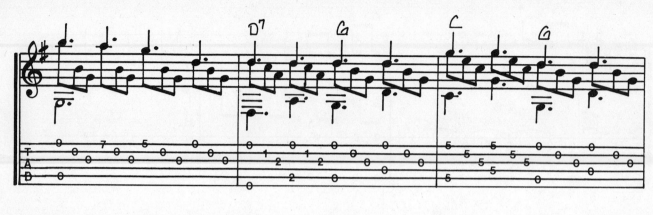

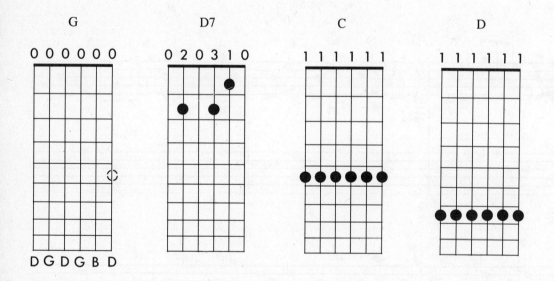

chapter 9
Using Barre Chords

UNDERSTANDING BARRE CHORDS

The concept of barre chords is simple, but the playing of them can be difficult for the beginner. Certainly, a large amount of good guitar music can be played with only open chords, but there is an even larger amount of good music that requires barre chords.

Any open chord that only needs three fingers and that is played in open position can be made into a barre chord. The first finger acts as a "movable capo," and the remaining fingers form the open chord above the barre as if it were the nut.

Only five of the twelve major chords can be played without barre chords (D, G, A, E, and C), and it only takes two *barre chord forms* to play all the rest. Barre chord forms are named for the open chord from which they are constructed; the A-minor barre chord form is shown below. When the Am form is moved to the first fret, it makes a B♭m chord, a Bm chord at the second fret, and a Cm at the third fret. Each successive fret to which the barre is moved raises the pitch a half step.

Am form   B♭m   Bm   Cm

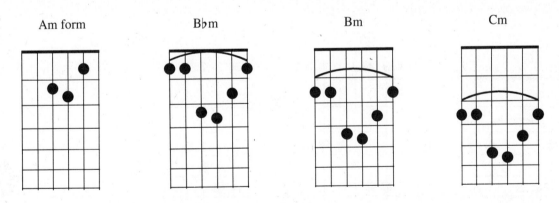

The general rule for all barre chord forms is the same. Each barre chord form produces a chord of the same type (major, minor, sixth, and so forth) at whatever fret it is played. The name of the actual chord produced by a barre chord form is obtained by counting up the chromatic scale the number of half steps to where the index finger forms the barre. The E-major barre form produces F major when the

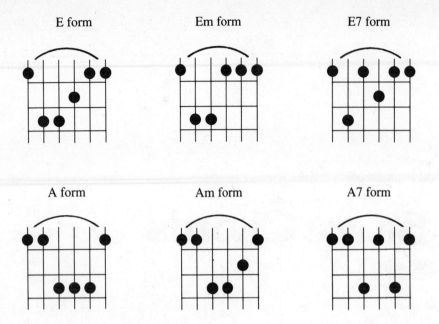

FIGURE 9.1 Common Barre Chord Forms

index finger is at the first fret, F♯ major when it is at the second fret, G major when it is at the third fret, and so on. The commonly used barre forms for the three basic chord qualities (major, minor, and seventh) are shown in Figure 9.1.

PARTIAL BARRE CHORDS

Many beginners find that full barre chords are too difficult to play, and advanced players need chords that can be more quickly executed and that do not tie up all the left-hand fingers. *Partial barre chords* can satisfy both demands. These are chords that require the use of a finger to fret more than one string but not all six. The basic E-form barre, often played as a full barre chord, is commonly found as either of two partial barre chords:

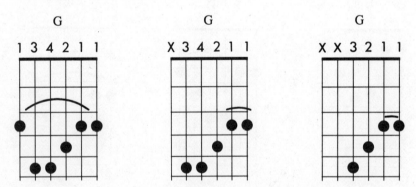

These partial barre forms can be moved to other frets as long as the correct number of strings are sounding. There are many partial barre chords that can be used to play other kinds of chords in place of the full six-string barre chords. They are extremely useful to the advanced player who is arranging melodies with accompaniment since these partial barre forms can offer a full chordal sound and still leave a spare finger with which to play a melody line against the chord.

Figure 9.2 shows several partial barre chord forms.

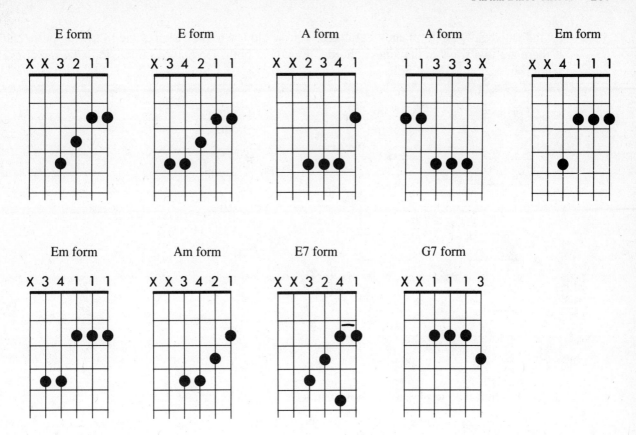

FIGURE 9.2 Partial Barre Chord Forms

Exercises: Barre Chords

1. Give the name of the chord produced when a barre form is played at the fret indicated.

Form	Barred at fret	Chord produced
E	2	F♯
E	4	_____
Em	3	_____
Em	5	_____
E7	7	_____
E7	1	_____
A	6	_____
A	3	_____
Am	2	_____
Am	7	_____
A7	5	_____
A7	8	_____

2. Indicate below the form and fret number you would use to play each of the following barre chords. If there are two ways to play these chords, give them both. Do not give any chords barred above the tenth fret.

Form	Barred at fret	Chord produced
_____	_____	B♭
_____	_____	D7
_____	_____	Am
_____	_____	F
_____	_____	E♭7
_____	_____	F♯ m
_____	_____	A♭7
_____	_____	G
_____	_____	C

3. Find a short way to play the F chord that uses four of the strings.

4. Find a short way to play the B♭ chord that uses five of the strings.

5. To improve your ability to form the barre with your index finger, play some three-chord songs in Open G tuning or Open D tuning. In Open G play the barre C and D chords at the fifth and seventh frets. As your hands get tired, switch back to the open chords for a rest.

6. Sometimes if a song has too many barre chords, you can transpose it to another key in which open chords can be used (see page 64). Suppose you found in a song book the following song in the key of B♭ with the chords as shown ("Pamela Brown," by Tom T. Hall, has these chords):

Key	Chords
B♭	B♭ F E♭ A♭ Gm F7

Transpose these chords to the key of E and see if you can eliminate all of the barre chords. If you still have one or more barre chords, transpose again to D, G, and A to determine how many barre chords must be used in each of those keys.

PLAYING BARRE CHORDS

It takes a great deal of practice to play barre chords effectively and requires building left-hand strength. The index finger forms the barre parallel to the fret and should be rotated slightly onto the fingerboard in order to fret all the strings clearly. You should check each string in the barre chord to make sure it is sounding clearly. If some are not, move the index finger across the strings about one-eighth of an inch in either direction. It is best to start out with songs that have just one barre chord so that the left hand does not become overtired.

"Polly Wolly Doodle" has two chords, and in the key of E it can be played with one open chord (E) and one barre chord (B). Play the E chord with the second, third, and fourth fingers. In moving to the B chord, keep the E formation and place the barre at the seventh fret with the index finger.

Song Performance Guide

CHORDS IN SONG: E   B

SINGING PITCH:

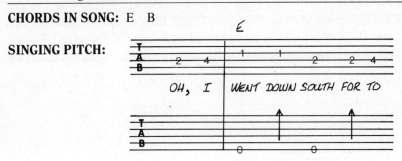

Polly Wolly Doodle

2. Oh, my Sal, she is a maiden fair, Singin' . . .
   With curly eyes and laughing hair, Singin' . . .
   (*Chorus*)

3. Oh, a grasshopper sittin' on a railroad track, Singin' . . .
   A pickin' his teeth with a carpet tack, Singin' . . .
   (*Chorus*)

4. Behind the barn, down on my knees, Singin' . . .
   I thought I heard a rooster sneeze, Singin' . . .
   (*Chorus*)

5. He sneezed so hard with the whooping cough, Singin' . . .
   He sneezed his head and tail right off, Singin' . . .
   (*Chorus*)

"I'm Goin' down That Road Feeling Bad" is a bluesy song that uses IV7, or A7, in place of the usual IV, or A, chord. Again, play the E with the second, third, and fourth fingers and lift up the fourth finger to play the E7. Then the A7 and B7 chords in the song can be played with the movable E7 barre form at the fifth and seventh frets, respectively.

Song Performance Guide

CHORDS IN SONG: E   E7   A7   B7

SINGING PITCH:

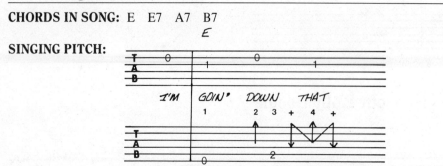

I'm Goin' down That Road Feeling Bad

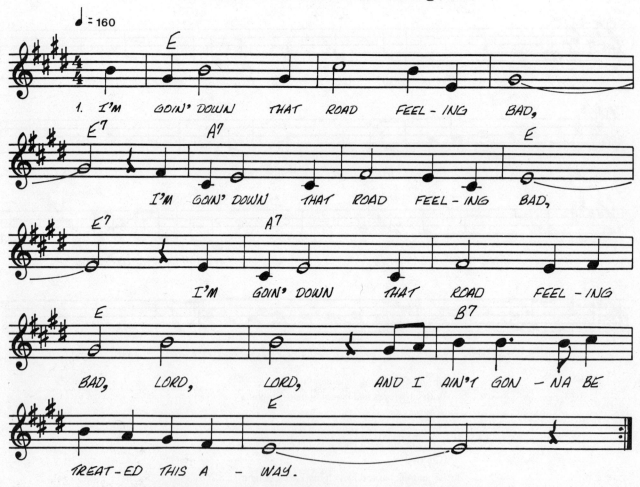

2. I'm goin' where the climate suits my clothes, ___ (3 times) (Lord, Lord),
   And I ain't gonna be treated this a-way. ___

3. I'm lookin' for a job with honest pay, ___ (3 times) (Lord, Lord),
   And I ain't gonna be treated this a-way. ___

4. These <u>five</u>-and-dime-store <u>shoes</u> hurt my <u>feet</u>, ___ (3 times) (Lord, <u>Lord</u>),
   And I <u>ain't</u> gonna be <u>treated</u> this a-<u>way</u>. ___

5. It takes <u>eighty</u>-dollar <u>shoes</u> to fit my <u>foot</u>, ___ (3 times) (Lord, <u>Lord</u>),
   And I <u>ain't</u> gonna be <u>treated</u> this a-<u>way</u>. ___

6. I'm <u>down</u> in the <u>jailhouse</u> on my <u>knees</u>, ___ (3 times) (Lord, <u>Lord</u>),
   And I <u>ain't</u> gonna be <u>treated</u> this a-<u>way</u>. ___

7. I'm <u>goin'</u> where the <u>burgers</u> taste like <u>steak</u>, ___ (3 times) (Lord, <u>Lord</u>),
   And I <u>ain't</u> gonna be <u>treated</u> this a-<u>way</u>. ___

8. I'm <u>goin'</u> where the <u>water</u> tastes like <u>wine</u>, ___ (3 times) (Lord, <u>Lord</u>),
   And I <u>ain't</u> gonna be <u>treated</u> this a-<u>way</u>. ___

9. I'm <u>leavin'</u> if I <u>never</u> come <u>back</u>, ___ (3 times) (Lord, <u>Lord</u>),
   And I <u>ain't</u> gonna be <u>treated</u> this a-<u>way</u>. ___

10. I'm <u>goin'</u> down that <u>road</u> feelin' <u>bad</u>, ___ (3 times) (Lord, <u>Lord</u>),
    And I <u>ain't</u> gonna be <u>treated</u> this a-<u>way</u>. ___

"Michael Row the Boat Ashore" uses one barre chord, F♯m, in the key of D. Although the barre chord comes quickly, the song moves slowly and there is time to prepare for it.

Song Performance Guide

CHORDS IN SONG: D G F♯ m Em

SINGING PITCH:

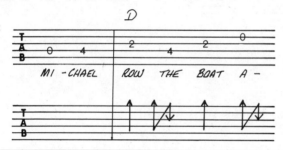

Michael Row the Boat Ashore

2. Sister, <u>help</u> to trim the <u>sail</u>, Hallelu<u>jah</u>,
Sister, <u>help</u> to trim the <u>sail</u>, Hallelu<u>jah</u>!

3. Jordan's <u>River</u> is chilly and <u>cold</u>, Hallelu<u>jah</u>,
Chills the <u>body</u>, but warms the <u>soul</u>, Hallelu<u>jah</u>!

4. Jordan's <u>River</u> is deep and <u>wide</u>, Hallelu<u>jah</u>,
Meet my <u>mother</u> on the other <u>side</u>, Hallelu<u>jah</u>!

5. If you <u>get</u> there before I <u>do</u>, Hallelu<u>jah</u>,
Tell my <u>people</u> I'm a-comin' <u>too</u>, Hallelu<u>jah</u>!

"I Never Will Marry" is a modernized version of an old ballad that uses the relative minor chord, Bm, in the key of D, played at the second fret with the Am barre form.

Song Performance Guide

CHORDS IN SONG: D A7 G Bm Em

SINGING PITCH:

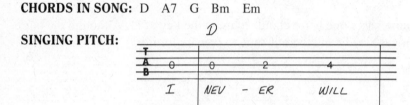

I Never Will Marry

1. SOME SAY THAT LOVE IS A GENT - LE THING, BUT IT
ON - LY BROUGHT ME PAIN, _____ AND THE
ON - LY ONE I E - VER LOVED IS
GONE ON THAT EV' - NIN' TRAIN. _____

2. I cried, I cried like a baby,
   Lay awake all night till dawn; __
   "I'm leaving you, darling," was all he said,
   "Don't count the days I'm gone." __ __ __ __
   (Chorus)

3. There's changes in the sailing winds, __
   Change in the deep blue sea; __
   Changes in my true love's heart,
   But never a change in me. __ __ __ __
   (Chorus)

There are many variations of "Wayfaring Stranger." This one, in the key of Am, features an F chord in the chorus. A staccato rhythm can be employed with the use of the barre forms of the Am and Dm chords by releasing pressure and muting the strings.

Song Performance Guide

CHORDS IN SONG: Am Dm F C E

SINGING PITCH:

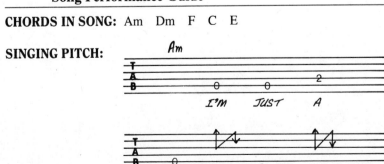

Wayfaring Stranger

♩ = 112

Am

1. I'M JUST A POOR   WAY - FAR - ING STRAN - GER,

Dm   Am

A TRAV - 'LIN' THROUGH   THIS WORLD OF WOE. _____

_____ BUT THERE'S NO SICK - NESS, TOIL OR DAN - GER, _____

Dm   Am

IN THAT BRIGHT LAND   TO WHICH I GO. _____

F   C

I'M GO - ING THERE   TO SEE MY FA - THER,*

F   E

_____ I'M GO - ING THERÉ   NO MORE TO ROAM,

Am

_____ I'M JUST A - GO - ING O - VER JOR - DAN, _____

Dm   Am

_____ I'M JUST A - GO - ING O - VER HOME.

*2. mother
 3. brother

"Railroad Bill" is usually Travis-picked. It is presented here in the key of A to give you an opportunity to use the A7-form and the A-form barres.

Song Performance Guide

CHORDS IN SONG: A C#7 D E7

SINGING PITCH:

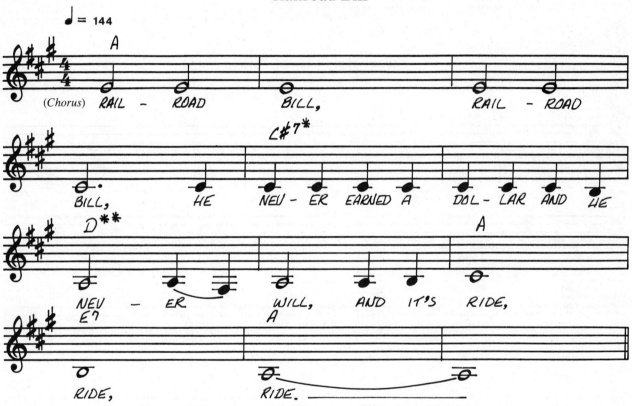

Railroad Bill

♩ = 144

(Chorus) RAIL - ROAD   BILL,   RAIL - ROAD

C#7*

BILL,   HE NEV - ER EARNED A DOL - LAR AND HE

D**   A

NEV - ER WILL, AND IT'S RIDE,

E7   A

RIDE,   RIDE.

*A7-form barre.
**A-form barre.

1. Railroad Bill, Railroad Bill,
    Lightin' big cigars with a twenty dollar bill
    And it's ride, ride, ride. ___
    (*Chorus*)

2. Railroad Bill's a mighty mean man,
    Shot the lantern from a brakeman's hand,
    And it's ride, ride, ride. ___
    (*Chorus*)

3. Railroad Bill is mighty bad,
    Shot at his Ma but he hit his Dad,
    And it's ride, ride, ride. ___
    (*Chorus*)

"Sweet Betsy from Pike" will help you to practice making a quick change to and from the F chord, which you should try to play as an E-form barre at the first fret. If this is too difficult, then practice other songs in this chapter until the barre chords seem as easy as playing first-position chords.

Song Peformance Guide

CHORDS IN SONG: C G Am D7 F

SINGING PITCH:

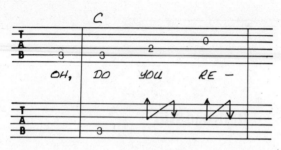

Sweet Betsy from Pike

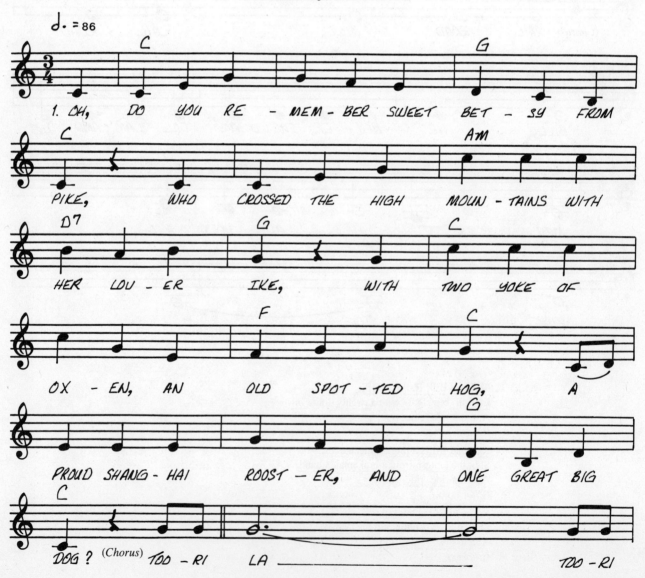

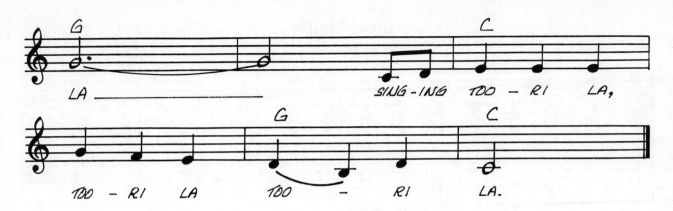

LA _____   SING-ING   TOO - RI   LA,
TOO - RI   LA   TOO - RI   LA.

2. One morning quite early they camped on the Platte,
Nearby a stream with a green shady flat.
Betsy sore-footed lay down in repose,
While Ike sat and smiled at his Pike County Rose.
(*Chorus*)

3. They camped on the prairie one bright starry night.
They broke out the whiskey and Betsy got tight.
She danced and she hollered all over the plain,
And showed her bare bum to the whole wagon train.
(*Chorus*)

4. The Shanghai ran off and the cattle all died.
The last strip of bacon this morning was fried.
Ike looked discouraged, Betsy looked mad,
The dog drooped his tail and looked awfully sad.
(*Chorus*)

5. They soon reached the desert where Betsy gave out.
In the dust and the sand she lay rolling about.
Ike he ran to her in awful surprise,
Saying, "Please get up, Betsy, you'll get sand in your eyes."
(*Chorus*)

6. Ike and Sweet Betsy attended a dance.
Ike wore a pair of his Pike County pants.
Betsy got decked out in ribbons and rings.
Ike said, "Betsy, you're an angel, but where are your wings?"
(*Chorus*)

7. Ike and Sweet Betsy got married, of course.
Ike, being jealous, sued for divorce.
Betsy got angry and started to shout,
"Get lost, you big lummox, I'm glad you backed out."
(*Chorus*)

Left-Hand Damping with Barre Chords

Barre chords have more uses than just being an effective way to play certain chords. On an electric guitar, for example, the open strings have a tone that is considered by many to be less desirable than the fretted-string sound, and many players will use barre forms of all chords for this reason. Barre chords are extremely useful in rhythm playing. Since the left hand is touching all the strings, the sounding of the chord can be stopped instantly at any desired moment simply by releasing pressure on the barre until the strings are no longer fretted but are muted or deadened. In this way chords can be cut off or "chopped," and much crisper, bouncier, and more precise rhythms can be defined than with open chords.

ROCK AND BLUES WITH BARRE CHORDS

Many rock and blues guitar players use barre chords extensively, partly because they use the electric guitar and partly because certain guitar rhythm figures demand it. Most rock and blues songs were written by guitar players, who use barre chords as a central part of the guitar sound of the songs. Also, many of the rhythms generated in rock and blues guitar require damping effects that can only be obtained with barre chords.

"Blues Shuffle" is an example of a guitar arrangement that uses barre chord figures. A repeating bass line moves through each chord change, and a barre form is needed for the A7 and B7 chords to keep the bass figure consistent. This type of rhythm is extremely common and can be played in many tempos. The right hand uses all downstrokes, either with the thumb or a pick, and plays only the bass strings. In blues, eighth notes written ♫ are usually played with a rhythmic feeling of ♩♪.

Blues Shuffle

The barre chord forms presented in Figure 9.3 are derived from the open chords given in Figure 10.4 (page 225). They can be moved anywhere on the neck to produce chords with different roots. The root-note position is marked in each chord with an *R* to assist in locating and naming the chords produced at each fret. Other barre forms are possible, but these are the most common and convenient forms of these chords.

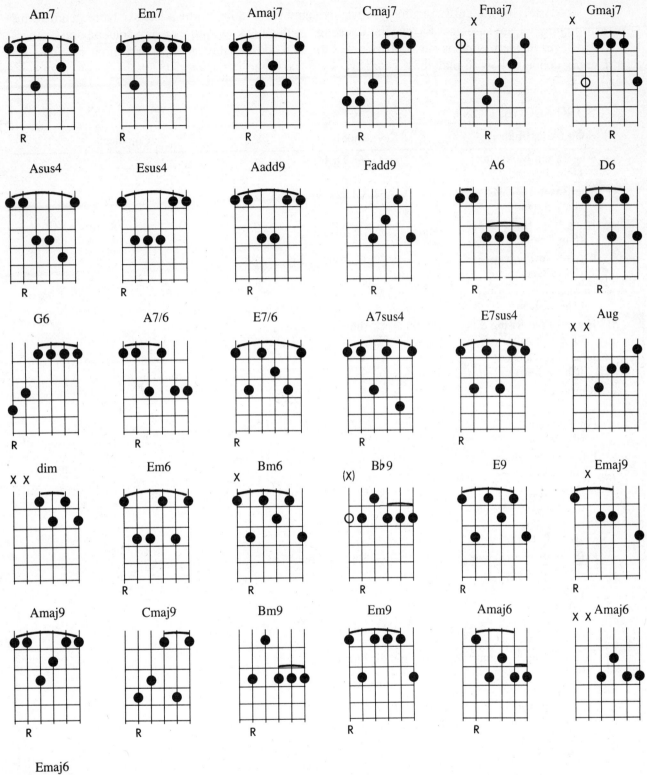

FIGURE 9.3 More Barre Chord Forms

Mastery of the guitar requires the use of many barre chord forms. The six barre chord forms in Figure 9.1 are sufficient for playing the songs in this book as well as many contemporary songs. However, modern popular music often makes use of a considerably larger variety of chord types. An introduction to how to play these chord types will be found in Chapter 10.

SONG SUGGESTIONS

Song (Artist/Author)	Key: Chords	Comments
Angel from Montgomery (John Prine)	G: G, C, D, F	
The Boxer (Paul Simon)	C: C, G, F, Am	
Bring It on Home to Me (Sam Cooke)	E: E, A, B7	Barre A, B7
City of New Orleans (Steve Goodman)	C: C, G, Am, F, Em, D, B♭	
Desperado (The Eagles)	G: G, C, D, Cm, G7, Em, A7, Bm, B7	
House of the Rising Sun (The Animals)	Am: Am, C, D, F, E	
Johnny B. Goode (Chuck Berry)	E: E, A, B7	Blues shuffle with barre chords
Kansas City	E: E, A, B7	Blues shuffle with barre chords
Lay Lady Lay (Bob Dylan)	A: A, C♯m, G, Bm, E, F♯m	Barre A, G also
Love Has No Pride (Eric Kaz)	G: G, Bm, Em, A7, C, D, Am7	
Mr. Bojangles (Jerry Jeff Walker)	C: C, C/B, Am, Am/G, F, G, D7	
Pamela Brown (Tom T. Hall)	E: E, A, B7, C♯m, D	
Puff, the Magic Dragon (Peter Yarrow)	G: G, Bm, C, Em, A7, D7	
The Rose (Amanda McBroom)	C: C, F, G, Em, Am, Dm	
Someday Soon (Ian Tyson)	G: G, Em, C, Bm, D, Am, D7	
Take Me Home, Country Roads (Danoff/Nivert/Denver)	G: G, Em, D, C, F	
Teach Your Children (Graham Nash)	D: D, G, A7, Bm	
Tennessee Stud (Jimmie Driftwood)	D: D, C, D, G, B♭, A	

chapter 10
Expanding Melody
and Chord Technique

PLAYING SCALES

Most musicians attempt to improve their technique by playing scales. Playing scales is probably the quickest route to overcoming the maximum number of barriers in acquiring left-hand guitar skills. A major scale can be played by moving up one string in the appropriate W–W–H–W–W–W–H (or 2–2–1–2–2–2–1) fret movement (see Chapter 11 for more information on scale theory). However, scales can be played with less left-hand movement by keeping the left hand in the same position and moving across several strings in the same area of the fingerboard.

Scale Playing: Right Hand

Scale playing can be done with any of the right-hand picking methods; it is good practice to play the scales in as many different ways as you can. Play them first with all downstrokes of the thumb, using either your bare thumb or a thumbpick. Many jazz, country, and blues players use the thumb for melody playing and move surprisingly fast.

With a flatpick try playing the scales slowly and evenly, using nothing but downstrokes. Then try using all upstrokes (this is harder). The greatest flexibility and speed comes with alternating down-up or up-down strokes. This takes a while to master but is essential for a melody player.

Using the fingers is a technique most associated with classical players, but can be used effectively by anyone. Try playing the scales using just upstrokes of the index finger. Then try using just the middle finger and just the ring finger. It is very common to play scales by alternating the index and middle fingers.

Scales can be played very fast and smoothly by alternating the thumb and index finger. It is good practice to play the scales with thumb-index as well as with thumb-middle and thumb-ring.

Playing Open-Position Major Scales

The word *position* is used to indicate where on the fingerboard something is to be played. Since the four fingers of the left hand can comfortably span a distance of four frets, each such four-fret segment is called a position. The first four frets, including the open strings, are called the *first position* or sometimes *open position* or *nut position*. Notes occurring on the first fret of any string are fretted with the index finger; notes in the second, third, and fourth frets of any position are fingered with the second, third, and fourth fingers, respectively. There are many exceptions, but this is a good general rule.

To find scale fingerings on the guitar, you simply need to know the names of the pitches on the fretboard and the names of the tones in the scales. The notation and open-position fret diagram for the C-major, G-major, and E-pentatonic blues scales are shown in Figure 10.1. Practice each of these scales in both upward (as pictured) and downward directions.

The pitches of some of the scale degrees in blues lie in between the frets of the guitar. These pitches are called "blue notes" and are found at the third, fifth, and seventh degrees of the major scale. The "blue" third in E will lie between G and G♯, and can be played on the guitar by bending or stretching the string. The "blue" fifth lies between the fifth and the flat fifth, while the "blue" seventh lies between the seventh and the flat seventh. Because of the need for bending strings, most blues scales are played in higher position on the neck, since strings are harder to bend near the nut. Try bending the B string while pressing on the eighth fret. Raise the pitch of G by pushing the fretted string toward the G string. (See page 236 for an explanation of the construction of the pentatonic blues scale.)

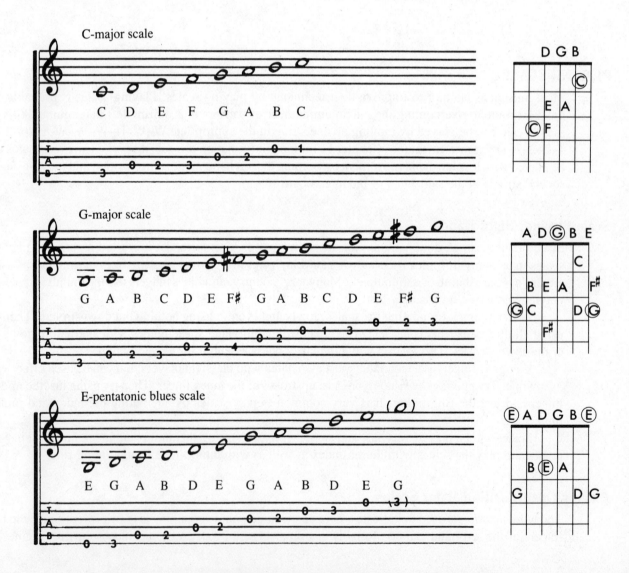

FIGURE 10.1 Open-Position C-Major, G-Major, and E-Pentatonic Blues Scale Fingerings

Playing Closed-Position (Movable) Scales

There are many different fingerings for major scales since the same notes can be played on different strings. In addition to the first-position open versions of the scales are the closed-position scales, so named because they have no open strings. Like the movable barre chords, these scale forms are movable and can be played with the same fingering at different positions on the neck to obtain different scales. Some of the closed-position scales are easier to master than others since some will require the fingers to span a four-fret interval and others may require five-fret reach. The "C" and "F" movable major scale forms are shown in Figure 10.2. These can be performed with just a four-fret reach, and they enable you to play a different major scale at each fret. The forms are named according to the scale that would sound if the first-finger notes were open strings and played in first position. This is analogous to the manner in which barre chord forms are named according to the name of the open chord that is formed above the index-finger barre. In Figures 10.2 and 10.3 the tonic note of each movable major scale form is shown as a solid circle. Movable pentatonic blues scale forms for G and E are given in Figure 10.3. These scales are played on guitar as far as they can without stopping at the tonic note. This extended scale develops hand position and a knowledge of the fingerboard. Practice each scale carefully, and move through the different forms at different positions to extend a given scale up to fingerboard.

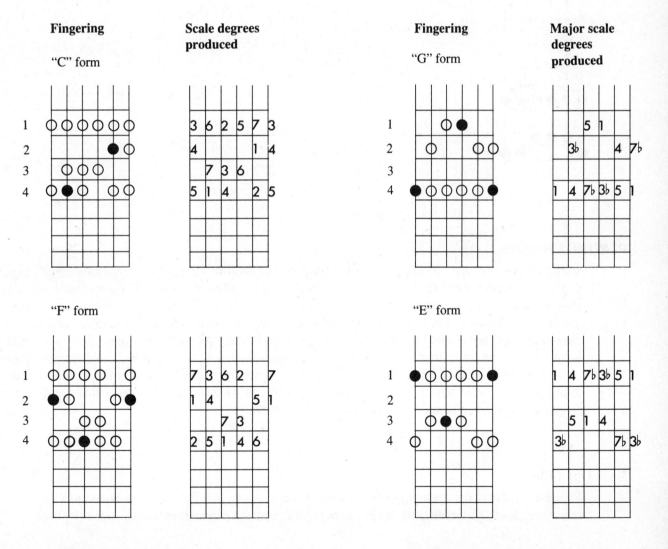

FIGURE 10.2 Movable Major
Scale Forms in C and F

FIGURE 10.3 Movable Pentatonic Blues
Scale Forms in G and E

Exercises: Playing Scales

1. Play an E♭-major scale using the movable C scale form.

2. Play a B♭-major scale using the movable F scale form.

3. Draw the open-position scale diagrams for the keys of D, A, and E.

4. Draw the movable major scale forms for G and B♭.

5. Draw the movable pentatonic blues scale forms for B♭, C, and D.

6. Improvise a melody over the twelve-bar blues progression

A	A	A7	A7
D7	D7	A	A
E7	D7	A	E7

by playing an E form of the blues scale at the fifth fret. This scale fingering played at the fifth fret will produce an A-pentatonic blues scale.

PLAYING CHORDS

Although the basic open chords presented in Chapter 3 will allow you to play a large number of songs, there is an obvious need for having a more complete knowledge of chords. The three basic types of chords—major, minor, and seventh—will suffice for harmonizing most simple melodies, but much guitar music involves more complex chords. There are twelve major chords, twelve minor chords, and twelve seventh chords, yet the open chords from Chapter 3 only total fifteen of these thirty-six fundamental chords. Learning to transpose and use a capo (see Chapter 12) can help you avoid learning some of the harder chords for a while, but eventually you will need to expand your chord repertoire in order to play more complex music. There are also many different ways to play each chord that use different fingerings. These can be used to create varied tone colors.

More Open Chords

Figure 10.4 shows the open-position versions of some chords that can easily be added to your chord repertoire. Many of these chords appear in popular music and can be found in various song books.

Major chords

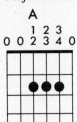 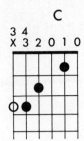 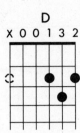 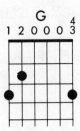

A — 0 0 2 3 4 0 (1 2 3)

C — X 3 2 0 1 0 (3 4)

D — X 0 0 1 3 2

E — 0 2 3 1 0 0

G — 1 2 0 0 0 3 (4)

Minor chords

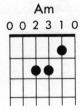 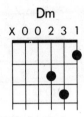

Am — 0 0 2 3 1 0

Dm — X 0 0 2 3 1

Em — 0 2 3 0 0 0

Dominant-seventh chords

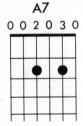 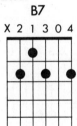 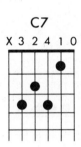 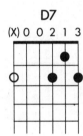 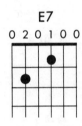 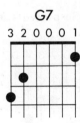

A7 — 0 0 2 0 3 0

B7 — X 2 1 3 0 4

C7 — X 3 2 4 1 0

D7 — (X) 0 0 2 1 3

E7 — 0 2 0 1 0 0

G7 — 3 2 0 0 0 1

Minor-seventh chords

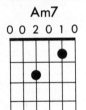 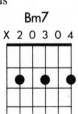 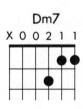 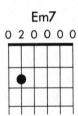 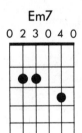 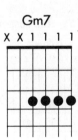

Am7 — 0 0 2 0 1 0

Bm7 — X 2 0 3 0 4

Dm7 — X 0 0 2 1 1

Em7 — 0 2 0 0 0 0

Em7 — 0 2 3 0 4 0

Gm7 — X X 1 1 1 1

Augmented chords

 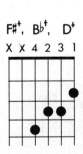 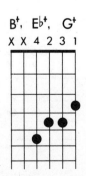

E^+, Ab^+, C^+ — X X 3 1 2 0

A^+, $C\#^+$, F^+ — X X 4 2 3 1

$F\#^+$, Bb^+, D^+ — X X 4 2 3 1

B^+, Eb^+, G^+ — X X 4 2 3 1

FIGURE 10.4 Open Chords

Diminished chords

D°,A♭°,B°, F°   E♭°, A°; C°,F#°   E°,B♭°,C#°,G°
X X 0 1 0 2   X X 1 3 2 4   X X 1 3 2 4

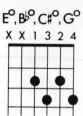

Major-seventh chords

Amaj7   Amaj7   Cmaj7   Dmaj7   Emaj7   Fmaj7   Gmaj7
0 0 2 1 3 0 0 0 1 1 1 4 3 4 2 0 0 0 X 0 0 1 1 1 0 3 1 2 0 0 X 3 4 2 1 0 2 X 0 0 0 1

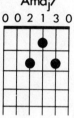

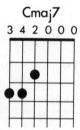

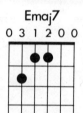
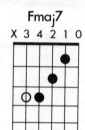
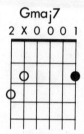

Suspended-4 chords

Asus4   Csus4   Dsus4   Esus4   Fsus4   Gsus4
0 0 2 3 4 0 X 3 4 0 1 1 X 0 0 1 3 4 0 2 3 4 0 0 X X 3 4 1 1 3 X 0 0 1 4

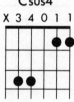

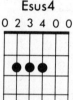

Seventh suspended-4 chords

A7sus4   D7sus4   E7sus4   G7sus4
0 0 2 0 4 0 X 0 0 2 1 4 0 2 0 3 0 0 3 X 0 0 1 1

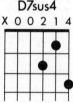

Sixth chords

A6   C6   D6   E6   F6   G6
0 0 1 1 1 1 X 4 2 3 1 0 X 0 0 2 0 3 0 2 3 1 4 0 X X 3 2 4 1 1 2 0 0 0 0

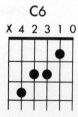
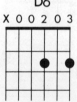

Seventh chords with added sixth (7/6)

A7/6
0 0 2 0 3 4

E7/6
0 2 0 1 3 0

G7/6
2 1 3 0 0 0

Minor-sixth chords

Am6
0 0 2 3 1 4

Bm6
0 2 0 1 0 4

Dm6
X 0 0 2 0 1

Em6
0 2 3 0 4 0
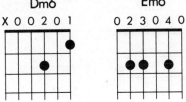

Gm6
3 1 0 0 4 0
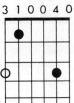

Major-sixth chords

Amaj6
0 0 2 1 3 4

Cmaj6
3 4 1 2 0 0
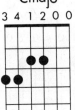

Dmaj6
X 0 0 4 1 1
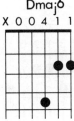

Emaj6
0 3 1 2 4 0
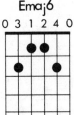

Fmaj6
X 2 3 1 4 0
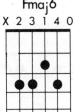

Gmaj6
2 1 4 0 3 0

Minor-major–seventh chords

Ammaj7
0 0 3 1 2 0

Dmmaj7
X 0 0 2 3 1

Emmaj7
0 2 1 0 0 0

Added-ninth chords

Aadd9
0 0 1 4 2 0

Aadd9
0 0 2 3 0 0

Cadd9
X 3 2 0 4 0
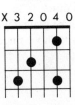

Dadd9
X 0 (3) 2 1 0
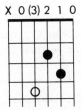

Eadd9
0 2 3 1 0 4

Fadd9
X 0 3 2 1 4

Gadd9
3 2 0 1 0 4

Dominant-ninth chords

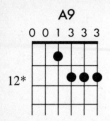
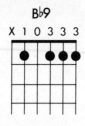
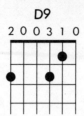
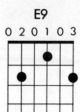

Minor-ninth chords

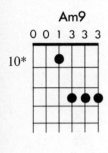
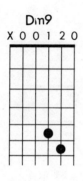

Major-ninth chords

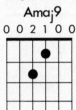
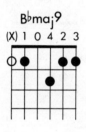
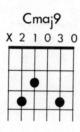
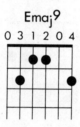
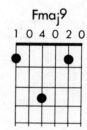
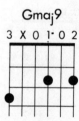

*The number to the left of the chord diagram indicates the fret number for chords played in higher positions on the neck.

Exercises: Playing Chords

1. Have a friend play several of the chords from Figure 10.4 for you. Identify the chord type of each, concentrating on the major, minor, and dominant-seventh chords first. Gradually have other chord types added, and identify each.

2. Repeat Exercise 1, but this time reverse roles with your friend.

3. There are several possibilities for playing barre chords in addition to the six given in Chapter 9 (page 206). Look through Figure 10.4, and find chords that can be played with the second, third, and fourth left-hand fingers. Some chords that can be played with those fingers and barred up the fretboard include Am7, Em7, and Amaj9. Can you play any others?

PART II
Special Topics

Part II of this book is concerned with aspects of the guitar that are informational in nature rather than skills to be learned. Understanding theoretical concepts enhances the enjoyment of music making and makes it easier to understand and communicate musical ideas. Chapters 11 and 12 explain scales, chords, chord progressions, keys, and transposing, with an emphasis on how they apply to the playing of songs on guitar. Chapter 13 surveys the information needed to purchase and maintain a guitar, and Chapter 14 gives useful ideas on how to create arrangements and accompaniments for music that is not systematically notated. Some scholars and musicians feel that the process of composing and performing one's own material is an important part of the folk guitar experience. Chapter 15 explores some of the practical and philosophical issues involved in writing and performing your own versions of songs. And the final chapter is a historical overview of the acoustic steel-string guitar in the United States. It follows the development of the styles and the evolution of the music and the repertoire through most of the important players and groups, and provides an outline for understanding the various stylistic idioms as well as a discography so that aspiring guitarists may learn from their predecessors.

chapter 11
Theory of Scales, Keys, and Chords

NAMING MUSICAL PITCHES

The concept of musical pitch relationships that is common to virtually all musical systems is the *octave*. The octave is something that occurs in nature and represents the number 2. The pitch of a vibrating string is raised an octave if the string is shortened by half; likewise, the pitch is lowered an octave if the length of the string is doubled. Pitches an octave apart have a frequency ratio of 1:2 and are so musically consonant that they are given the same musical name.

In Western culture the octave has been divided into twelve equal intervals called *semitones*, *half steps*, or, on the guitar, *frets*. The interval of two frets is called a *whole tone* or a *whole step*. The first seven letters of the alphabet together with the sharp (♯) and flat (♭) symbols are used to name the twelve divisions of the octave. A sharp symbol placed next to a letter name means that the "sharped" note has been raised one half step higher than the "unsharped" note with the same letter name; the flat symbol similarly lowers the pitch one half step. Thus, G♯ is one half step higher in pitch than G, and B♭ is one half step lower in pitch than B. The succession of semitones in the octave is called the *chromatic scale*, and it represents the names of all the pitches produced by all the keys of the piano or the frets of the guitar. The chromatic scale is shown on the keyboard in Figure 11.1.

Notice that the white keys of the piano receive letter names and have no accidentals (sharps or flats) and that the black keys have letter names with sharps and flats. The pitch between A and B has two names: sometimes it is called A♯, and sometimes it is called B♭. Notice also that there is no sharp or flat between B and C and between E and F. Many important concepts in music theory require that these notes' chromatic names be used.

Figure 11.2 shows the names of the notes on the guitar fingerboard. Notice that the succession of notes on each string follows the chromatic scale. Notice also that the twelfth fret is an octave above the open string. The twelfth fret divides the string into two equal halves.

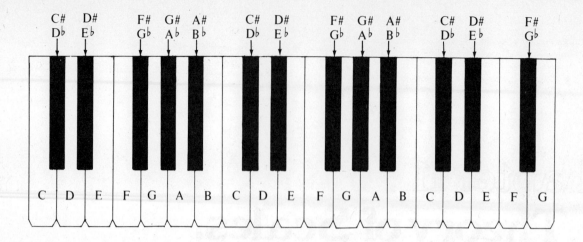

FIGURE 11.1 The Keyboard

SCALE STRUCTURE
The Major Scale

Most songs do not use all twelve pitches of the chromatic scale in their melodies: the most common songs primarily use only seven. These seven pitches are arranged sequentially in a pattern known as the *major scale*, the familiar do–re–mi–fa–sol–la–ti–do. The major scale uses tones from the chromatic scale in a specific pattern of whole steps and half steps: W–W–H–W–W–W–H, where W is a whole step and H is a half step. Each whole step is equal in size to two half steps (Figure 11.3).

Each tone of the scale can be referred to as a *scale degree*. In the C-major scale, C is the first scale degree and so on:

Name of tone:	C	D	E	F	G	A	B	C	D	E
Scale degree:	I	II	III	IV	V	VI	VII	VIII	IX	X
								(I)	(II)	(III)

Note that there is always a whole step between successive pitches of the major scale except between the third and fourth scale degree and between the seventh and eighth scale degrees. A different major scale can be built on each of the twelve chromatic tones of the octave, and each of those scales is named after the pitch on which it starts.

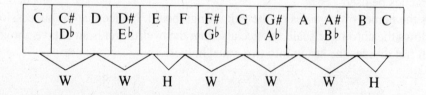

FIGURE 11.3 Construction of the C-Major Scale

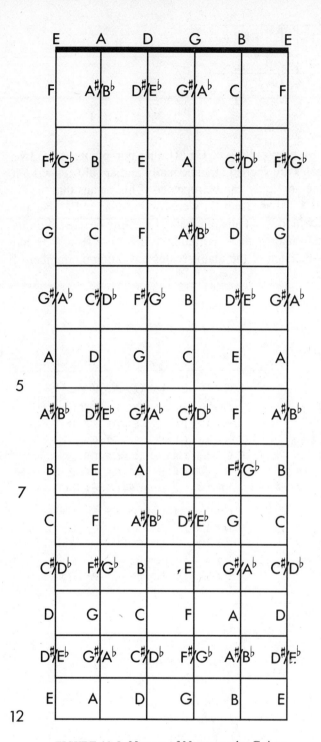

FIGURE 11.2 Names of Notes on the Guitar

Naming the Major Scales

If we apply the W–W–H–W–W–W–H pattern to each of the twelve pitches in the chromatic scale, twelve different major scales can be built. The scale on the note C is called the C-major scale: it has the notes C–D–E–F–G–A–B–C. A C scale has no sharps or flats in its notation. The major scale that starts on G requires one sharp for the seventh scale degree.

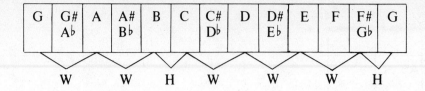

But should that note be called F♯ or by its *enharmonic* spelling of G♭? (Enharmonic notes have two different letter names but are the same pitch.) Scales are spelled alphabetically and are always written in such a way that every letter is used once before any letter can be repeated. This means that the G-major scale can only be written G–A–B–C–D–E–F♯–G because if G♭ were used instead of F♯, then the last three notes of the scale would read E–G♭–G, which is not an alphabetical spelling because it omits the letter F and repeats the letter G. Similarly, a D-major scale is written D–E–F♯–G–A–B–C♯–D and an F-major scale is written F–G–A–B♭–C–D–E–F. Each of the major scales has a unique number of sharps or flats. See Figure 11.4.

Scale	Number of sharps or flats	Notes altered	Tones of scale
C	0	0	C –D –E –F –G –A –B –C
G	1♯	F♯	G –A –B –C –D –E –F♯–G
D	2♯	F♯–C	D –E –F♯–G –A –B –C♯–D
A	3♯	F♯–C♯–G♯	A –B –C♯–D –E –F♯–G♯–A
E	4♯	F♯–C♯–G♯–D♯	E –F♯–G♯–A –B –C♯–D♯–E
B	5♯	F♯–C♯–G♯–D♯–A♯	B –C♯–D♯–E –F♯–G♯–A♯–B
F♯	6♯	F♯–C♯–G♯–D♯–A♯–E♯	F♯–G♯–A♯–B –C♯–D♯–E♯–F♯
G♭	6♭	B♭–E♭–A♭–D♭–G♭–C♭	G♭–A♭–B♭–C♭–D♭–E♭–F –G♭
D♭	5♭	B♭–E♭–A♭–D♭–G♭	D♭–E♭–F –G♭–A♭–B♭–C –D♭
A♭	4♭	B♭–E♭–A♭–D♭	A♭–B♭–C –D♭–E♭–F –G –A♭
E♭	3♭	B♭–E♭–A♭	E♭–F –G –A♭–B♭–C –D –E♭
B♭	2♭	B♭–E♭	B♭–C –D –E♭–F –G –A –B♭
F	1♭	B♭	F –G –A –B♭–C –D –E –F

FIGURE 11.4 Summary of Tones in Major Scales

Exercises: Major Scales

1. Play a major scale on the guitar on the bass E string by starting with the open string and going up the fingerboard according to the major scale pattern of half steps and whole steps.

2. Play a different major scale on the bass E string by starting at the first fret. What is the name of this scale? At what fret does the scale end? How many frets above the starting note is the final note of the scale?

3. Play a major scale on the D string starting at the second fret. What is the letter name of this note? What is the name of this scale? Play another scale starting with the open high E string. What name does this scale have? Compare the sound quality of this scale to the scale that started at the second fret of the D string and also to the scale that started on the open bass E string.

4. When guitarists play scales, they generally do not play all the notes on just one string since it is faster to cross to the next higher string. By referring to the fretboard diagram in Figure 11.2 (page 233), find a way to play the E-major scale that starts at the open bass E string but that doesn't use

any notes above the fourth fret. The final note of this (one octave) scale should be the same as the note that was at the twelfth fret of the bass E string. This new note will be on what string and at what fret?

5. Write out the names of the notes in an E♭-major scale. How many flats or sharps are there?

6. Write on the treble staff the notes of the A-major scale:

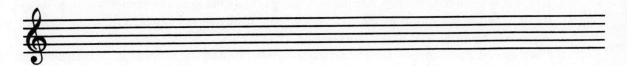

7. Write on the treble staff the notes of the A♭-major scale:

Modal, Minor, and Blues

There are other seven-tone scale systems called *modes* that are closely related to the major scale and that are the foundation of what is called modal music. The modes have Greek names and can be derived from the major scale by having each scale degree become the tonic tone for a different mode. The major scale is actually a mode itself (Ionian) and follows the familiar pattern of whole steps and half steps: W–W–H–W–W–W–H. The *Dorian* mode can be found by starting on the second scale degree of the major scale and proceeding through one octave, thus resulting in a new scale pattern of W–H–W–W–W–H–W. Since a C-major scale is C–D–E–F–G–A–B–C, a D Dorian scale with D tonic would be D–E–F–G–A–B–C–D. The modes and their scale structures are shown in Figure 11.5 along with an example of each mode constructed from each of the degrees of the C-major scale.

Mode	Built on major scale degree	Scale tones/Structure
Ionian (major)	I	C – D – E – F – G – A – B – C W – W – H – W – W – W – H
Dorian	II	D – E – F – G – A – B – C – D W – H – W – W – W – H – W
Phrygian	III	E – F – G – A – B – C – D – E H – W – W – W – H – W – W
Lydian	IV	F – G – A – B – C – D – E – F W – W – W – H – W – W – H
Mixolydian	V	G – A – B – C – D – E – F – G W – W – H – W – W – H – W
Aeolian (minor)	VI	A – B – C – D – E – F – G – A W – H – W – W – H – W – W
Locrian	VII	B – C – D – E – F – G – A – B H – W – W – H – W – W – W

FIGURE 11.5 Structure of the Modal Scales

All of the modes in Figure 11.5 share the same tones and thus would all have the same key signature. When two scales (or modes) have different tonic tones but use the same seven notes, they are referred to as *relative* keys or relative scales. C Ionian (major) is the relative key of A Aeolian (minor) because both scales use the tones A, B, C, D, E, F, and G. D major and E Dorian are relative scales because they both use the seven tones D, E, F♯, G, A, B, and C♯.

The most widely used modes are Ionian (major) and Aeolian (natural minor). In the natural-minor scale the seventh tone is often raised a half step to create the *harmonic minor* scale: A–B–C–D–E–F–G♯–A. The practice of raising the sixth and seventh scale degrees produces the *melodic minor* scale in the ascending form: A–B–C–D–E–F♯–G♯–A.

Several styles of guitar music rely heavily on other modal inflections. Mixolydian and Dorian modes are very common in traditional and bluegrass music, and the Phrygian mode is used in Spanish and Flamenco music. The Lydian mode is being increasingly employed in rock music.

The blues scale is extremely prevalent in American guitar music. It appears to be a hybrid of an African pentatonic (five-tone) scale and the major scale. There are no half steps in the pentatonic blues scale, which has a pattern of half steps WH–W–W–WH–W. Three half steps is equal to a whole step and a half step and is written as WH. A blues scale in C would be

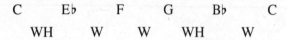

Exercises: Modal, Minor, and Blues Scales

1. If there is a piano available, play each of the seven modes on the white keys as they are given in Figure 11.5 (page 235). First play the C-major (Ionian) scale, and then the D Dorian, E Phrygian, F Lydian, and so on. Listen to the differences. Play the scales in both ascending and descending order.

2. Write the letter names of the notes for each of the modal scales, starting them all on G.

3. Play the first five notes of an Aeolian scale. What other modal scale has the identical first five notes?

4. Play the first five notes of an Ionian (major) scale. What other modal scale has the identical first five notes?

5. Write the notes of a pentatonic blues scale starting on E.

KEYS

One of the most important ideas in music—and one of the most difficult to define—is *key*. The term *key* includes the concepts of scale, the relationship among the scale tones, and the harmonic tension and release properties of chords. A given song can exist in any key. Changing the key of a song merely puts it at a different pitch level while keeping intact all other relationships.

One of the most noticeable properties of a key is the scale upon which it is based, and the most important aspect of the scale is the role of its first note and its final note—the *tonic*. The basic nature of scales seems to cause this gravitation toward the tonic, and the melodies constructed around particular scales most frequently come to rest on the tonic. The melodic activity is at a point of least tension and greatest stability and finality when it resolves to the tonic. When melodies do not end on the tonic note of the scale, the ear tends to hear them as unfinished. The notes of the major scale seem to gravitate to the tonic, even if it is not one of the notes in the melody. If a song in G major began in the middle of a G scale, for example, and went on for some time without the note G in the melody, the ear would still discern that the note G was the tonic and that resolution of melodic activity would lead to the G. The tonic note is sometimes called the *key center*.

FIGURE 11.6 Relative Tonic Tones for Major, Mixolydian, Dorian, and Minor Scales for Each Key Signature

Determining the Key

One of the basic steps in determining the key of a song is to find the scale tones that are used in the melody. If the song is written on the staff, then this information is much easier to obtain than if you are just listening to it. On the staff a group of sharps or flats at the beginning of each line of music, called the *key signature,* will indicate which tones are being used. A song in the key of G major would use the notes from the G-major scale as the basis for its melody. Since the key signature for the key of G major has one sharp, F♯, the melody of the song would be much more likely to have an F♯ than an F♮. The key signatures for the other keys are shown in Figure 11.6. Minor, Dorian, and Mixolydian scales have the same twelve key signatures as the major keys, they use the same scale tones as major scales, but they have different tonic tones.

Keys that have the same number of sharps or flats in the key signature and utilize the same scale tones but have different tonics are called *relative* keys. This relativity among scale tones is shown in Figure 11.7. The seven pitches are A, B, C, D, E, F, and G; however, each different scale has its own tonic tone and a particular set of intervallic relationships that give it its identity. The letters W and H in Figure 11.7 stand for the whole- and half-step distance between scale degrees. *Parallel* keys are built on the same tonic pitch; for instance, C major, C minor, and C Mixolydian are parallel keys.

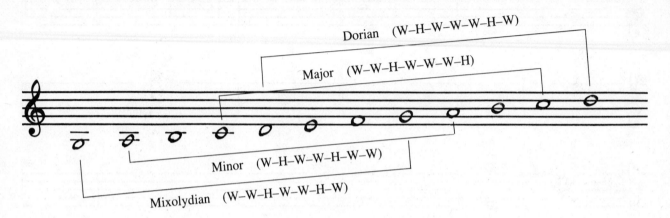

FIGURE 11.7 Tonic-Tone Derivation for Four Relative Scales

After you have looked at the key signature and have determined the scale tones used in the song, the next clue to look for is the *final note* of the song. Because the key signature alone can only narrow the possibilities for the key of the song, additional pieces of information must be used in conjunction with knowledge of the scale tones. The key note, or tonic, being the note with the least amount of melodic tension, will most likely be the final note of a song. The tonic note also commonly occurs at the end of sections of a song such as verses or choruses. A song in the key of G major will probably end on the note G; and while a song in E minor will have the same key signature (and, therefore, the same pitches) as G major, it will most likely end on the melody note E. Likewise, a song in D Mixolydian will have the key signature from G major, but will probably end on the note D.

The third and usually conclusive clue to the key of a song is the *final chord*. Just as the melodic activity of a song tends to come to rest on the tonic note, so does the harmonic activity come to rest on the tonic chord. The chord built on the tonic note is also likely to occur at the end of sections of the song or anywhere the chord movement of the song seems to be "at rest." Thus a song in G major will have the scale tones G, A, B, C, D, E, F♯, and will probably come to rest on the melody note G and on a G-major chord. A song in E minor would have the same scale tones and would probably end with the note E and with an E-minor chord.

When the key signature, final note, and final chord of a song all agree, then it is safe to conclude that the key has been determined. If there is disagreement that cannot be explained by the song being major, minor, Dorian, or Mixolydian, then perhaps the song has a "trick" ending that purposely leaves an unresolved feeling. Hearing the song will allow you to determine if the final note or chord is not the one that will create a feeling of resolution at the end of the piece.

Exercises: Keys

1. Determine the key of each of the songs in a song book. Check the key signature, final chord, and final note.

2. Put on a record or turn on the radio, and try to find the tonic note to the song that is being played. This means that your guitar will have to be in tune with the record or the radio. It

should not matter if your guitar is a fret or two sharper or flatter than the source. Just make sure that some note on your guitar is in tune with some note in the song you are listening to; then you can find the tonic note. This will be easier if you are listening to country and western music or pop music rather than avant-garde or classical music, because the latter two are more likely to change keys in the middle of the piece or be ambiguous.

3. "Old Joe Clark" (page 127) is often played in a major key with inflections from the Mixolydian scale. It has a lowered seventh tone when compared with the parallel major scale. What would the key signature be for this song if the Mixolydian tonic note were C?

4. Find the key in which each of the following excerpts is written. Check the key signature, final chord, and final note.

CHORD STRUCTURE

Since the guitar is most easily accessible as a chording instrument, a working knowledge of chords is essential to a guitarist. A *chord* may be defined as three or more tones played simultaneously. There are many different kinds of chords and many different ways to play each chord on the guitar. There are also many series or progressions of chords that need to be identified and understood.

Intervals

The building blocks of chords are intervals. An interval is the distance between two notes which may be played either consecutively or simultaneously.

The name of an interval is derived from the number of letters encompassed by its spelling. The distance from A up to B is called a second because only two letter names, A and B, are encompassed by the two notes. C up to G is a fifth because there are five letter names encompassed by the two notes (C, D, E, F, and G). Intervals may also descend. The distance from D down to A is a fourth (D, C, B, and A).

Intervals are further identified by their types. The three basic intervallic qualities are perfect, major, and minor. Combined with the name of the interval, these qualities of intervals are determined by the specific number of half steps they contain. For instance a major third is made up of three letter names which are separated by a distance of four half steps (C to E, for example) while a minor third, which is also made up of three letter names, contains only three half steps. See Figure 11.8 for a list of perfect, major, and minor intervals above the note C.

Two other intervallic qualities should be mentioned. An augmented interval is one half step larger than a perfect or major interval. A diminished interval is one half step smaller than a perfect or minor interval.

Interval quality and name	Half steps	Number of letter names	Example
Perfect unison	0	1	C–C
Minor second	1	2	C–Db
Major second	2	2	C–D
Minor third	3	3	C–Eb
Major third	4	3	C–E
Perfect fourth	5	4	C–F
Perfect fifth	7	5	C–G
Minor sixth	8	6	C–Ab
Major sixth	9	6	C–A
Minor seventh	10	7	C–Bb
Major seventh	11	7	C–B
Perfect octave	12	8	C–C
Minor ninth	13	9	C–Db
Major ninth	14	9	C–D

FIGURE 11.8 Table of Ascending Intervals

Exercises: Intervals

1. Write one note to form the following intervals:

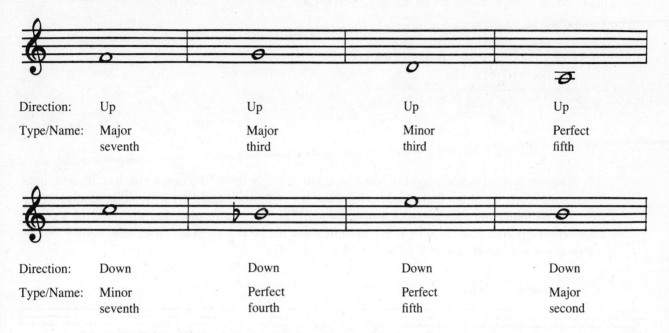

Direction:	Up	Up	Up	Up
Type/Name:	Major seventh	Major third	Minor third	Perfect fifth

Direction:	Down	Down	Down	Down
Type/Name:	Minor seventh	Perfect fourth	Perfect fifth	Major second

2. Listen to the difference between a major third and a minor third as played on your guitar. Listen to a major sixth and a minor sixth. Is there a consistent difference between major and minor intervals?

3. Play a major second above C and then a major ninth above C, and compare them. What are the letter names of the notes in each of the intervals?

4. Play intervals of a unison through a perfect fifth. Start with the open B string and the fourth fret of the G string (this is a unison) and then play the open B against successively higher notes on the G string. When you reach the ninth fret on the G string, you can continue to play the higher notes on the high E string.

Triads

The simplest chords, called *triads,* are made up of just three notes. The *major triad,* also called the major chord, is made up of two intervals: a major third and a minor third. Thus a C-major chord has the notes C–E–G in it, with C–E being the major third and E–G being the minor third. Major chords can also be thought of as being made up of the first, third, and fifth notes of the major scale.

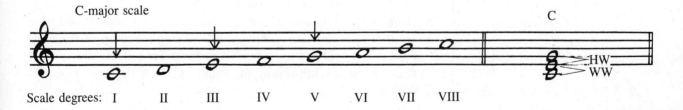

Scale degrees:	I	II	III	IV	V	VI	VII	VIII

Another way of constructing a major chord is simply to count the half steps between the root and third of the chord, and then between the third and fifth. The root, third, and fifth are so named because of their intervallic distance above the root of the chord. The note E is a third above C, and G is a fifth above C. Chords are spelled using every other diatonic scale degree, which is the same thing as every other letter: C D E F G. The formula for a major chord is simply WW–WH. That is, there are four half steps between C and E, and there are three half steps between E and G. The F#-major chord would, therefore, be spelled F#–A#–C#.

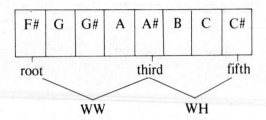

The *minor triad* is made up of a minor third plus a major third. The minor chord is often thought of as being made up of the first, third, and fifth notes of a minor scale or, more colloquially, as the first, flatted third, and fifth notes of a major scale. The formula for deriving the notes of a minor chord from any root pitch is WH–WW. Both of these methods lead to the same note names. An E-minor chord is E–G–B, and a C-minor chord is C–Eb–G.

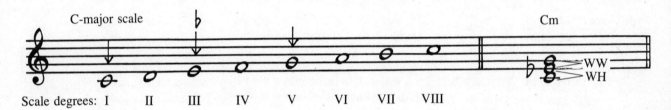

Exercises: Triads

1. What notes are produced on each string in the open-position C-major chord in Figure 10.4 (page 225)?

2. Compare the A-major chord and the A-minor chord as played on guitar. What is the difference? Compare the E-major chord and the E-minor chord. What note of the chords is different (root, third, or fifth)?

3. An E-minor chord has what notes in it? Look at the E-minor chord given in Figure 10.4 (page 225), and give the letter name of the note produced on each string. Do this with other chords.

Four-Note Chords

The most common four-note chords are the seventh chords, of which there are several types. They are formed either by adding another third to a triad or by adding as the fourth note an interval of a seventh above the root of a triad. Both ways produce the same fourth note.

The most familiar seventh chord is the *dominant seventh,* which is constructed by adding a minor third on top of a major triad. It is also commonly thought of as being made up of the root, third, fifth, and flatted seventh of the major scale. The intervallic formula for a dominant-seventh chord is WW–WH–WH. Thus, a C dominant-seventh chord, abbreviated C7, has the notes C–E–G–Bb, and the G7 has the notes G–B–D–F.

The *major-seventh* chord has a major third added to the major triad and can be thought of as being made up of the first, third, fifth, and seventh notes of the major scale. The intervallic formula for this chord is WW–WH–WW. The C major-seventh chord, abbreviated Cmaj7 or sometimes Cma7, has the notes C–E–G–B, and the D major-seventh chord (Dmaj7) is spelled D–F♯–A–C♯.

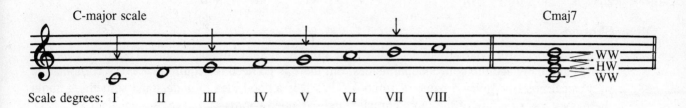

When a minor third is added to a minor triad, a *minor-seventh* chord results, which contains the first, flatted third, fifth, and flatted seventh notes of the major scale. The intervallic formula for this chord is WH–WW–WH. The D minor-seventh chord, abbreviated Dm7, is D–F–A–C, and C minor-seventh chord, abbreviated Cm7, is C–E♭–G–B♭.

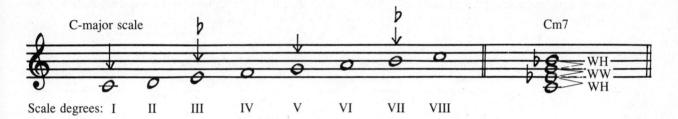

Exercises: Four-Note Chords

1. What are the notes in a D7 chord? What are the notes in a Dmaj7 chord?
2. Look at each of the dominant-seventh chords given in Figure 10.4 (page 225). Write down the name of the note produced on each string in the A7, G7, and E7 chords from bass to treble. Compare this to the notes that are in the major triads. On which string is the seventh played in each of the chords? Does the seventh tend to be in the bass or the treble?

Augmented and Diminished Chords

An augmented triad is made up of two major thirds; a diminished triad consists of two minor thirds. Three minor thirds form a four-note diminished-seventh chord. The intervallic formula for the augmented triad is WW–WW; the formula for the diminished-seventh is WH–WH–WH. Augmented and diminished chords are found much less often than major and minor chords. The C diminished chord, abbreviated C°, is spelled C–E♭–G♭, and the C augmented chord (C⁺) is spelled C–E–G♯. A diminished triad can be thought of as being made up of the first, flatted third, and flatted fifth of the major scale; an augmented triad may be thought of as being made up of the first, third, and sharped fifth of the major scale.

The diminished triad is rarely used in guitar chording. The diminished-seventh chord is normally used rather than the triad.

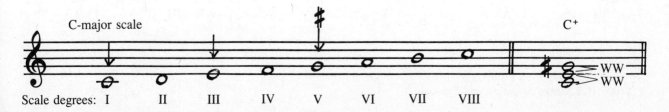

Scale degrees: I   II   III   IV   V   VI   VII   VIII

Other Chords

There are dozens of types of chords, each with a different structure and sound. The more common chords gradually acquire conventional names, but there is no need to require that every combination of musical notes be given a name or symbol. Thus it is a good idea to understand something about the names and structure of the more complex and extended chords.

The traditional way to describe chords is in terms of intervals. But for many of the complex chords this becomes a cumbersome method. So the chords given in Figure 11.9 have their structure explained by giving the note positions on the major scale in addition to the intervallic formula. This is the way many folk, jazz, and rock players keep track of the structure of the chords since it requires only knowing the formula for the chord and the major scales. Common symbols and names for the chords are given also. Even though they are rarely found, the exotic chords at the end of the list are shown only because they illustrate the way in which the chord symbol and name indicate the structure of the chord.

Chord name	Chord symbol with A root	Notes in relation to major scale	Intervallic formula between chord tones	Number of half steps
Major	A	1–3–5	WW–WH*	4,3
Minor	Am	1–3b–5	WH–WW	3,4
Dominant seventh	A7	1–3–5–7b	WW–WH–WH	4,3,3
Minor seventh	Am7	1–3b–5–7b	WH–WW–WH	3,4,3
Augmented	A⁺	1–3–5♯	WW–WW	4,4
Diminished	A°	1–3b–5b	WH–WH	3,3
Major seventh	Amaj7 or Ama7	1–3–5–7	WW–WH–WW	4,3,4
Diminished seventh	A°7	1–3b–5b–7bb(6)	WH–WH–WH	3,3,3
Suspended 4	Asus4 or Asus	1–4–5	WWH–W	5,2
Seventh suspended 4	A7sus4 or A7sus	1–4–5–7b	WWH–W–WH	5,2,3
Sixth	A6	1–3–5–6	WW–WH–W	4,3,2
Dominant sixth	Adom6 or A7/6	1–3–5–6–7b	WW–WH–W–H	4,3,2,1
Sixth suspended	A6sus	1–4–5–6	WWH–W–W	5,2,2
Minor sixth	Am6	1–3b–5–6	WH–WW–W	3,4,2
Major sixth	Amaj6	1–3–5–6–7	WW–WH–W–W	4,3,2,2
Minor–major seventh	Ammaj7	1–3b–5–7	WH–WW–WW	3,4,4
Add 9	Aadd 9	1–3–5–9	WW–WH–WWWH	4,3,7
Minor add 9	Am9	1–3b–5–9	WH–WW–WWWH	3,4,7
Dominant ninth	Adom9 or A9	1–3–5–7b–9	WW–WH–WH–WW	4,3,3,4
Minor ninth	Am9	1–3b–5–7b–9	WH–WW–WH–WW	3,4,3,4
Dominant eleventh	A11	1–3–5–7b–9–11	WW–WH–WH–WW–WH	4,3,3,4,3
Minor eleventh	Am11	1–3b–5–7b–9–11	WH–WW–WH–WW–WH	3,4,3,4,3
Minor 7/11	Am7/11	1–3b–5–7b–11	WH–WW–WH–WWWH	3,4,3,7
Thirteenth	A13	1–3–5–7b–9–11–13	WW–WH–WH–WW–WH–WW	4,3,3,4,3,4
Seven flat nine	A7/9b	1–3–5–7b–9b	WW–WH–WH–WH	4,3,3,3

*W = whole step; H = half step.

FIGURE 11.9 Chord Structure and Symbols

Exercises: Augmented, Diminished, and Other Chords

1. A C dominant-ninth chord contains the 1–3–5–7♭–9 notes of the C scale. What are these notes? Find these notes on your guitar in order, beginning with the root on the bass E string.

2. What are the notes in a B diminished-seventh chord?
What are the notes in a G♯ diminished-seventh chord?
What do you notice about the notes in these two chords?

3. How many differently pitched diminished-seventh chords exist?

4. How many differently pitched augmented chords exist?

Inversion and Doubling

Up to this point it has been assumed that chords have been played with the root in the bass. We have not investigated what happens when the notes that make up a given chord are rearranged. The rearrangement of notes in a chord is called *inversion*; there are several ways to invert chords to obtain different sounds. Since major triads have only three different note names in them, when a six-string guitar chord is played, there is repetition of the same notes in different octaves. Repetition of notes in a chord is called *doubling*. The combination of doubling and inversion requires special consideration with respect to how they are fingered on the guitar. A few basic rules about inversion and doubling can help every aspiring guitarist.

The most important note in a chord is the lowest-pitched one, or the bass note. Since it controls the sound of the chord much more than any other note, it is of the utmost importance to play chords with well-chosen bass notes. There are names given to the different ways of arranging a chord so that the different notes are in the bass. A triad with the root in the bass is called a *root-position chord*. When the third of the triad is in the bass, this is called *first inversion*. When the fifth is in the bass, this is called *second inversion*.

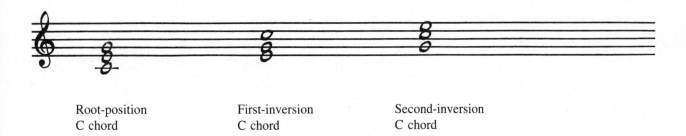

Root-position   First-inversion   Second-inversion
C chord   C chord   C chord

As we saw earlier, more complex chords may be built upon triads, and although it is possible to have a seventh chord in *third inversion* with the seventh note in the bass or a ninth chord in *fourth inversion* with the ninth note in the bass, these are rare. Most discussions of inversion just deal with the root, third, or fifth in the bass.

Most chords are given in chord charts with root bass. Although there is no special symbol for inversion that specifies exactly how the chord is built, there is a very convenient way of indicating the bass note in a chord. The *slash symbol, /,* such as G/B, indicates that a G chord is to be played with a B bass note. This notation appears frequently in song books and in popular literature. Here are some examples of inverted and doubled chords with their structure and resulting chord tones labeled. Bass tones are indicated with an arrow.

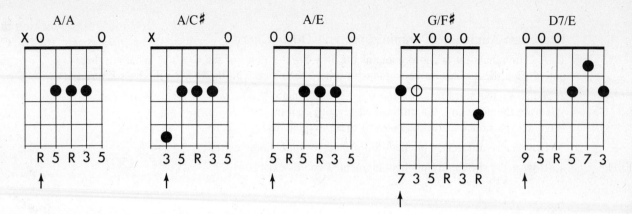

The slash-system notation is a good way of letting you know, without complicated explanations, what notes are in the bass. A G major-seventh chord in third inversion is simply written G/F♯, and a D dominant-ninth chord in fourth inversion is written D7/E.

G chord tones

G   = R (root of chord)

B+ = 3 (third of chord)

D   = 5 (fifth of chord)

C chord tones

C+ = R (root of chord)

E+ = 3 (third of chord)

G   = 5 (fifth of chord)

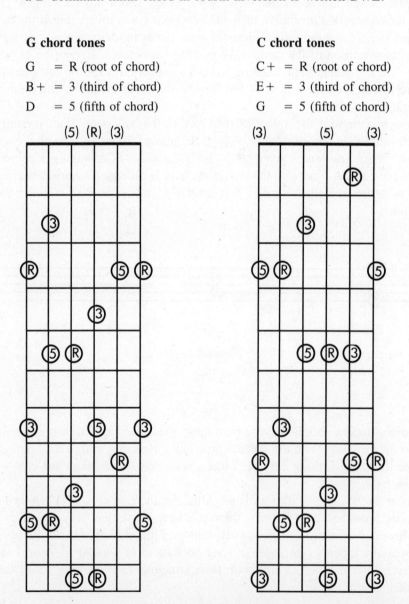

FIGURE 11.10 Tones of the C and G Chords on the Guitar Fretboard

Sometimes a performer will want to move a bass line against a static chord. Fingerpicking these progressions allows the right-hand thumb to bring out the bass line. For instance C/C, C/B, C/A, C/G, F/F, G7/G, C/C is an effective progression.

A good way to visualize all of the different inversions of a given chord is to draw a twelve-fret chord diagram and locate each tone of a given chord everywhere it occurs on the fretboard. Figure 11.10 shows the position of each chord tone on the guitar fretboard for the G-major and the C-major chords. Study them carefully and look for these recurring patterns.

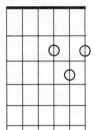 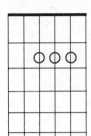 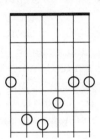 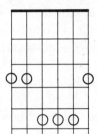 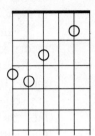

Exercises: Chord Inversions

1. How do you play a D-major chord in first inversion?

2. How do you play a C-major chord in first inversion?

3. Find the chord fingering for B7 in second inversion and A7 in third inversion.

4. Find a way to play a G chord with the chord tones R, 5, R, 3, 5, R sounding on the sixth through first strings, respectively.

5. Is Am7/C different than C6?

6. On the top three strings of the guitar there are several ways to play major chords of three notes, as shown below. For each of these assign the correct chord tone produced on each of the three treble strings. What is the inversion of each chord?

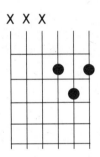 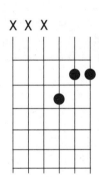 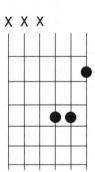

7. Make a fingerboard diagram, like that shown in Figure 11.10, for an E-minor triad. Then find three ways to play an E-minor chord, keeping the bass E, B, and high E strings open.

CHORD PROGRESSIONS

To the modern guitar player, a chord progression is one of the most important pieces of information about a song. Studio players are very often given only a chord progression, with measures marked out with chord symbols. They are then expected to create their own arrangement on the spot. Rhythmic cues can be picked up from the rest of the band, and the actual choice of what chord inversions to play and what lead notes to use is part of the working knowledge of the players. Most studio players think in terms of the changes and can be depended on to create interesting and recordable guitar parts with no other information. This type of creativity is possible in styles such as blues or bluegrass because there are well-defined musical conventions which can be applied to the song by someone familiar with that style.

Many songwriters write their songs over a chord progression, the rhythm and melody being secondary elements in the creation process. And when learning a song from another player or a record, many guitarists master the chord changes first. Even beginning guitar players must learn how to find chords to accompany familiar tunes, thus developing a concept of harmonization at a very early stage in their musical growth.

Understanding and identifying common chord progressions are an important part of the music-theory knowledge a guitarist needs, and because of the nature of the instrument it is not necessary to discuss the chord changes and harmonic movement in terms of voice leading and four-part harmony. Instead, chords are named according to their root and type. In traditional song books chords are sometimes labeled with roman numerals (I, IV, V, I). Each Roman numeral represents a chord built on a scale degree. Chord progressions are sometimes written as Arabic numbers (1, 4, 5, 1). Guitarists should recognize both numerical chord notation methods.

Chords derive their names from the steps of the major scale. Figure 11.11 gives the names of each scale degree.

The *primary chords* are those that are built on scale degrees 1, 4, and 5. Chord changes are by no means restricted only to primary chords, although there are many instances of songs that contain only these three chords.

The pattern of chord changes in a song is usually referred to as the *chord progression*.

I–V–I Progressions

Musically, this is the simplest and most fundamental chord progression. It uses two of the primary chords: the piece shifts from the *tonic chord*, or I chord, to the *dominant chord*, or V chord, and then returns to the tonic chord. The simple, two-chord songs in this book are most often I–V–I songs. This naming of the progression provides a good way to discuss the harmonic structure of the song independent of a particular key. There are D–A–D and G–D–G songs, but they are both referred to as I–V–I songs. The V chord is commonly a V7 chord, because the addition of the seventh tone above the root of the chord strengthens the resolution or return to the tonic chord. An A chord is stable by itself. But an A7 chord contains an element of harmonic tension, and this tension is best

C-major scale

Chord:	I	II	III	IV	V	VI	VII	VIII (I)
Scale degree:	1	2	3	4	5	6	7	8 (1)

FIGURE 11.11 Names of Scale Degrees

resolved by returning to the D chord. Try playing these two forms of the A chord and listening for this difference. Likewise, an E7 chord resolves to an A chord, and a D7 to a G.

I–IV–V Progressions

The IV chord, or *subdominant chord*, the next most important chord in a major key, is built on the fourth degree of the major scale. It is the third primary chord and, with the I (tonic) and V (dominant), can provide the harmony for numerous songs. In the key of C, F is the IV chord. Together these three chords use every note in the major scale.

Sometimes the IV chord appears without the V chord in a two-chord song. "Rye Whiskey" (page 47) and "Kookaburra" are two examples of I–IV–I songs. This progression does not have the finality of the V–I resolution. Listen to the D–G–A7–D progression and then to the G–C–D7–G progression, and compare the sound. It is a good idea to think of these as I–IV–V7–I progressions and to be familiar with this progression in every key.

There are many songs that can be played in any key with just the I, IV, and V chords, and when you hear players speak of knowing only three chords, this is what they mean. In fact, any melody that comes from the major scale can be accompanied effectively with just the I, IV, and V chords. Many early country players such as Woody Guthrie and Maybelle Carter used almost entirely I–IV–V progressions for songs that are commonly done with other chords. This is a good place to start when you want to write a song or to find the chords to a song you have heard.

Primary chords are not the only chords that are found in each key, but they are the chords that are the most stable. Chords with notes in them other than the scale notes will tend to pull away from the key and its scale. There are many such chords that can lead the song away from the key center as well as other chords that can bring about a return. Since the "easiest" chord changes do not involve the chords that pull out of the key, the most common chord changes involve the primary chords. Many chords can be built using only the natural tones of the major scale. Figure 11.12 gives the chord types that use only scale tones found in the major scale of a key along with the scale degree on which each chord occurs. This figure is based on the C-major scale.

Chord type	Scale degrees	Examples from key of C
Major	I, IV, V	C, F, G
Minor	II, III, VI	Dm, Em, Am
Seventh	V	G7
Major seventh	I, IV	Cmaj7, Fmaj7
Minor seventh	II, III, VI	Dm7, Em7, Am7
Sixth	I, IV, V	C6, F6, G6
Minor sixth	II	Dm6
Major sixth	I, IV	Cmaj6, Fmaj6
Ninth	V	G9
Major ninth	I, IV	Cmaj9, Fmaj9
Minor ninth	II, VI	Dm9, Am9

FIGURE 11.12 Chords That Use Only Diatonic Scale Degrees

Exercises: Playing Chord Progressions

1. Look through a song book to see how many of the songs use just the I, IV, and V chords.

2. Learn to hear the I, IV, and V chord changes. Have a friend play some chord changes in different keys, and practice naming the I, IV, and V chords as they are played.

3. Using some melodies that you are familiar with, such as "Red River Valley," "Clementine," "The Old Gray Mare," "This Old Man," or "This Land Is Your Land," try to harmonize them with only I, IV, and V chords. Compare the results you obtain with the chords that you find for the same songs in books. You will notice that the chords for given songs can vary from one book or source to another and that the chords you used are just as "right" as the ones in the book.

Secondary-Dominant Chord Progressions

Although many common chord progressions involve only the primary chords, frequently there are instances in which a song will leave the original scale and key briefly and then return. Probably the most familiar progression to do this uses what is called the *secondary dominant* for the fifth scale degree (II7). It is the dominant of the dominant, or the V of V, and it resolves most naturally to the dominant. In the key of C it is the D7 chord. Many songs use the C–D7–G7–C progression. This is only a transient harmonic movement, not a key change. But there is a very real temporary pulling away from the tonality of the original key, especially if the secondary-dominant chord is sustained for any period of time. The secondary-dominant chord has a striking and recognizable sound, particularly when found in its usual form of I–II7–V7. Play "Home on the Range" (page 69), and listen to the II7 (E7). The I7 (D7) also functions as a secondary dominant going to the IV chord (G).

A logical extension of the secondary-dominant concept is the chain of dominants, in which the resolution of one secondary dominant becomes the dominant seventh in yet another progression. These dominant chains tend to "jump" out of a key and then return through the chain of resolutions. The secondary-dominant chord's resolution to the dominant is the simplest example, but the chains can go on much longer. There are many ragtime songs that feature C–E7–A7–D7–G7–C progressions. "Five Foot Two," "Swinging upon a Star," and "Salty Dog" all employ dominant chains. Other progressions also appear with different kinds of extended chords built on a root progression that follows the dominant chain pattern. It is not uncommon in jazz, blues, and ragtime to find songs that have minor chords or ninth chords in place of dominant sevenths. Such progressions often have a similar root movement, such as C–E7–Am7–Dm7–G or C–Bm7–Em9–A7–Dm7–G6/7–C.

Twelve-Bar Blues Progressions

A basic folk-song structure is the twelve-bar blues, comprised of a repeating harmonic pattern twelve measures in length. The blues is invariably played in $\frac{4}{4}$ time. A diagram of its unaltered chord progression is shown below:

I	I	I	I
IV	IV	I	I
V	IV	I	V

This is the basic root progression, frequently played just this way but often with the seventh added to the I and V chords when leading to IV and I, respectively. Also, the IV chord is often played as a IV7, giving the music a characteristic "blues" sound:

I	I	I	I7
IV7	IV7	I	I
V7	IV7	I	V7

Another common alteration is to insert a IV chord in the second measure:

I	IV7	I	I7
IV7	IV7	I	I
V7	IV7	I	V7

Other substitutions, especially in the more modern and urban blues styles, include sixth and ninth chords, usually as extensions of the IV and V chords:

I	I	I	I7
IV9	IV9	I	I
V9	IV9	I	V9

I6	I6	I6	I6
IV6	IV6	I6	I6
V6	IV6	I6	V6

Often you will find just one or two of these ninth and sixth chords in the progression rather than exactly as shown above. The ninth chords most commonly used are dominant-ninth chords, and the sixths are usually 7/6 chords (a dominant-seventh chord with an added sixth).

Every guitarist should know the chord progressions for the twelve-bar blues in the five guitar keys (C, G, D, A, E), since for many musicians the blues is common ground. If a rock musician and a country musician meet, usually the only thing they can both be sure of knowing is a twelve-bar blues; likewise nearly every jazz, classical, bluegrass, or swing musician has enjoyed playing twelve-bar blues. There are different tempos that are used, but the chord progressions are the same.

Another feature of the twelve-bar blues that should be noted is the *turnaround*, the name given to measures 11 and 12. As the name implies, it returns the progression to the beginning. The many variations of the turnaround are usually identified by a walking bass root line that connects the I and the V chords. The turnaround is also used as the passage that starts a blues song. Some turnarounds, shown below, can be played as melodic bass notes on the guitar.

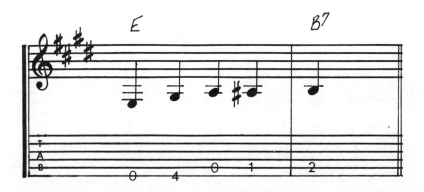

Try inserting these turnarounds into the last two measures of "Ramblin' on My Mind."

Ramblin' on My Mind

Robert Johnson

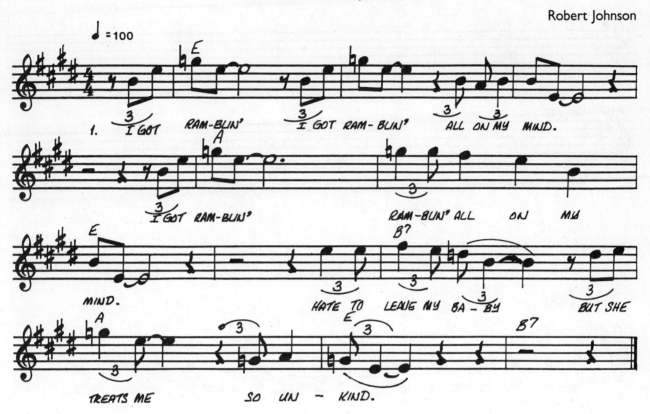

2. I got <u>mean</u> things I got <u>mean</u> things all on my <u>mind</u>. ___
   Little <u>girl</u> little <u>girl</u> I got mean things all on my <u>mind</u>. ___
   Hate to <u>leave</u> you baby, but you <u>treat</u> me so un<u>kind</u>. ___

3. Run <u>down</u> to the <u>station</u> catch the first mail train I <u>see</u>. ___
   Run <u>down</u> to the <u>station</u> catch the first mail train I <u>see</u>. ___
   I got the <u>blues</u> about Miss So and So and the <u>child</u> got the blues about <u>me</u>. ___

4. I'm leaving <u>early</u> this <u>morning</u> with my arms folded up and <u>cryin'</u>. ___
   I'm leaving <u>early</u> this <u>morning</u> with my arms folded up and <u>cryin'</u>. ___
   I hate to <u>leave</u> my baby but she <u>treats</u> me so un<u>kind</u>. ___

5. I got <u>mean</u> things I got <u>mean</u> things all on my <u>mind</u>. ___
   I got <u>mean</u> things I got <u>mean</u> things all on my <u>mind</u>. ___
   I got to <u>leave</u> my baby but she <u>treats</u> me so un<u>kind</u>. ___

"Sweet Home Chicago" by Robert Johnson, page 161, is a blues standard that is usually done as a twelve-bar blues, even though Johnson's original is a bit irregular in meter.

"Drop" Chord Progressions

Songs written in the Mixolydian mode often use a 1–VIIb–I cadence. In A Mixolydian the root notes of these chords are A–G–A. The difference between Mixolydian and major is the flatted-seventh scale degree, giving rise to the VIIb symbol, indicating its difference from the major VII. The Mixolydian tonic (I = A), and subdominant (IV = D) are identical to the I and IV chords in the parallel major key of A. The distinctive, fresh quality of Mixolydian comes from using a G chord (the "drop" chord) instead of the normal V, or E. Compare the two lines of the chorus of "Old Joe Clark," below, with those that appear in the complete song, which follows.

Old Joe Clark

2. Joe Clark had a violin,
   Played it all the day,
   Never did he fiddle around,
   All he'd do is play.
   (*Chorus*)

3. Old Joe Clark, he had a house,
   Twenty stories long,
   Ev'ry story in that house
   Was sung to a little song.
   (*Chorus*)

4. Old Joe Clark he had a dog,
   A blue tick hunting hound,
   Once a month they'd both get drunk
   And stagger home from town.
   (*Chorus*)

5. Old Joe Clark he had a cat,
   Meanest cat around,
   Sharpened his claws on the side of the barn,
   Pulled the whole thing down.
   (*Chorus*)

6. Old Joe Clark he had a cat,
   Not like any you've seen,
   Carried off that muley cow,
   My that cat was mean.
   (*Chorus*)

7. Old Joe had a muley cow,
   Knew it when she's born,
   Took a jaybird half a year
   To fly from horn to horn.
   (*Chorus*)

Exercises: Chord Progressions

1. Write out the chord progression for "East Virginia," below, with four measures per line.

2. Add secondary dominants or substitute chords to "East Virginia." Play your version. Is it successful?

East Virginia

2. Well, her <u>hair</u> was dark of <u>col</u>or,
   Cheeks they <u>were</u> a rosy <u>red</u>.
   On her <u>breast</u> she wore white <u>lil</u>ies,
   Where I <u>longed</u> to lay my <u>head</u>.

3. I'd rather <u>live</u> in some dark <u>hol</u>ler
   Where the <u>sun</u> would never <u>shine</u>,
   Than for <u>you</u> to love an<u>oth</u>er,
   And to <u>know</u> you'd never be <u>mine</u>.

4. I don't <u>want</u> your greenback <u>dol</u>lar,
   I don't <u>want</u> your silver <u>chain</u>;
   All I <u>want</u> is your love, <u>dar</u>ling,
   Say that <u>you'll</u> be mine a<u>gain</u>.

HARMONIZATION

Harmonization is concerned with deciding which chords will sound correct when played with a particular melody. This topic comes up a great deal among folk guitarists since they tend to look at music from a chordal point of view. It is easy to ask what chords go with a given melody, but hard to answer. If it is a song that has been written and popularized by a particular artist, then specific chord changes were used that would be considered the "correct" ones. However, musically speaking, there are many ways to harmonize a given melody.

Different harmonizations create different effects. A bluegrass musician's version of a song would no doubt be very different from a jazz musician's version. The object is to find the appropriate accompaniment for the situation. Once you have established the key and the tonic note of a piece, you need a "skeleton" arrangement. This is most often provided by the I, IV, and V chords. There are also a number of common chords, especially the minors and sevenths, that, when combined with the I, IV, and V chords, will allow you to devise an accompaniment that will be very effective. The verse from "Home on the Range," below, will serve as an illustration.

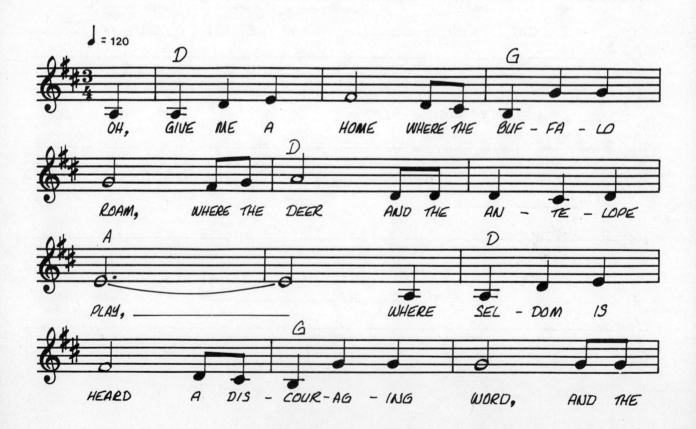

If you were to strum the chords given above and sing the melody, it would not sound wrong, but it could be improved upon. Substituting the V7 (A7) for the V (A) and inserting a I7 (D7) between the I (D) and IV (G) adds a good deal, since dominant-seventh chords accentuate these changes. Also, the addition of the secondary dominant, or II7 (E7) chord, between the I (D) and the V7 (A7) is very common, and with this done you have an arrangement such as might be found in a song book. Note the changes in the version below:

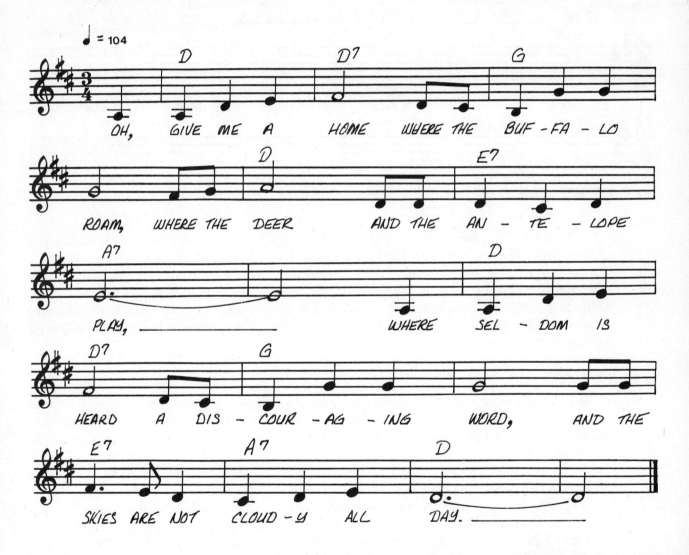

Other chord progressions and substitutions could be made, such as a diminished chord or a minor chord in place of the IV. Here is a more sophisticated arrangement, one that might be used by a cocktail pianist.

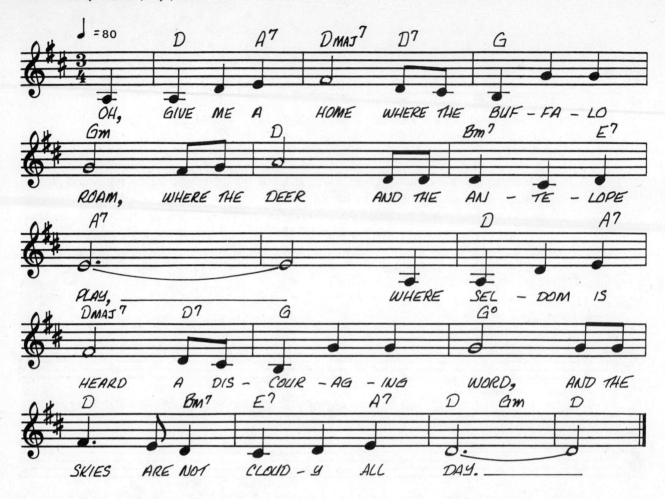

There are many other ways to harmonize this tune; this discussion is meant only to show some of the possibilities. It is a good idea to look at as many song books and as much sheet music as you can, and compare the arrangements of the songs to what you are used to hearing. You will be in for some surprises! The only way to learn to harmonize is to do it and to look at what has been done, rather than trying to apply rules and formulas. The more songs you know and the more chord progressions you have identified, the easier it will be for you to learn new songs and to rearrange familiar ones.

MODULATION

Some songs stay in one key throughout, and others move from one key to another as part of their structure. Songs with "built-in" key changes are said to *modulate*. Modulation is different from transposing in that when a song with a modulation is transposed, the modulation remains intact as part of the song's internal structure.

The basic idea of modulation is to make the music more interesting by musically "shifting gears." Modulation can be done smoothly and unnoticeably or suddenly and dramatically.

Perhaps the most common modulation is to the key of the dominant, such as from C to G or from D to A. Many well-known songs, such as "San Antonio Rose," will have the verse in one key and the chorus in another. The most common way to modulate from a key to its dominant is by means of the II7 or secondary-dominant chord, which resolves logically into the dominant chord. For example, a D7 chord greatly smooths the shift from C to G. If you wanted to return to the key of C, then the dominant of C—namely, G7—would lead you back. Likewise, a song could shift from the key of C to the subdominant key of F with the help of a C7 chord, and a G7 would return the song to the original key of C.

Modulations to the key of the dominant or subdominant or other "nearby" keys such as the relative minor can be achieved easily. But if you were to shift further away from the original key center, you might need an intermediate progression of chords to smooth out the transition.

A very common modulation that occurs in popular music, usually between verses of a song, is accomplished by going up a whole step, such as from C to D or from G to A. It is sometimes done with an intermediate chord. The change from G to A might be facilitated with an E7 chord, a G♯ chord, or even a B♭ chord, for example. Some songs will modulate up a half step with no intermediate chord. Many songs do this to increase excitement and suspense. Sometimes these modulations are accompanied by a change in tempo.

The most frequent use of modulation in popular music today is as an arranging tool, to "spice up" a relatively simple song. Nashville-style country songs often feature such modulations. Understanding the process of modulation can be a great help to a guitar player who plays by ear and who wants to figure out the chords to a pop song.

Exercises: Harmonization and Modulation

1. Above the staffs of "Amazing Grace," below, are two, three, or four chords written for each harmonic change. Try each of the chords given for each position, and determine which ones you prefer.

2. Select the set of chords you prefer from the choices given for "Michael Row the Boat Ashore":

3. Play an A7 chord for eight beats, and listen to it. Is it stable, or does it need resolution to another chord? Play a D chord following the A7 chord. Then play A7 followed by Em. Which produced the strongest sense of resolution?

4. Play the D7 chord for eight beats. What chord should follow the D7 to create the strongest sense of resolution? Can you find anything in common with the root movement in Exercise 3?

5. A moving line in the treble strings can create different forms of the same chord. Play the following chord progression, and listen for the descending chromatic line on the B string.

D / Dmaj7 / D7 / D6 / Em / A7

6. Play "Tom Dooley" (page 24) starting in the key of C. Modulate to the key of D on the third verse and then to the key of E on the fifth verse.

7. Guitarists can create harmonic movement by sliding fingerings up and down the fretboard. Try moving the open D chord up two frets, then down one fret, then down one more fret, which brings the fingering back to the original position for the D chord. Try moving the A-minor chord fingering up two frets, then up two more frets.

8. Move the open E chord up one fret, then down to the original position. With the proper strum, this harmonic movement hints at a Phrygian cadence so characteristic of Flamenco music.

9. Play the E chord fingering up five and seven frets while droning the other strings. Compare this to the E–A–B7 progression.

chapter 12
Transposition and Capos

TRANSPOSITION

Transposition is one of the most useful theoretical concepts for a performing musician. Singers may say that a song is in too high a key for their vocal range and that it would be easier to sing if it were shifted down in pitch. Guitarists may find the chords of a piece easier to play in one key than in another. It is then that *transposing* or *transposition*—the shifting of the pitch level of a song from one key to another—comes in handy. When a song is transposed, even though its pitch level changes, all of the internal relationships of the notes are kept constant; the structure, form, and "essence" of the song remain unchanged.

Transposing Melodies

Transposing the melody line of a song is basically a mechanical process of shifting each note up or down the same distance in half steps. A shift up from the key of Eb to the key of G would necessitate moving each note up the distance between Eb and G, or four half steps. That distance can be measured by using a chromatic-scale ruler, pictured in Figure 12.1.

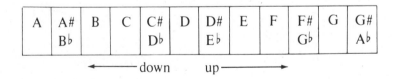

FIGURE 12.1 Chromatic Scale

Count the intervals between pitches when determining the number of half steps between the two pitches. For instance, the distance between B and C is one half step and there are two pitches involved. Begin counting on zero (0) when computing the distance. The number of half-step intervals between D and F is three: D = 0, D♯ = 1, E = 2, and F = 3. The distance from G♯ to A is one half step; this requires going from the end of the "chromatic-scale ruler" back to the beginning of the twelve pitches, but remember that these pitches can be repeated over many octaves.

Exercises: Counting Half Steps

1. Find the number of half steps in the following intervals:

    B up to E _____   F down to D _____

    B♭ up to F _____   E♭ down to B _____

    G up to F _____   A down to G _____

2. Transpose the following melody from the key of F major to the key of D major. You should move each note down three half steps because that is the distance between the two keys.

Transposing Chords

Transposing chords is basically the same process as transposing melodies in that the pitch level of the chords must simply be shifted up or down the correct distance in half steps. First find the distance in half steps that the key is to shift up or down. From C to E would be up four half steps, and from F♯ down to E would be down two half steps. Next, shift the letter name of the chord this distance, making sure you follow the correct sequence of pitch names in the chromatic scale. Last, keep the chord type or symbol the same. Minor chords in the original key transpose to minor chords in the new key; major chords stay major chords; seventh chords stay seventh chords; augmented major-ninth chords stay augmented major-ninth chords; and so on. The chord quality must remain the same after the transposition. Study the following example.

Old key:	F major	Chords:	F,	Gm,	C7,	Dm6
Transposed key:	D major	Chords:	D,	Em,	A7,	Bm6

Exercises: Transposition

1. "Wildwood Flower," on page 152, is written in the key of G, a key that may be too low for singing. Transpose the chords of this song to the key of A, and then sing the song.

2. Transpose "Wildwood Flower" to the key of C. Which key—G, A, or C—is most comfortable to sing in?

3. Suppose you found a song in a song book with two flats in the key signature. What major key would it be in? Suppose that it had the chords given below, which were too hard to play, and you wanted to transpose the song to the key of G. What would the new chords be?

Key	Chords				
B♭	E♭	F7	B♭	Gm	Cm7
G					

THE CAPO

The *capo* is a strap or clamp that can be affixed to the guitar at any fret to shorten all six strings at once. It can be used as an easy way to transpose songs by allowing you to play the chords for a song in one key while sounding in a higher-pitched key. When a capo is placed on the fretboard of the guitar, it functions as the nut (see page 2), and all fingerings should be fretted the same distance from the capo as normal fingerings are fretted above the nut.

D-chord fingering
without capo

D-chord fingering with
capo placed at third fret

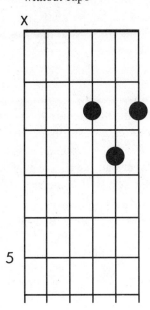

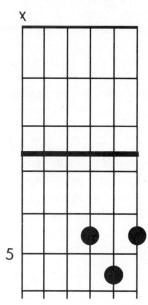

There are many types of capos, some of the more common of which are shown in Figure 13.21 (page 281). The simple elastic-strap capos are suitable for use on nylon-string guitars or on steel-string guitars with very light-gauge strings. The double-strap elastic capos and the various buckles, clamps, and threaded-screw mechanisms are designed to provide the extra force needed to clamp down heavier-gauge steel-string and twelve-string guitars.

The theory of the capo is simple. By shortening all the strings a certain amount, it raises the pitch of every note played an equal distance. If you have a capo on the first fret and play a song in the key of D major as if there were no capo, your song would sound one half step higher, in E♭. Moving the capo up to the second fret would put you in E. Likewise, playing in G with a capo on the fifth fret would place you five half steps higher, in C. The capo can only be used to raise the pitch of songs, and it cannot be moved during a song. It is most frequently employed by singers who want to sing in a key that suits their voice but who prefer to play the guitar in one of the easily accessible guitar keys—D, A, G, E, or C. By playing in the comfortable keys for the guitar and using the capo, you can perform songs that actually sound in any of the keys.

For example, if you play a song with the chords for the key of A but you would like to sing it in B, where would you put the capo? Answer: on the second fret. Placing the capo at the first fret would raise it to B♭, and placing it at the second fret would raise it to B.

As another example, suppose you want to sing a song in E♭, and you have a song book that gives the chords in E♭, but they are too hard to play.

Key: E♭   Chords: B♭7,   E♭,   A♭,   Fm

Transpose the chords of the song to a playable key just below the desired key—namely, D.

    Key: D   Chords: A7,   D,   G,   Em

Then put the capo on the first fret, and play the chords for D. The capo will cause the song to sound in E♭.

  As a final example, if you know a song in G but want to play it with a friend who sings it in F, how can you use a capo to help you? Since F is below G, using a capo won't help much. You would have to capo on the tenth fret in order to play in G and sound in F. It is a common mistake to count backward and think that having a capo on the second fret will do it. Since you are playing in G, having a capo on the first fret raises you to A♭, the second fret to A, and so on up to F on the tenth fret. Your only recourse would be to transpose the song to a key *below* F, such as E, and then capo one fret back up to F.

Cross-Keying

When there are two guitar players, the capo can be used as a way to get a nice duet sound. The capo changes the timbre and flavor of the guitar, especially when it is placed in a higher position on the neck. The difference in tone between a guitar played with no capo and one played with the capo on the seventh or eighth fret is remarkable; you can use this to your advantage. One player can play a song with no capo, and the other can play with a capo, but playing chords in a different key so that the sound is in the same key as the first player's. This is called *cross-keying*.

  For example, if a song has the following chords in G—G, C, D7, and Am7—then the first guitar player would play in G with no capo. The second guitar player would transpose the song to D, using the chords D, G, A7, and Em7. Then that player would put on a capo at the fifth fret, which would bring the pitch back up to the key of G.

Problems with Capos

Capos tend to throw off the tuning of the guitar when they are clamped on, especially on the bass strings. There is little that can be done about this, although some capos seem to cause less tuning distortion than others. The amount of tuning distortion depends on the guitar and on how heavy the gauge of the strings is. Lighter-gauge strings seem to have fewer problems.

  There are many who feel that the capo is a crutch and that it interferes with "proper" guitar playing. They like to call capos "cheaters." It is true that the capo can be overused and that it can prevent a guitar player from exploring the sounds that are obtained by performing in many keys, but it is unquestionably a valuable tool. Skilled guitarists can use a capo to obtain sounds that are otherwise unachievable, and beginners can use it to expand the range of music accessible to them.

Exercises: Capo Transposition

1. If you played a song in C but wanted to sing in E♭, where would you place a capo?

2. If you found the following song in a song book and wanted to sing it in its original key but found that the chords were too hard to play, where would you place a capo and what chords would you play?

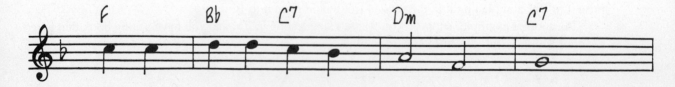

3. Suppose that you and a friend were going to play a song in G, but your friend was going to play in G normally, and you were going to play the chords for the key of D and put a capo on so that you, too, would actually be sounding in G. Where would you put the capo? If your friend played the chords given below, what chords would you play?

Your friend:	Gmaj7	B7	Am6	C	Am/F♯
You:	_____	_____	_____	_____	_____

4. People who play twelve-string guitars usually keep them tuned down at least two frets below standard pitch to reduce the tension on the neck that can damage the guitar if left at standard pitch. Usually these people also use a capo to restore the instrument to standard pitch. Suppose that you were playing a twelve-string guitar that was tuned down one whole step below pitch (D–G–C–F–A–D). Where would you put a capo to be at standard pitch? If you were playing with a friend who had a six-string guitar at normal pitch, and he was performing a song in B♭ by playing it in G with a capo on the third fret, where should you put your capo? In what key should you play?

5. Play and sing "Wildwood Flower," page 152. The range of the melody is probably low for singing. Where would you place the capo so that it sounds in the key of A as you play in the key of G? Play the song again, this time so that it sounds in D . Where did you place the capo?

6. Play "Red River Valley," page 38, with a friend who is playing the song in D. If you put your capo at the fifth fret, what chords should you play? If you play the C, F, and G7 chords, where would you put the capo?

chapter 13
Owning a Guitar

TYPES OF GUITARS

Guitars come in a bewildering array of sizes, shapes, woods, styles, and prices. It is a good idea to know something about the range so that you can select the instrument that best suits your needs.

Electric Guitars

Two fundamental types of guitars are the *acoustic guitar,* which creates sound without the aid of an amplifier, and the amplified *electric guitar,* which uses a magnetic pickup to convert the vibrational energy of the strings to an electric signal that is then sent to an amplifier. Electric guitars come in two basic types: *solid-body* guitars (Figure 13.2), which have no resonating chamber and are scarcely audible without the amplifier, and *hollow-body* electric guitars, which are audible without an amplifier. A more recent type of amplified guitar is an *acoustic-electric* guitar, which is an acoustic guitar fitted with a piezoelectric crystal pickup (see "Amplifying Acoustic Guitars," pages 282–284) that translates vibrational energy into electrical current. It features a more "natural" sound than normal electric guitars.

The electric guitar in Figure 13.5 has a *cutaway,* a concave shape where the body meets the neck, to allow easy access to the high frets. Some electric guitars have a double cutaway, where the body is concave on both sides of the neck. There are acoustic guitars built with a cutaway, although this is less common.

Acoustic Guitars

The two basic kinds of acoustic guitars are the *nylon-string guitar* and the *steel-string guitar;* the names are self-explanatory. It is essential to realize that these are two entirely different types of guitars. Nylon-string guitars (Figure 13.3) are more lightly constructed and can be severely damaged by the greater tension of steel strings. These guitars have a sweeter, softer tone, and require less physical force to play. They are generally used by classical and Flamenco guitarists, although some popular artists (Willie Nelson, Chet Atkins, Jerry Reed, and José Féliciano among others) use them, too.

There is no danger in putting nylon strings on a steel-string guitar, but the tone will suffer immensely. The steel-string guitar is designed for the larger amount of vibrational energy that is emitted from the steel strings.

266

It is sometimes hard to tell if a particular guitar was intended for nylon or steel strings. In general, nylon-string guitars are smaller and lighter, and the neck joins the body at the twelfth fret. Steel-string guitars are heavier and have a fourteen-fret neck and a pickguard. The best way to tell if a guitar was designed for steel or nylon strings is to look at the tuning gears. Since it takes more revolutions of the gears for nylon strings to make tuning adjustments, the cylinders that the strings wind around have a much greater diameter. Steel-string guitars have winding barrels about one-half the diameter of those of nylon-string guitars, the steel-string guitar barrels usually measuring about $\frac{3}{16}$ inch to $\frac{1}{4}$ inch across (see Figure 13.1).

Types of Steel-String Guitars

There are many different types of steel-string guitars since playing styles and the design of the instrument are undergoing rapid evolution. The *flat-top acoustic guitar* has, as its name implies, a flat top and usually a round sound hole, and is by far the most common kind of steel-string guitar today. It comes in many different sizes and body styles, and in several different kinds of wood. The most common body shape is the "dreadnaught" or D-series body pioneered by the C. F. Martin Company (Figure 13.4). The larger guitars have more bass response and volume but are harder to hold and play. The smaller guitars have a more delicate tone, and may require less force to play.

It is now unusual to see an *arch-top acoustic guitar* (Figure 13.5), which was far more common in the 1930s and 1940s than it is today. It is made like a violin, with a carved top, and usually has f-holes like the violin. Arch-top guitars are most popular among swing and jazz guitarists. They are usually very big and were originally used primarily for rhythm purposes in big bands and orchestras. Most arch-top guitars are electric and are favored by players for their warm, natural tone. Good arch-top guitars are very expensive since they are hand-carved. No doubt this contributes to their scarcity.

The *twelve-string guitar* (Figure 13.6) is a very common type of steel-string guitar. It has six pairs of strings tuned in unisons and octaves: the two treble pairs of strings are usually tuned in unison, and the four lower pairs of strings are tuned an octave apart. This creates a big, rich, full sound while still allowing normal chord fingerings.

An interesting member of the steel-string guitar family is the *resonator guitar* or *Dobro* (see Figure 13.7). The metal resonator, a mechanical speaker used in place of the sound hole, was developed around 1925 by the Dopera brothers. Resonator guitars were made until World War II with both Dobro and National trademarks. Full-scale production of resonator guitars was not reinstituted until 1971. Wooden-bodied resonator guitars are usually called "Dobros" and are favored by country and bluegrass players, who hold them in their laps and play them with a steel bar instead of the left-hand fingers. The metal-

FIGURE 13.1 Peghead Comparison: Nylon-String and Steel-String Guitars

bodied Dobros, often called *National steel guitars,* are used by blues and bottleneck-style players. Although the resonator was originally invented as a means of amplification, the unique tone it imparts to the guitar sound has made it the choice of guitarists who play with a metal or glass "slide." Both styles involve gliding the smooth surface of the slide over the strings rather than pressing the strings to the fingerboard with the fingers.

HINTS ON CHOOSING A GUITAR

1. Select an instrument in the right price range. While there are such things as bargains, in general guitars are not the kind of things you can buy in secondhand stores or at yard sales. The person who sells you the instrument is often well aware of its value. But it may take twice as much money to buy an instrument that is only 20 percent better. Very cheap instruments are usually hard to play and do not produce enough tone to inspire you to keep playing. Likewise, the extremely expensive instruments that cost well over a thousand dollars often feature fancy inlay, gold-plated tuners, and decorative work that do not increase their musical value. The lower-priced guitars have been improving in quality due to mass production and mass marketing, and it is now possible to buy an affordable and a good-sounding guitar. Professional-quality guitars are expensive, but instruments of only slightly lower quality can be found for far less money.

2. Select the body style and wood that are best suited to your needs. Steel-string guitars come in many shapes and sizes and kinds of wood. Almost all guitars have a spruce top, and the back and sides are usually rosewood, mahogany, maple, or koa. Rosewood- and maple-backed guitars tend to have a deeper, warmer, and more bass-rich sound, while mahogany and some koa guitars have a brighter and crisper sound often favored by melody players. Dreadnaught-shaped guitars and jumbo bodies have a bigger sound that has more bass and projects farther than the smaller-bodied guitars, but they are harder to hold and play. There are many varieties of small-bodied guitars that have remarkable tone and volume as well as good bass response. Try as many kinds and sizes of guitar as you can to see how they feel and what they sound like.

3. Find an instrument with a tone you like. Guitars, even from the same manufacturer and the same year, can sound remarkably different. Listen for bass and treble responses, balance of volume between the bass and the treble, as well as the overall resonance and clarity. The sound of an instrument depends a good deal on the strings. Guitars are often shipped with cheap factory strings that do little for the tone of the instrument.

4. Be aware of the brand name of a guitar. A brand-name instrument can always be resold, and with a guitar made by an established company you will have the backup of a warranty.

5. Have someone who knows guitars look at the instrument before you buy it. There are many things that seem to be problems that are not serious, and there are serious things that can be easily overlooked. Cracks or scratches in the finish, for example, do not affect the tone while cracks in the wood do. If a tuning knob is broken or a string is missing, it is a simple matter to remedy the problem, although it may make the guitar unplayable at the moment.

6. If there is no way to get a professional opinion on the instrument before buying it, the inexperienced person can still check a few crucial things. Cracks in the wood, especially in the top, are not hard to spot. If you are not sure if something is a crack,

FIGURE 13.2 Solid-Body Electric Guitar

FIGURE 13.3 Nylon-String Guitar

FIGURE 13.4 Dreadnaught Guitar

FIGURE 13.5 Arch-Top Guitar

FIGURE 13.6 Twelve-String Guitar

FIGURE 13.7 Metal-Body Resonator Guitar*

push down on one side of it, and see if the crack will catch a fingernail. Cracks are very likely to occur in the top near the bridge and in joints between any of the pieces of wood that make up the back and sides. Look very carefully to see if the neck has been broken off. A thin line will show either at the peghead, which is a common place for breaks, or at the heel, where the neck joins the body. A guitar that has had the neck broken may appear to be in good shape but may never be able to be tuned properly. Also check the intonation of the guitar. (See "Troubleshooting," page 271.) A guitar with an improperly placed saddle, very old strings, or a warped neck will often have faulty intonation. To check it, compare the twelfth-fret harmonic of each string to the fretted twelfth-fret note on each string. They should be the same pitch, although the B string may vary slightly. Also check each string, and play each note at each fret to listen for rattles and buzzes. If

*DOBRO is a registered trademark of O.M.I. Co., Inc. Used by Permission.

some frets rattle and others don't, the fingerboard may have bumps or indentations and this may be expensive to fix. It is often easier to fix a guitar in which the string rattles at every fret. Try to pluck the string with constant force when checking the various notes. It is very common for guitars to play well up to the twelfth or fourteenth fret, where the neck joins the body, and then to rattle since the fingerboard attached to the body may swell due to the pressure from the more porous wood underneath.

CARING FOR A GUITAR
Guitars and Weather

Guitars are usually made of wood, and, like anything made of wood, they must be protected from the elements. Most environmental problems with the guitar come from rapid changes in temperature or humidity. Wood tends to swell and contract with heat, cold, and moisture, and the different kinds of wood that make up the different parts of the instrument will react differently. This can cause cracking, warping, and glued joints to loosen. Ideally, wood should be well seasoned before it is used to make guitars, and instrument builders generally control the climate in their shops when completing crucial steps of construction such as joining the neck to the body.

Climatic extremes can damage your guitar. If you leave your instrument in the trunk of a car on a hot day, you may return to find a guitar kit instead of a guitar. If the glue softens, the immense pressure of the strings can "spring" the whole guitar and pull the neck off the body. Intense cold usually damages the finish, since the wood and the finish react to temperature differently. A very cold guitar that is suddenly warmed will develop "weather checking," small cracks that form mosaiclike patterns in the finish (Figure 13.8). Weather checking is harmless to the sound of the instrument but detracts from its appearance. To prevent this, the guitar must always be warmed gradually, either by leaving it in the case once it is brought into a warm place or by fanning the top with the lid of the case. If the finish fogs when the guitar is brought into the warmer climate, put it back in the case and let it warm up more gradually.

Many people feel that humidity is an even greater danger to guitars than temperature. Rapid changes in humidity can cause warping and cracking since the wood will absorb moisture at different rates. (Some professionals have cases with built-in humidifiers and air conditioning, but this is impractical in normal situations.) In dry climates keep the guitar in the case when not in use, and keep a small, damp sponge in the case in a jar with some holes in the lid. There are several commercially available dehumidifiers that can be stored in the case or even inside the guitar.

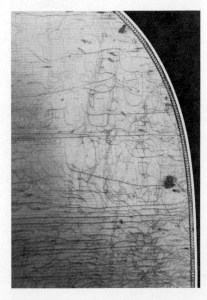

FIGURE 13.8 Weather Checking

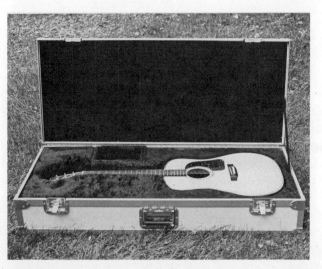

FIGURE 13.9 Custom-made Guitar Case

If there is a general rule about how to take care of a guitar with respect to the weather, it is probably this one: your guitar can survive whatever you can. You can spend half an hour or an hour outside on a cold day, or a few minutes in the trunk on a hot day, but not all afternoon or all night. The same with a guitar.

Each guitar should have an adequate case. There are four types of guitar cases. Soft-shell cases, made out of cloth, canvas, or leather, offer little protection. Cardboard and chipboard cases are relatively inexpensive and offer reasonable protection for less expensive instruments. Hard-shell cases can be expensive but are the only suitable means of protecting a valuable instrument. They are made out of wood, plastic, or fiberglass. If you own a very expensive instrument and if you travel a great deal by air, you might want to spend several hundred dollars on a custom-made case (see Figure 13.9). Custom-made cases are designed to withstand the rough treatment that airline baggage can receive.

Troubleshooting

Guitars require a certain number of adjustments and repairs, and although it is not necessary or advisable to do your own repairs, it is good to know when they need doing.

The body

The top of the guitar is responsible for most of the tone the instrument produces and is thus the most important part of the body. Early guitar makers found that even with the back and sides made of paper the guitar would sound reasonably good with a good top. Cracks in the top, which most often occur near the bridge, should be repaired quickly since they interfere with the tone of the instrument. If the top is not flat and is bowing up from the pull of the strings near the bridge, then a serious problem may result. The more the top pulls up, the more leverage it gives the strings to further pull it. Small "bubbles" in the top can be pulled down by a repair person and should be attended to since they can disrupt the ability of the guitar to be tuned properly. The back and sides of the guitar are less crucial in producing the sound, and small cracks, although they will not appreciably affect the sound, should be fixed before they become large cracks. If the joints between any of the pieces of the body become loose or separated, they should also be fixed quickly. Since repair shops have special clamps and glue for various jobs, these should not be attempted at home.

The finish of the body of the guitar protects the wood, and although the guitar may become scratched, dented, or discolored, it should not be refinished. Refinishing can seriously damage the tone of the instrument since in removing the old finish a small amount of wood from the top is necessarily removed in sanding. The top of a guitar is precisely fashioned to tolerances of very small fractions of an inch, and even the small amount removed in refinishing can dramatically alter the sound. If you would like a good finish on the guitar, take care of the old one.

The neck

The neck and fingerboard are the most accident-prone parts of the instrument and require the most adjustment. An unstrung guitar has a "reverse warp" and tilts backward. The tension of the strings pulls the neck up to the correct angle. When the strings pull the neck too far, it is called a *simple warp*. It is easily corrected on most steel-string guitars. A warped neck may not only make the guitar very hard to play by raising the action (the height of the strings above the fingerboard), it may also make the instrument impossible to tune. Most modern steel-string guitars are fitted with an adjustable *truss rod,* a threaded, reinforcing rod that lies inside the neck of the guitar (see Figure 13.10). A repair person can easily adjust the truss rod, usually for a very small fee.

The fingerboard should not be entirely flat, since the strings vibrate with greatest amplitude in their center and need room to clear the fingerboard. To check the warp of a guitar neck, any of several methods can be used. Sighting down the fingerboard can enable you to spot very large problems, and measuring the action can indicate whether or not a serious problem exists, although high action

FIGURE 13.10 Truss-Rod Nut

FIGURE 13.11 Compensating Saddle

may be due to too tall a bridge. On a steel-string guitar a straight edge laid along the fingerboard should leave a gap of about .005 inches to .015 inches above the fret at the middle of the fingerboard. This measurement can also be made by placing a capo at the first fret, pressing a string (fretting) at the twelfth fret, and measuring the clearance of the string above the sixth or seventh fret.

A simple warp is usually easily corrected, but more complex twists, bumps, and valleys in the surface of the fingerboard can be more of a problem. These are located by playing each fret of each string with a relatively constant force of the right hand and noticing if there is buzzing or rattling at some of the frets and not at others. If there is a bump, then the frets below that bump will rattle and the frets above it will not. If a fret is too low, the rattle may occur at just one fret. Correction of these problems may be accomplished by reseating a fret that may have worked its way out, leveling the frets, or removing all the frets and planing the fingerboard. All of these operations should be performed by a qualified repair person.

If the neck of a guitar ever breaks or if it separates from the body even just a small amount, serious consequences may arise—the guitar may be untunable afterward. A good repair person should be consulted immediately.

The peghead and nut

The tuning machines, located on the peghead, are common sources of trouble but are easily replaced. The small screws that sometimes hold the knobs on should be kept snug and tightened only with a thumbnail or a guitar pick. Open-gear tuners should be oiled occasionally. The nut should be tall enough so that the strings all clear the first frets when plucked open. If the open strings rattle and buzz and the fretted string does not, then the nut is too low. If the nut is too tall, then the strings will be too high above the first fret. If the strings clear the first fret by a great deal more than they clear the successive frets, the nut should perhaps be lowered or the grooves in it refiled. Again, these operations, though simple, must be done very carefully, since the grooves in the nut are cut in a specific fashion so that the string crosses the nut at a precise place and does not rattle in the groove.

The bridge and saddle

The *saddle* is the bone or plastic piece that rests in the saddle slot in the bridge. The cutting of the saddle slot and the carving of the saddle are among the final structural stages of building the guitar, and their placement and shape are critical to the *intonation,* or the ability of the guitar to produce the correct pitches. Together with the adjustments to the nut and fingerboard or truss rod, the adjustment of the saddle is part of what is called "setting up" a guitar. The frets are placed on the fingerboard before the placement of the saddle, and the saddle must be cut so that the strings line up correctly over the frets.

Fine adjustment to the intonation of acoustic guitars is often accomplished with a compensating saddle (Figure 13.11).

Rather than a straight piece of bone or plastic, the *compensating saddle* allows individual string lengths to be adjusted by individual beveling of each of six notches on the saddle.

The best way to evaluate the intonation of a guitar is to make sure that the twelfth fret of a guitar produces the same pitch as the twelfth-fret harmonic. (See pages 8–17 on tuning problems.) If the saddle is too high, it can be shaved, and if it is too low, it can be shimmed up. Both these operations require great care, and only qualified repair persons should perform them.

If the bridge angle is too severe, it can cause a loss of tone as well as the breaking of strings at the saddle. It may be caused by too tall a saddle or by incorrect placement of the holes for the bridge pins (this refers to a steel-string guitar only).

If the saddle, truss rod, and nut are adjusted properly, the guitar will produce musically correct pitches at each fret without rattling or buzzing and the action will be in a normal range. For a steel-string guitar, the bass E string should clear the twelfth fret by about ⅛ inch, and the treble E should be slightly lower—about 3/32 inch. Some players prefer higher or lower action, according to their choice of strings and their playing styles.

Rattles and buzzes

If your guitar makes rattling or buzzing sounds when you play it, try to locate their source. First, listen for the position of the sound—that is, try to determine if it is coming from the body, the fingerboard, or the peghead of the guitar. Also listen for the metallic sound of a fret buzz as compared to the nonmetallic sound that a wooden part may make. Rattles in the peghead are most often simply the loose ends of strings that have not been trimmed. Sometimes the screws that hold the tuning pegs together can come loose. If the grooves in the nut are not cut at an angle, the string can rattle in the groove. Rattles from the fingerboard are caused by loose or worn frets, too low action, or warped fingerboards. Rattles from the bridge and body can be due to loose pickguards, picks inside the guitar, string ends, loose braces inside the guitar, and even buttons or snaps on your clothing touching the outside of the instrument. Always look for the simplest explanation. Try reattaching the strings if the rattling persists, and look for loose wood joints. If nothing solves the problem, consult an expert.

STRINGS

Modern guitar strings are vastly superior in almost every way to their earlier counterparts. There are many different kinds of strings available to enable you to achieve the sound you want. The two basic categories of strings are nylon and steel.

Nylon Strings

Nylon strings first became available commercially after World War II and now have almost completely replaced the gut strings used previously. Nylon strings stay in better tune, do not fray, have better intonation, and are less prone to breakage than strings made out of gut. The treble strings are made from bundles of nylon filament, and the bass strings are wound with wire made from different alloys. The only significant differences between different kinds of nylon strings is in the quality and kind of wire used in the winding. Some nylon strings are now made with ball ends to facilitate attaching them to the guitar.

Steel Strings

There is a great variety of steel strings available, since the steel-string guitar is used for so many different sounds and styles of music.

Round-wound strings

This is by far the most common variety of steel string, due to its long life and brilliant tone. The high E and B strings and sometimes the G string are made from plain steel wire, and the bass strings have a steel core wound with wire. Again, the type of wire used to wrap the bass strings will vary considerably. Bronze-wound strings have a gold color and are probably the most brilliant sounding and also the most commonly used. These may contain varying amounts of brass or copper. Round-wound strings for the electric guitar use a winding that is magnetically responsive, such as steel or various nickel alloys.

Flatwound strings

Flatwound strings, as their name implies, are wrapped with a flat metal tape instead of the usual round wire. They do not have the long life and brilliant tone of the round-wound strings, but they greatly increase playing ease and reduce finger squeaking noises. Flatwound strings for an acoustic guitar are almost nonexistent. It is generally not advised to put flatwound strings on an acoustic guitar due to the extra tension they exert on the instrument. Flatwound strings are favored by jazz guitarists for their soft, muted sound and ease of playing. There are companies that manufacture "ground round-wound" strings, which have some of the smoothness of the flatwound strings and some of the brilliance of the round-wound strings. These strings are also called "polished" round-wound strings since they are made by grinding and polishing normal round-wound strings.

String gauge

The *gauge* or thickness of a guitar string can greatly affect both playing ease and tonal qualities. A thin or light-gauge string is tuned to a lesser tension than a heavy-gauge string tuned to the same pitch, and thus requires less pressure to fret than the heavy-gauge string. However, heavier-gauge strings produce more volume, sustain tones longer, and tend to have an extended life.

Sets of steel strings are sold by manufacturers according to the general thickness of the strings and usually carry the labels "light gauge," "medium gauge," "heavy gauge," and "extra light gauge." These names can mean different things from one brand of string to the next. If you find a brand that seems right, it is a good idea to make a note of the exact diameter of each string in the set. Figure 13.12 gives the average thicknesses of strings.

AVERAGE STRING GAUGES IN INCHES

	Heavy	Medium	Light	Extra Light
E	.014	.013	.011	.010
B	.018	.017	.015	.014
G	.028w*	.026w	.022w	.020w (.019)
D	.038w	.035w	.030w	.028w
A	.048w	.045w	.042w	.040w
E	.058w	.056w	.052w	.050w

*w refers to a wound string. The G string is sometimes plain.

FIGURE 13.12 Chart of Average String Gauges

Heavy-gauge strings are not recommended for any guitar since they tend to pull so hard that they damage the instrument. They are also harder to play. Extra-light-gauge strings are favored by rock players for their fast action and ease of stretching and bending. On an acoustic guitar extra-light-gauge strings do not produce enough vibrational energy to project well. They are, therefore, most commonly found on electric guitars. Many beginners start with light-gauge strings and later switch to medium-gauge strings as their hands gain more strength.

Guitars are usually made to be strung with either medium-gauge strings or normal light-gauge strings; if you want to use an extra-light or heavy gauge, your instrument may need some adjustment. The gauge of the string affects the height of the strings above the fingerboard, and the grooves cut in the nut and saddle are made to certain sizes. Very light strings may rattle and buzz if the strings sit too deep in the grooves and if the tension exerted does not pull hard enough on the neck to create sufficient playing action. This will require adjustments to the instrument that can be done by a repair person.

Compound wound strings

For those who prefer the tone of the steel-string guitar and the playing ease of the nylon strings, there is a type of string called the compound-wound or silk-and-steel string. These strings are designed to be put on a steel-string guitar, but have less tension and brilliance than the steel strings. Putting nylon strings on a steel-string guitar is not a good idea since the tone is so poor. Compound strings offer an excellent alternative.

CHANGING STRINGS

Some guitarists only change their strings when they break, and others change them every day. It depends on what kind of sound you want and how much energy and money you have. Manufacturers often recommend changing strings after every forty hours of playing time, which is a rough average figure based on all preferences and playing habits. There is an initial period when new strings have a "bright" and "crisp" sound, after which the strings will produce an acceptable, but slightly duller tone. Some players prefer the bright, very new strings, and change their strings after every eight hours or so of playing, and others prefer the duller sound. When strings get too old, they can lose their ability to produce musically correct pitches.

HINTS ON CHANGING STRINGS

1. It is best to replace an entire set of strings at once. However, that may be too expensive or too inconvenient. If you need to replace just one string, you may want to try putting an old one in its place, since one new string among five old ones can sound uneven.

2. When changing all of the strings, do them one at a time. Taking off all six and then replacing them subjects the guitar to unnecessary changes in stress.

3. Make sure you attach the strings properly at both ends. To attach most steel strings at the bridge, merely remove the pin, put the ball end of the string in, and replace the pin (Figure 13.13). If the guitar has a tailpiece, you will have to insert the string through a hole in the tailpiece.

To change nylon strings, you often need to tie a knot in the string at the bridge end. Some nylon strings come with a ball end that can be simply inserted in the hole in the bridge, but most often you need to tie the knot shown in Figure 13.14. Be sure that the point at which the string crosses itself (the pressure point) is on the vertical and not the horizontal part of the bridge.

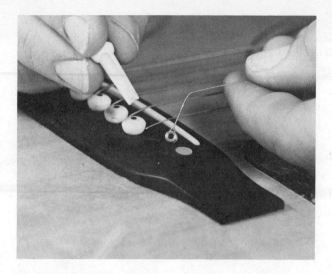

FIGURE 13.13 Attaching Steel Strings at the Bridge

FIGURE 13.14 Attaching Nylon Strings at the Bridge

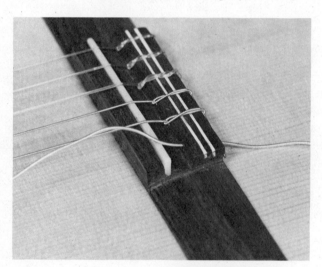

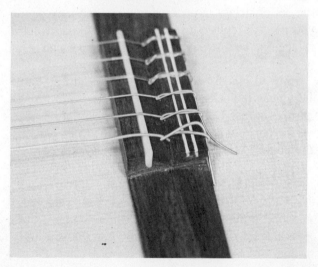

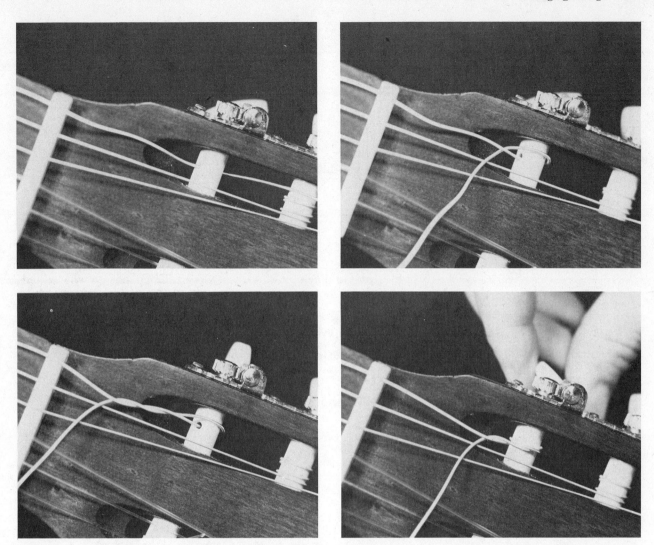

FIGURE 13.15 Attaching Nylon Strings at the Peghead

To attach the strings at the peghead, see Figures 13.15 and 13.16 for nylon-string and steel-string guitars.

To attach steel strings at the peghead, simply insert the string through the hole in the winding barrel (Figure 13.16a) and wind up the string (Figure 13.16b). Make sure the tuning gear is turning in the correct direction—that is, so that the string winds around the barrel from the inside out—clockwise for the treble strings, counter-clockwise for the bass strings (Figure 13.16c). To ensure even winding, take up the slack in the string as it is being wound by keeping it taut with the other hand (Figure 13.16d). Many players will put the loose end of the string back through the hole after the first couple of winds of the barrel to tie a knot and hold the string more securely. This is recommended on the unwound treble strings that are more likely to slip. The loose end of the string may either be coiled around the guitar or trimmed off. The trimmed ends of the strings can be very sharp and should be bent out of harm's way.

Some guitars do not have a hole in the winding barrel but have a slot instead. (This is typical of Fender guitars.) To attach strings to such a barrel slot, you should trim the string first, leaving an inch or so extra, and then insert the end of the string down into the center of the winding barrel from above. The string is brought out through the slot and wound around the shaft, with the end of the string still inside the winding barrel. This prevents string ends from snagging or injuring the fingers. In general, it is a good idea to wind strings on the peghead so that the string goes around the barrel one or two full revolutions.

4. Do not change the strings immediately before performing. New strings will stretch and be hard to tune for some time. Steel strings will stretch for an hour or so, and nylon strings may take days before they settle down. Lighter-gauge strings stretch more than heavier-gauge ones. You can hurry the stretching process by stretching them by hand after they are installed on the guitar. Pull on the string, taking care to stretch it evenly along its length. This can help you find out if the string is slipping at either end.

ACCESSORIES
Picks

It is not necessary to use a pick or plectrum to play guitar, nor is it wrong. It depends on what sounds you wish to produce. If you are studying classical guitar, you will most likely not want to use a pick. But if you are playing in a bluegrass band, you will not be able to do without one. Bare fingers, fingernails, flatpicks, fingerpicks, and thumbpicks are all useful in different situations.

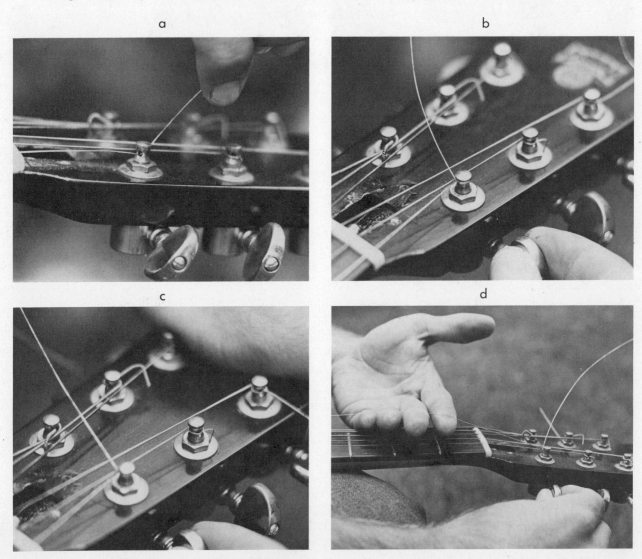

FIGURE 13.16 Attaching Steel Strings at the Peghead

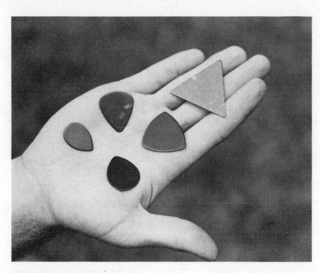

FIGURE 13.17 Flatpicks

Flatpicks

Flatpicks are usually made of plastic or nylon and come in a variety of sizes, shapes, and thicknesses (see Figure 13.17). Thin picks give a softer sound and are easier to manage, while heavier picks give a stronger tone and a wider dynamic range. Large picks are easier to hold than small ones, but are harder to move quickly and manipulate. Most players use a pick of medium thickness and medium size since this allows for maneuverability and produces the widest choice of sound.

HINTS ON USING A FLATPICK

1. *Select the type of pick that suits you.* Picks are available in a wide variety of sizes, shapes, and thicknesses. Thin picks are easy to manage at first, but hard to control for intricate playing. Heavy picks are hard to manage, but give a wide variety of sound. Nylon picks have a soft sound and do not break or wear down. If you are in doubt, use a medium gauge flatpick.

2. *Hold the pick properly.* There are several ways of holding a pick, but the two most common ones are shown in Figure 13.18. Be sure not to hold the pick too

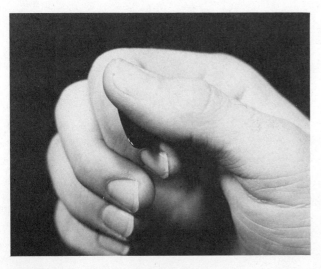 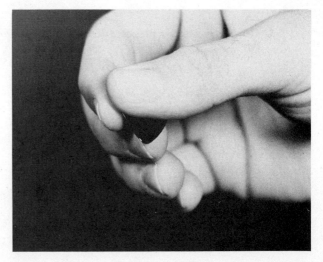

FIGURE 13.18 Holding the Flatpick

tightly. It takes a lot of practice to allow the pick to be held loosely enough for a good sound but firmly enough so that you don't drop it. Ideally, use a tight grip for picking single notes, and let the pick "flop" around for softer strumming.

3. *Strike the string properly*. How to strike a string properly is open to debate, but there are guidelines. Holding the pick at right angles to the string gives the clearest tone. Striking the string near the bridge gives a very different sound than striking it over the sound hole or the fingerboard. Try to vary what you do to add an assortment of tonal colors to the sound.

Fingerpicks and Thumbpicks

Fingerpicks

Fingerpicks have long been associated with banjo playing, although they are used by a large number of guitarists, especially steel-string acoustic players. They offer increased volume, speed, and agility at the expense of the more delicate tone of the fingernail or the bare finger. Nylon-string players rarely use fingerpicks since the nylon strings do not require as much force to play. Steel strings tend to tear up fingernails, especially in the heavier gauges.

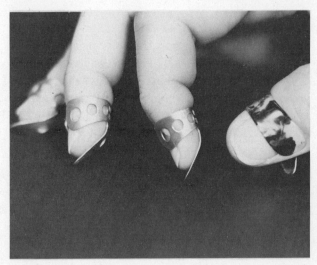

FIGURE 13.19 Fingerpicks

FIGURE 13.20 Thumbpicks

Fingerpicks are available in either plastic or metal. Metal fingerpicks last longer and are easier to fit to the fingers, while the plastic picks give a warmer, more natural sound. Plastic picks can be fitted to the size and shape of the fingers by immersing the picks in boiling water for a few seconds and then reshaping them before they cool. Metal picks are now available in a variety of thicknesses to help you obtain the tone that most suits your tastes. Figure 13.19 shows some metal and plastic fingerpicks.

Thumbpicks

Thumbpicks are worn by all styles of guitarists either with or without fingerpicks. Nylon and plastic thumbpicks seem to be the most common, although metal thumbpicks are available. Left-handed thumbpicks are hard to find. Figure 13.20 shows some common types of thumbpicks.

Capos

The capo (from the Italian *capotasto*) holds down the strings of the guitar either by clamping across all of them, as with the conventional capo, or by allowing you to select which strings are clamped, as with the variable Third-Hand capo. The capo is discussed in Chapter 12, and the Third-Hand capo is used in Chapter 8 for playing melodies and also in Chapter 7 and in Appendixes A and B.

There are many different clamping mechanisms available with different capos, and there is no agreement among players as to which is the best. In general, the simple, one-strap elastic capos are sufficient for nylon-string guitars, and the double-strap elastic and the clamp-type capos are used for steel-string and twelve-string guitars. Some common types of capos are shown in Figure 13.21.

Neck Straps

Since many guitarists play in a sitting position, a neck strap is not necessary. But it is a good idea to have one. Straps can be made to fit or can be purchased with an adjustable buckle. However, beware of buckles that have a tendency to scratch the finish of the guitar.

Some guitars come equipped with strap buttons on one or both ends for attaching a neck strap; if your guitar does not have them, it is a simple job to have them installed. It is not a good idea to tie the strap to the peghead of the guitar. Even though this is commonly done, it can pull unnecessarily on the neck and get in the way of the chording hand. The strap button on the neck side of the guitar

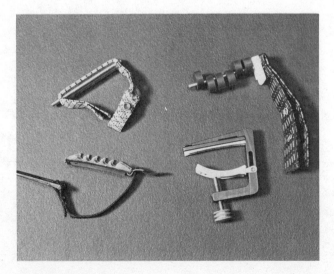

FIGURE 13.21 Capos

should be attached at the heel of the neck, as shown in Figure 13.22. There are neck straps available for classical guitars that do not require the installation of strap buttons and that hook into the sound hole and attach to the peghead.

String Winders

The string winder (Figure 13.23), a simple device, greatly expedites the string-changing process. The tuning pegs can be rotated much faster than with the fingers.

AMPLIFYING ACOUSTIC GUITARS

There are several ways to amplify the sound of an acoustic guitar. But it should be stated that the best amplification system is a good room and a quiet audience, and that no other method will ever result in a totally "pure" and "natural" sound.

Microphones

A good microphone probably gives the best "natural" sound of any amplification method, but it is also the most susceptible to the most common problem in amplification: feedback. Feedback is caused when the amplified sound from a speaker causes the vibrating object (the guitar, in this case) to vibrate further, which, in turn, causes more feedback. It is usually heard by the audience as a shrieking sound and can damage equipment and ears. Microphones come in two basic varieties: dynamic microphones and condenser microphones. Dynamic microphones mechanically convert the physical pressure of the sound waves into electrical impulses and have been the standard and most common microphones for many years. Condenser microphones and electret condenser microphones require line voltage or a battery, and use an electrical method of converting the sound waves into electrical signals. In general, condenser microphones are more sensitive and can be considered an improvement on the dynamic microphone except for the fact that they are much more fragile.

Microphones are further categorized according to the response pattern. A unidirectional microphone picks up sounds that lie in a narrow cone-shaped path in front of the microphone, while an omnidirectional microphone picks up sounds all around it. A unidirectional microphone is suited for use by a singer or an instrumentalist who wants to minimize feedback, since it is less likely to pick up extraneous sounds. The omnidirectional microphone is used much less often, since it is so prone to feedback. It is suitable when several performers use only one microphone. It is used more in

FIGURE 13.22 Strap Button and End Pin

recording than for amplification. A cardioid microphone is a recent development that is popular because it picks up sounds in a cardioid, or heart-shaped, pattern around the microphone. It not only picks up most of the sounds in front of it, but also enough from the sides so that more than one performer can use the same microphone.

Some guitars are more suited to one microphone than another, and in many cases not only is a good microphone needed, but also further tone adjustment or equalization. Equalization—or EQ— is no more than adjusting the tone in the same manner as you would adjust a common stereo's bass and treble. More sophisticated equalizers allow control of more than simply bass and treble, and many performers use an equalizer to emphasize or deemphasize certain parts of the sound spectrum. Most guitars, for example, need to have the bass response lowered since common microphones are designed for vocal use.

A further classification of microphones refers to the type of signal that is generated. High-impedance microphones cost less, have shorter cords, and are more susceptible to picking up noises such as motors or radio stations than low-impedance microphones. The word *impedance* refers to the electrical resistance of the signal. The impedance of the microphone should always match that of the amplifier. Impedance adapters are available that simply plug into the jack of an amplifier to accommodate the desired type of microphone. Many PA systems are built to accommodate either kind of input.

Pickups

The magnetic pickup was invented about fifty years ago and is the means by which electric guitars produce their sound. This type of pickup relies on a magnetic field around the string to produce an electrical signal when the string vibrates, and is much less prone to feedback problems than a microphone. The tone of the signal produced comes directly from the sound of the strings rather than the body of the guitar. The bodies of electric guitars are made of the densest materials that are practical so that they absorb the least amount of the energy of the string. The idea of an acoustic guitar is to transfer the sound of the strings through the bridge to the body and then have the wood and the air create interesting resonances with the sound of the strings to make the final sound. Electric guitars do the opposite, and the manufacturers try to make the bodies absorb the least amount of sound and thus preserve greater sustaining power in the notes. (For this reason electric guitars have movable bridges, since there is no concern for whether or not the sound is weakened as it passes over the bridge to the body.)

FIGURE 13.23 String Winder

There are a number of electric pickups that can be easily snapped into place or permanently mounted on an acoustic guitar to give it an electric-guitar sound. Of course, the guitar will not be able to sustain tones as well as a solid-body electric guitar and will be more prone to feedback, but it will produce a sound much louder than that generated with a microphone. With proper selection of pickup and guitar, and with proper equalization, this kind of pickup can produce an "acoustic" and "natural" sound.

A newer type of pickup, sometimes called a contact pickup, has come into widespread use in recent years. It can be attached quickly to any vibrating surface, and converts the vibration into electricity with a piezoelectric crystal that creates electric current when it is bent or distorted in shape. These pickups can be built into the bridge of the instrument and can pick up the vibration of the wood rather than simply the strings themselves, as in the case of the magnetic pickup. Contact pickups give a substantially louder sound than a microphone, and without feedback, although the sound is still not as loud as with a magnetic pickup.

Amplifiers

The signal generated by a pickup or a microphone is very weak and must be amplified before it can be heard through a speaker. Most such signals are first sent through an equalizer or mixed with other signals before the final product is sent to the speaker. A mixer is used to combine the signals from more than one microphone or instrument and to allow independent adjustment of each channel's volume and equalization. The "mixed" signal is then sent to the amplifier and on to the speakers. Guitar amplifiers are usually single units that contain volume and tone controls, an amplifier, one or more speakers, and perhaps a mixer. Professionals often have separate components for better maintenance and control over the sound.

chapter 14
Learning from Recordings, Other Players, and Song Books

A large part of the typical learning process for a folk guitar player involves studying records, other players, and instruction materials that are not specifically designed for folk guitar players. In fact, nearly all modern folk guitarists, including many professionals and recording artists, have learned this way. Certainly, it is more precise and straightforward a process simply to learn to read music. But such a method is not useful for playing the many kinds of guitar music that are not written down. Perhaps in the future arrangers and publishers will have sorted through the guitar's repertoire and will have organized the study aids, but for now the popular guitarist must learn to work from sources of information other than the printed page. The most common source of information about the music and lyrics of a song is the commercially produced record.

LEARNING FROM RECORDINGS

The number of guitarists who read music is small as compared to the number of guitarists overall. There are two reasons for this. You must go through several steps to translate musical notation into something playable on the guitar. Although some of the fingering problems are solved with guitar tablature, tablature is effective in conveying only the simplest rhythms. And even more guitar "illiteracy" is due to the fact that very little of the stylistic performance practice of the instrument has been notated accurately.

Many guitarists performing today have learned much of what they know from recordings. Music can be learned from recordings in much the same manner that a spoken language can be learned without the written language. Recordings are not good or bad learning tools, but may be the only way of obtaining information about certain music. Let's assume, for example, that you want to learn to play guitar like Bob Dylan. Even if you read music well, you will have to study the recordings since Dylan's style is not transcribable. Likewise, most song books contain piano arrangements that are not an accurate reflection of the tunes as played by the artists.

Although a certain amount of what can be learned from a recording depends on the ear of the listener, there are patterns and ground rules that can be followed.

Rhythm and Meter

The first things to listen for in recorded music are the rhythm and meter. Listen for repeated rhythmic phrases and for the overall "swing" of the music. Practice clapping out the rhythm or strumming it on the guitar. One of the goals of rhythm study is to develop your memory so that you can re-create the rhythm of a particular song as needed. Ask yourself whether the beats are combined into groups of two, three, or four.

Song Structure

The organization of a song is very important, and it is good to make a note of how many verses, choruses, and sections a song has. Capital letters are usually used to notate this. A song that has a verse-chorus-verse-chorus structure would be an ABAB song. Each distinct unit is given a letter name. A song with two verses, a chorus, two more verses, another chorus, a bridge, and a final chorus would be AABAABCB. Introductions are not usually given a letter, nor are final sections, called codas or "tags," unless they are lengthy.

Key

When the rhythm and song structure are established, the next thing to determine is the key (see pages 236–239). This is usually given by the final chord and the final note of the piece. Normally, the final chord and note of sections of a song will give the key; it may not be necessary to wait until the entire song is finished. Find the keynote on your guitar, and check to see if the chord with that name works also. This requires having your guitar tuned to the recording. A record player with a variable pitch control is very handy. It is only necessary to have your guitar in tune in some key with the record. (If you determine that the key on the record was F from your guitar, have a reference note such as that from a tuning fork to make sure that the real key was not E and your guitar a fret sharp.)

Lyrics

Writing down the words to a song can help you get a temporal impression of the structure of the song. Verses and choruses can be identified, and the words can be written down with spaces between the lines to help you find the chord changes and notate them where they occur.

Chord Changes

Finding the chord progression can be easy or difficult, depending on the complexity of the song, how good your ear is, and your knowledge of chords. Learning to identify common chord progressions is an extremely useful skill (see page 247), and knowing their sound can save you large amounts of time spent figuring out chord changes. Learn the characteristic sound of each type of chord by comparing the major, minor, minor-seventh, and other types of chords given in Chapter 10. Each chord type has a distinct quality that can be identified with practice. Write the chord changes down above the words where they appear or in a chord chart with the measures of rhythm marked out with the chord changes. Often several chords will "work" in a given part of an arrangement; there are also chords that may only occur very briefly, such as passing chords. Always try the primary chords first in the key you are in, and listen for key changes (page 258).

Neck Position

With careful listening, especially to acoustic guitars, you can tell if the chords are being played high on the neck or near the nut. There is a certain tonal quality, or timbre, associated with each position that can be identified. Learn to listen for capos, too. A guitar with a capo, especially one placed high on the neck, has a different timbre than a guitar without a capo (see page 263).

Open Strings and Open Tunings

Open strings have a sound of their own and can help you identify the chords and the key. If you are listening to a blues song that you thought was in E♭ and you hear a low tonic bass note, then either your guitar is tuned sharp or the guitar on the recording is tuned low. Hearing the open strings can also help you spot capos as well as open tunings. Most players tune to the various open tunings (pages 156–163) by loosening certain strings, and if you hear a bass note that is pitched lower than any notes on your guitar, chances are there is an open tuning involved. Knowing the key can help you locate the tuning since there are only a few common tunings. Harmonics also give an indication that there are open strings, although jazz and classical players occasionally produce harmonics on fretted pitches with the right hand.

Melody

Learning a melody by ear can be easy or hard, again depending on the song and your ear. There is no secret to doing this: find the first note, then the second, and so forth. If you are not going to play the melody on the guitar, then you only need to learn the melody in order to sing it. Some people play the records at a slower speed (and, therefore, in a different key) since it is easier to hear the pitch changes. It is interesting to compare printed notation of songs with the recording; very often the rhythmic elements of the melody are greatly simplified in the printed version. Complex rhythmic movement involves melody notes being sung ahead of or behind the felt impulse of the beat and syncopating groups of two or three notes. Melody pitches are often different from those notated. You may have to work hard to learn a melody from recordings, but it is excellent ear training. This process gets easier with practice, as does the task of finding guitar fingerings for sequences of notes that can be played several ways.

Tone and Dynamics

This is one of the things that can be easily learned from a recording but hard to interpret from a printed page. Listen for the different tones produced by flatpicks, fingerpicks, fingernails, and bare fingers, as well as for the different sounds that come from playing near the bridge or over the sound hole or fingerboard. Bending strings, vibrato, hammering-ons, trills, and other stylistic devices are much more easily learned from a recording than from sheet music.

Be Realistic

It helps to know something about the players on the record. Don't try to play pieces that are too difficult for you, but don't be afraid to listen to good players. Consult the song books and sheet music if you are having trouble with the chords or words, and try to hear the artists in concert or to find other players who know those artists' music.

LEARNING FROM OTHER PLAYERS

Much of today's guitar music is getting so technically sophisticated that it is not always easy for a beginner to learn what is needed from recordings. The best source of information is another person who already knows the pieces you're interested in. There are a number of ways to go about learning from other players.

Watch and listen to other players. This is the main thing to do. You can learn a great deal by watching good, bad, and intermediate players. Many times you can learn more from beginners or intermediate players than from a star. If you meet players who are not famous, you can ask questions and get them to show you some of what they do. They are usually more than glad to oblige.

Play with other people as often as possible. You can learn a tremendous amount by performing with other people, whether they are as able as you or not. Take turns showing the chords to songs with a friend. Your sense of rhythm is really put to the test in these situations, and you can learn about other people's approaches to the same songs and rhythms. If you want to learn to play lead guitar, play rhythm for a more experienced performer. Lead players love it when someone is willing to play rhythm for them.

Take lessons. It is a good idea to know what you want to learn so that you can find a teacher who is right for you. Music stores almost always have a teaching staff, and many professionals offer lessons. It is easier to learn from someone if you have heard him or her play and can ask the right questions. Some players, though, are just players and cannot describe what they do. But there are many excellent musicians who both play and teach. Learning from a good teacher can save you a lot of time and keep you from having to figure everything out the hard way.

USING SONG BOOKS AND SHEET MUSIC

Song books and sheet music can be a valuable source of information and can give you an overall, if not accurate, outline of the words, chords, and melody of a song. Even so, you will have to decide how to voice the chordal accompaniment, what right-hand techniques to use, and what musical material to use for the introduction, coda, and breaks (instrumental interludes—see Chapter 8).

There are two basic types of song books: the artist song book that features songs by a particular person or group and the collection song book. Either of these types of song book may be notated as lead sheets in which the words, chord, and melody of the song are presented on one musical staff; or they may be notated as piano reductions on a grand staff in which the words, chords, and melody are given along with a completely written-out left- and right-hand piano part. There are also a limited number of instructional-style song books that show you how to play like a particular artist. Unless the artist is well known and has many admirers, this latter kind of book is rare. Song books are generally written by and for piano players and may or may not have accurate information on the guitar part, even if there is no piano on the original recording. If you look at the Jimi Hendrix song book, you will find not only a piano score, but guitar chords that have virtually nothing to do with the way Jimi Hendrix played the guitar! It is very common for song books to feature songs in such keys as B♭ and E♭ even though the original version was done in a common guitar key such as G or D. The chord symbols given are often incorrect, incomplete, misleading, or inappropriate. What should you do?

As mentioned above, you can look for the instructional-style song books that are usually written by admirers of the original artist and are not the normal output of the artist's publisher. But these are not common. Then, again, if you have time, you can wait, because the music publishers seem to be producing better guitar editions of the song books every year. The music-publishing industry is well established, and the patterns and practices in the publishing of sheet music in many cases predate the relatively new surge of popularity of guitar-based music. The last and best option is to keep an open mind, keep your wits about you, and get what you can from the sheet music. It is for the most part intelligently done, but by people with a different outlook on music than the guitar player who reads the book. Song books are certainly a good place to obtain the lyrics of songs, and the lead-sheet notation usually gives an accurate version of the melody. Many guitarists do wonderful things by adapting piano scores for guitar, although this usually consists of an arrangement of the song that reflects the knowledge and tastes of the arranger rather than those of the artist.

Most folk guitar players buy song books to obtain the lyrics and the chord symbols above the staff, which enables them to work out a "skeleton" arrangement based on a knowledge of what the recording sounded like. Folk singers then manage to make their own arrangements of popular songs that do not reflect accurately either the exact style of the recording artist or of the arrangement in the song book. This process is difficult to explain, although it clearly exists and is used by a large number of guitar players. However, such "re-creative" activity may be responsible for perpetuating the great popularity of the guitar as a means of musical expression. Guitar players seem as likely, if not more likely, to inject their own moods, feelings, and stylistic nuances into what they play than other, more schooled musicians. This may simply be a consequence of the learning process through which each player has gone.

Song books may or may not tell you very important things about the guitar music. Many songs are recorded with a capo, and many different tunings of the guitar are used. If the guitar chords as written in the song book don't sound quite right, it may be that the person who wrote them out for the publisher was not aware of the fact that the artist used a capo or a different tuning. These things can be figured out by careful listening to the recording. The chord symbols given may have the correct name, but they may not produce sounds heard on the recording. Guitar players, when asked to play a G chord, will normally play something that uses all six strings. But, it is not uncommon to find song books that show only four-string chords, even for chords like G, Em, or A7.

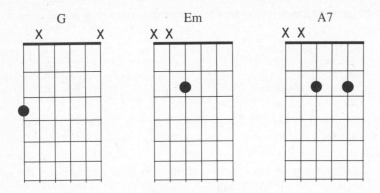

This practice of showing only four strings may be a throwback to the days of ukelele chords, which predated guitar chord symbols and used only four strings (since the ukelele has only four strings), or it may reflect the chord notes in the piano arrangement. The latter may also explain the frequent occurrence of chords in places where no guitarist would put them. Some song books have from six to eight chords in the space of one or two measures, probably reflecting a piano cadence that the arrangement contains. But these are impossible to play or awkward sounding on guitar.

HINTS ON USING SONG BOOKS AND SHEET MUSIC

1. Always try first to play the arrangement as it is written. Just because some song books are poorly done doesn't mean they all are.

2. Learn as much as you can about the artist whose material you are playing. Knowing something about the artist's skills and style can help you to know if the song book's information is accurate. Going to concerts is a good way to clear up questions about how a song is played.

3. Check the chord diagrams, and see if they are realistic. If the book says to play a G chord, you may be better off playing the usual G chord; but, on the other hand, you may get the desired sound by using an inversion. This means that you not only need to know a good, full version of most chords in case the one in the book is just a four-string chord, but you also need to know something about chord theory in order to construct a "stripped down" version of a chord that may be essential but too hard.

4. Play the song in a realistic key. Transpose the song, if necessary, to suit your voice and guitar ability or to get it in a key that sounds like the record. Some songs

are, in a sense, untransposable if they feature some chord voicing that can only be played in a particular key. But in general, transposing is one of the things that you have to do most often.

5. Check to see if there are too many chords. One limitation of many song books is that "overzealous arrangers" sometimes write excessively sophisticated chords in simple songs to make the songs more "interesting." Sometimes just leaving these chords out is the best thing to do. Your ears, taste, and musical intelligence are the only guide. Do not be afraid to perform the song differently than is written; but do not oversimplify things either, if you can help it. The chords in the song book may be an attempt to combine what several different instruments are doing on the recording, and this may or may not be what you want.

6. Beware of song books that are designed more for fans than players. You can pay a lot of money for music and just get pictures and biographical information on the artist. Some publishers stretch each verse of a song out on a separate page instead of combining verses in a shorter arrangement with repeat signs. You think you are getting a lot of music in a one-hundred-page song book, and then you find that there are only a dozen songs!

7. Keep an open mind, and learn what you can anywhere you can learn it.

ARRANGING SONGS

The songs in this book are usually written out in lead-sheet notation and were chosen to represent a variety of types of songs that guitarists may want to learn. Some are easy, having few chord changes, and others are moderately difficult in that they require bass runs, more advanced chord changes, or melodic playing. Guitarists must create arrangements that are compatible with the spirit of the songs and that are within their technical prowess. Some things to keep in mind when creating arrangements are the introduction, the strum or fingerpicking pattern, the number of times the chorus is sung, instrumental interlude or break possibilities, the coda, and the factors of tension, release, climax, and resolution.

The introduction of a song has several purposes. It sets the mood of the song, conveys a feeling and a sound picture, and begins the song. The easiest way to create an introduction is to play through the primary chords of the key in which the song is written. The basic strum or fingerpicking pattern that is used throughout the song can supply the rhythmic element in the introduction. If the song is based upon chords other than the primary chords in the key, then chord progressions from the song itself might form the introduction. If you can play melody, one phrase of the song may make a good introduction or the last phrase of the song may lead easily into the first sung words. Church organists often begin hymns for congregational singing by playing the last four measures of the melody. The introduction can aid the singer by subtly indicating the first singing pitch.

You must decide on a strum or fingerpicking pattern to use while accompanying the melody of a song. Chapters 3, 4, and 6 will help you develop this decision-making ability.

If you are performing a song with many verses, interest can wane if the chorus is sung after every verse. Consider deleting the chorus between some of the verses if this is the case. If you have the technique, you might consider playing an instrumental version of one verse and/or chorus. Chapter 8 explains how to play Carter-style and Travis-style melodies. Instrumental breaks can increase the listener's interest by providing variety of sound.

The coda should bring the song to an effective conclusion. Sometimes the material in the introduction can be repeated, or it might be changed to reflect the conclusiveness needed at the end of a piece.

The performer should always be aware of the tension and release factors in the song. Dynamics of the melody and accompaniment must be carefully planned. The text will reveal the best clues as to where in the song a slight increase or decrease in tempo might be needed or where a dissonant sound will jolt the listener into a feeling of anticipation or closure. Voice inflection and changes in vocal quality can effectively portray the differences between narration and first-person lines or between lines suggesting calmness and pathos. These changes might also be conveyed through timbre differences on the guitar by playing close to the bridge or close to the fingerboard, by using fingers, fingerpicks, or flatpicks, by employing different techniques to play the strings, or by choosing to pluck different spots on the strings. The tension and release that are part of each phrase in the song will combine to form an overall structure of climax and resolution. The sense of resolution may have the characteristic of victory, sorrow, timelessness, or satisfaction, and each must be conveyed through the musical devices of tempo, dynamics, melody, harmony, and timbre. These elements form the "pigments" of the guitarist's "palette."

Listen to your favorite artists to learn how they solve these problems, and work out your own solutions. Try to play in a manner that conveys to your audience the expressive intent of each song.

chapter 15
Communicating through Performing and Writing Songs

ON PERFORMING

Although many people play instruments solely for their own pleasure and satisfaction, it can be argued that the greatest joy of playing music is to communicate with others. This does not mean that everyone must be a professional performer; it does mean that music in its complete form was meant to be heard. It seems to be easier to play in front of friends than strangers, and often those guitarists who find themselves in a social environment that accepts and encourages music progress the fastest toward performing competence. It is probably safe to say that playing for others is something that can be learned and that although some points in the learning process may seem traumatic, it is worth the aggravation. Professional performers often feel that those rare times when everything goes right and there is total communication with the audience more than make up for all the frustration of the bad experiences. Here are some suggestions on how to make your early performing experiences enjoyable and effective.

1. *Be prepared*. Only choose material that you can play well, and practice it for more than just a few days. Short practice sessions that are spread out over a long period of time usually work better than a marathon session that occurs the night before a performance.

2. *Start the song right*. A suitable introduction to a song can give you the initial singing pitch and can establish the meter and the rhythm.

3. *Think about the song*. When performing, concentration is essential. If your mind drifts to other things, the song may suddenly stop and you won't know where to begin again. If the song has a story, think about the story line or put yourself in the role of the characters in the song. This will help you present the song properly since the listener will only be involved in the song if you are. Understanding your material and knowing something about the origin of the song or its meaning can help you remember the song and can enhance your ability to communicate its musical content.

4. *Present the song properly.* If the song depends on a story line, make sure the words are audible and pronounced correctly. Don't let the final vowels or consonants of the words trail off so that they become unintelligible, and don't play the guitar so loudly that the lyrics aren't heard. Be aware of the effect the song is intended to convey; if it is a sad song of lost love, don't shout out the lyrics and pound on the guitar.

5. *Do not mentally leave the role of performer to criticize your performance.* After you have finished performing, it is fine to analyze how you did, but while your presentation is under way, simply do it. Some performers flinch, tighten their muscles, or utter mild oaths when they are not satisfied with some aspect of their performance. Needless to say, this detracts from the overall impact and is distracting.

6. *End the song effectively.* A piece of music needs the qualities of suspense, development, climax, and resolution. A good ending, whether dramatic or simple, will leave the proper impression on the listener and can greatly affect the way that the entire song is interpreted. Know at the beginning how you are going to end the song so you can prepare and build toward that ending.

ON WRITING SONGS

Although it is not necessary to write songs since there are more good songs in existence than any person can ever learn, many musicians view writing their own songs as an expressive and creative alternative to learning popular music or studying formal music. A large part of the guitar's popularity seems to be due to its image as a tool for self-expression, and there is no way to be more self-expressive than to write your own music. Many successful songwriters have learned their craft without benefit of formal training; many others, however, have studied composition and find their training invaluable.

Anybody can write a song. Whether the song is good or not is a different and possibly irrelevant issue. Simplicity is often the key to a song's being good or memorable, and extensive musical knowledge is not needed to create noteworthy songs. If you want to write a song, then you probably will. Once you feel creative, try to stay in that mood, capitalize on it, and be productive. Keep those currents of creativity flowing. Becoming judicial and trying to decide whether or not your song is good while you are writing it can distract you from the compositional process. And lack of notational skills shouldn't stop you from writing because your song can be recorded and written out later by someone else.

How does a song get written? Some composers simply sit down with a guitar and begin to play anything that comes into their heads, working the melodies out of the chord progressions. Others prefer to start with the words. Paul Simon has stated that he thought the best songs come from simultaneously creating the words and the music.* Here are some ideas on how others write and on how you may add a new dimension to your music by writing your own songs.

1. *Getting creative ideas flowing.* Many writers have methods that work for them, and all writers have periods when nothing works—the dreaded "dry spells." Every method works for somebody, and some method works for everybody. Studying people, watching television, reading books, and doing other activities can give you ideas for songs. A common tool for many writers is distraction. If you are sweeping a floor or driving a car, sometimes your mind will take off by itself. Many writers will sit by a window and watch activity on the street, a fire, clouds, or an ocean for visual distraction that can lead to clear creative thinking. If you can get your mind going, like leafing through a magazine, then you may land on an idea that would make a good song. Try many things, and see what works for you.

2. *Finding the music.* Most writers write with an instrument, usually the guitar or piano. The guitar is easier to carry around, but the piano offers more musical variety. A voice is fine, also; some of the best songs are written with no instrument. Many writers feel that a song should pass the "whistle test" and be singable or hummable without any accompaniment. Words often suggest melodies or at least melodic rhythms. If you have some lyrics and need a tune, try to find a tune that lets the

words be sung in a natural way. Many composers write over chord changes and start with a progression that captures the mood of the song they want to create. This is extremely common and sets up the rhythm and style of the song. The chord changes will suggest all kinds of melodies, and many times the notes in the melody will come from the chords themselves.

3. *Making the words and the tune compatible*. Words that are spoken or read are different in nature than words that are sung. A simple word can take on a great deal of meaning when it is sung a certain way. You can try to set already existing words to music, or you can write words to fit a particular tune, but it is not easy to arrive at a finished product that sounds natural. For this reason, many writers like to find the lyrics—or at least key parts of the lyrics—at the same time that they find a tune to go with them. This seems to be almost a trademark of pop songwriting, where songs are built around catchy words or phrases, called "hooks." The hook is usually repeated frequently and is intended to be the most memorable part of the song, the part that someone remembers after hearing the song once. Usually the melody that goes with the hook is as important as the actual lyrics, and the two are often written simultaneously.

4. *Keeping track of what you have written*. One of the hardest parts of writing songs is maintaining concentration and keeping a certain mood long enough to write about it. It is very common for a good idea to come along and suggest itself, only to have the inspiration vanish before the mechanics of the song are finished. Most writers carry a notebook, and many work with tape recorders to save ideas for another time. The meter and rhyme patterns of a song can be worked out after the original concept for the song is done; likewise, when ideas are flowing, it is often good to write them down so the mechanics can be worked on later.

5. *Protecting your songs with a copyright*. The 1976 Copyright Act makes it easy to obtain a copyright for musical compositions since it is now permissible to submit the songs on a tape instead of the lead-sheet notation that had been previously required. A simple form can be obtained from the Office of Patents and Copyrights of the federal government. (Form PA is applicable to creative works of the performing arts and is available free from the Copyright Office, 2111 Jefferson Davis Highway, Crystal City, Virginia 22202.) The copyright protection extends for a period of fifty years after the death of the composer. A folio of songs can be copyrighted, too, a lesser expense than copyrighting individual songs.

There are numerous books and publications dealing with songwriting, and there are probably as many rules, methods, and patterns to songwriting as there are songwriters. As with most writing, it is important to do it often and to experiment with different kinds of material. Ballads and narratives, blues, humorous songs and parodies, love songs, patriotic songs, seasonal songs, country songs, personal songs, songs of lost love, sea chanteys, prison songs, religious songs, political and protest songs—these are just a few of the kinds of songs you might try your hand at.

One last thought, from Woody Guthrie, seems to be appropriate. "The fancier it is the worse it is. The plainer it is the easier it is, and the easier it is, the better it is—and the words don't even have to be spelt right."*

*Paul Simon, *The Songs of Paul Simon* (New York: Knopf, 1972), p. x.

*Alan Lomax, Woody Guthrie, and Pete Seeger, *Hard Hitting Songs for Hard-Hit People* (New York: Oak Publications, 1967), p. 19.

chapter 16
Overview of the Acoustic Steel-String Guitar in the United States

The modern guitar probably originated in Spain. It certainly found its first home there. The European guitar tradition has a long history, with its roots in the lute playing and storytelling of the early troubadours and court musicians. Outside of Spain, however, guitar playing primarily remained a pastime for the upper classes, and the guitar's widespread appearance in the native music of the United States appears to have been due to the Spanish influence in the southwest and Gulf Coast regions. The British and other west European settlers who populated the early colonies brought mostly fiddles with them; early colonial music shows almost no trace of guitars. The slaves in the South brought with them from Africa a tradition of plucked stringed instruments, and apparently, when they came into contact with the guitar, they instantly adopted it. The earliest observations of guitars in folk music of the United States came from travelers to the South in the late 1800s who found the blacks playing them in churches, in convict camps, and at social gatherings. The guitar was being used to accompany the new music that was being molded out of the traditions of the field hollers, work songs, dance tunes, and spirituals. This comes as a surprise to those of us who, noting the prevalence today of the guitar in the predominantly white popular and country music, had assumed that it had a long history there.

THE GUITAR IN BLUES MUSIC

The early 1900s found the guitar in the saloons, streets, and churches of New Orleans, Memphis, and other areas with large black communities. With the first recordings in the 1920s of early blues music came the first familiar names of American guitarists. Blind Lemon Jefferson was a street minstrel whose many recordings in the 1920s made him a great deal of money and earned him celebrity status. At the same time other so-called Delta blues artists began to be heard outside their native culture. Charley Patton, Son House, Blind Blake, Kokomo Arnold, and Scrapper Blackwell typified this style, which usually consisted of singers accompanying themselves on the guitar, with the voice and guitar often interacting in a "call and response" manner. The "bottleneck," or slide guitar, made its first appearance in this period, since it could be used to mimic the slurred notes, gliding melodies, and falsetto leaps of the blues vocal style. The early fingerpicking styles typified by Blind Blake and Scrapper Blackwell are sophisticated even by modern standards, and the drive and complexity of this very early guitar music surprises many guitar students who had associated fingerpicking with the urban folk musicians of the 1960s.

Most blues historians agree that the culmination of the Delta blues style was with Robert Johnson (1914–1938). Almost nothing is known about Johnson's life or untimely death (he was probably murdered), but he left behind a legacy of about three dozen recordings that are as fresh today as they were when they were recorded. His rhythmic changes, exciting singing style, and driving, slashing bottleneck guitar have inspired countless blues and rock musicians, and many of his songs have become rhythm-and-blues as well as rock classics.

The depression of the 1930s caused a heavy migration of blacks from the South to the urban areas of the North, and they brought their music and their guitars with them. Since the smoky bars of Chicago were too noisy for the solo Delta blues style, in the 1930s and 1940s a new, urban blues sound was born. T-Bone Walker led a Texas-based blues movement, but the major focus of this music was in Chicago. Muddy Waters is credited with being one of the first and most important of the Chicago bluesmen; together with Big Bill Broonzy, Tampa Red, Elmore James, and others he helped create an exciting sound. The electric guitar took the place of the quieter acoustic guitar of the Delta blues; drums, bass, harmonica, and sometimes piano or washboard filled out the blues band. This is the music that was later adopted by white musicians and the recording industry and that was to become rock-'n'-roll. The blues-based rock-'n'-roll bands that sprang out of England and urban white America in the 1950s and 1960s were basically playing music derivative of the much earlier Chicago blues style. The Memphis-based rockabilly sound popularized by Elvis Presley, Jerry Lee Lewis, and Carl Perkins was also a direct outgrowth of the black blues sound that emerged a decade earlier.

THE GUITAR IN JAZZ

One of the first jazz groups in New Orleans was led by guitarist Charlie Galloway in 1894, but the appearance of the guitar as a melodic voice in jazz music did not occur until after the introduction of the electric guitar. Eddie Lang, who recorded extensively in the 1920s, is usually credited with being the first to use the guitar as a solo instrument. He was trained as a classical guitarist but chose instead to play swing and blues music; he was heard backing up many of the popular singers of the day. But it was Charlie Christian who at a very young age joined Benny Goodman's band and who was the first guitarist to really exploit the capabilities of the electric guitar as a way to play melodic, hornlike lines. He died at the age of twenty-three, but not before pointing the way to a new use for the guitar, which had, by virtue of its lack of volume, been used only for rhythm purposes in the bands and swing orchestras of the day.

The other early pioneer in jazz guitar was, oddly enough, a French gypsy named Django Reinhardt (1910–1953). Reinhardt lost the use of the third and fourth fingers on his left hand as a result of a fire but still was able to develop an as yet unequaled virtuoso guitar style. His astonishingly fast runs, superb taste, and swinging rhythm with the Quintet of the Hot Club in Paris in the 1940s were an inspiration to many to use the guitar as a versatile jazz solo instrument.

Modern jazz guitarists owe their roots to Lang, Christian, and Reinhardt, and also to the generation of "bebop" guitarists that emerged in the 1950s, primarily in New York. Wes Montgomery was the best-known exponent and pioneer of the style, and other great players such as Joe Pass, Herb Ellis, Kenny Burrell, Tal Farlow, Barney Kessel, and Howard Roberts came out of this era. The bebop style is characterized by a smooth, mellow, electric-guitar sound, played almost exclusively on a hollow-body guitar. Complex, extended chords are used widely, and chord-melody solos are common, as are fast, single-note passages. The use of octaves in melody passages, first developed by Wes Montgomery, is a typical feature of the style. It is a sad comment on popular music that in the late 1950s and early 1960s these creative and skilled musicians were put out of work by the new, raw sound of early rock-'n'-roll, or, by virtue of their ability to read music, they went into the studio to play the guitars on the new recordings! Fortunately, there has been a resurgence of interest in recent years in the jazz and bebop guitar styles, and many young players are emerging and reaching a mass audience. George Benson has topped the pop charts as a jazz guitarist, and players involved in the jazz-rock fusion such as John McLaughlin, Larry Coryell, and Pat Metheny are using the guitar in unprecedented instrumental settings.

THE GUITAR IN COUNTRY MUSIC

The guitar in country music has an even shorter history than the guitar in blues and jazz. It initially appeared on recordings of early string-band music when the first "hillbilly" records were made in the 1920s but generally played a supportive role to the fiddle and banjo.

However, some of the early string-band guitarists, notably Riley Puckett of the Skillet Lickers and Roy Harvey of Charlie Poole's North Carolina Ramblers, began to develop new ways of accompanying string-band music and showed traces of skills probably learned from their black neighbors. Riley Puckett's use of syncopated bass runs instead of strummed chords was probably the earliest notion of what was to become modern bluegrass guitar.

At the forefront of the new country-music recording scene were Jimmie Rodgers and the Carter Family, both discovered and recorded by Ralph Peer in the 1920s. They were among the first country artists to really sell large numbers of records and reach a mass audience on the radio, and they featured the guitar both as an accompanying instrument and as a solo instrument. The original Carter Family consisted of A. P. Carter, his wife Sara, and his sister-in-law Maybelle. At a very early age, Maybelle developed a finger-picking melody style (see page 169) that provided the rhythm and the melody for the tunes. The trio blended their voices around Maybelle's guitar and autoharp playing, and recorded hundreds of traditional ballads, hymns, and adaptations of all kinds of songs that fit into Maybelle's instrumental style. Many now familiar songs such as "Will the Circle Be Unbroken" and "Wabash Cannonball" found their way into the folk tradition through the Carter Family, and Maybelle's guitar style was adopted by nearly all the country players of the day.

Jimmie Rodgers (1897–1933) was the first of a long line of charismatic country music "stars." Known as the "Singing Brakeman," he won the hearts of early audiences with his unique blues-influenced singing, yodeling style, and relaxed stage personality. He is usually referred to as the "father of modern country music" although his style was heavily derivative of the blues music he encountered while working on the railroad. His yodeling, original songs, and guitar-accompaniment style were widely copied. He performed in a Panama hat and a white cotton suit, singing about trains, cowboys, women, and gambling, and was largely responsible for the popularizing of the image of the singing cowboy in country and western music.

Historians tell us that virtually no cowboys played guitar or even owned guns. But the interest in the singing cowboy started by Jimmie Rodgers spawned a huge movement in American culture, giving rise to a large crop of Hollywood singing "cowboys." Gene Autry, Tex Ritter, and Roy Rogers were the best known of this group, and their appearances in the movies with fancy outfits, polite, smiling personalities, and guitars set off a love affair with the public that persists to this day. The new generation of country-music recording artists, including Ernest Tubb, Hank Snow, and Roy Acuff, also adopted the cowboy image and vastly popularized the use of the guitar without ever playing much more than very basic guitar music. Hank Williams probably represented the artistic pinnacle of the guitar-playing country singer who sang honestly about the world around him, and who spoke directly to his audience with simple, emotional songs. Hank Williams died at age twenty-nine in 1953, but his timeless songs and "white man's blues" that told of love, shame, sadness, and fun laid the groundwork for modern "honky-tonk" and country music.

THE GUITAR IN BLUEGRASS MUSIC

The term *bluegrass music* is relatively new, coined to describe the music of Bill Monroe and his Bluegrass Boys. Monroe was from Kentucky and named his group for his home state. Bill and his brother Charlie were widely known in the 1930s as a guitar-mandolin duet called the Monroe Brothers (Bill played mandolin). But it was when Bill left to form his own group around 1940 that bluegrass music is considered to have originated. Monroe's music grew out of the string-band tradition of the southern mountains, but he infused it with his own blend of black blues, the ragtime music of the 1920s, and a strong dose of the gospel harmony singing style. It was with the addition of Earl Scruggs to the band around 1945 that idiomatic bluegrass is considered to have originated, although the basic sound was anticipated a few years earlier by J. E. Mainer's Mountaineers and Charlie Poole's North Carolina Ramblers. Scruggs's banjo style provided the spark that made the bluegrass sound complete and exciting. Monroe settled on the instrumental format that remains virtually unchanged to this day: a five-piece group consisting of banjo, guitar, mandolin, fiddle, and string bass. Monroe used his mandolin to inject the music with a powerful, complex rhythmic drive, and he created a dynamic mandolin solo style as well as a new form of ensemble music.

The guitar remained a rhythm instrument for many years in bluegrass music, with Lester Flatt's backup style and famous "G run" setting the pace for players. The guitar could not compete in speed or volume with the banjo, mandolin, and fiddle that provided the instrumental solos, although occasional guitarists would perform in the Maybelle Carter style. It did not always blend with the driving bluegrass style, and it was probably not until George Shuffler, who played with the Stanley Brothers, began playing lead guitar on the recordings that the idea of solo bluegrass guitar originated. The guitarists were usually the singers in the bands, and since there were three lead instruments in the ensemble already, there was no pressure on them to develop solo guitar styles.

The prevalence today of the guitar as a lead instrument in bluegrass music is probably due to Arthel "Doc" Watson. Blind since childhood, he managed to develop the ability to match notes with fiddlers and banjo players by means of very rapid flatpicking. He first came to public attention in the early 1960s, when folklorist Ralph Rinzler brought him out of his native North Carolina to the folk festivals. Audiences were stunned by his ability; it suddenly became clear that there was such a thing as bluegrass lead guitar. Watson says he got the idea from banjo player Don Reno and studio whiz Grady Martin, but his skill and originality were undeniable. Clarence White, who played with the Kentucky Colonels in the mid-1960s, did some impressive early bluegrass lead-guitar work before joining the Byrds to play electric guitar. Norman Blake has kept a low profile for many years, performing as a soloist and working in recording sessions, but his bluegrass flatpicking is a paragon of taste, melody, and smoothness. Dan Crary, Tony Rice, and Mark O'Connor now typify the awesome expertise of the modern bluegrass guitarists who are developing new techniques and infusing the style with new influences.

THE GUITAR IN FOLK MUSIC

It has been the consistent ability of guitarists to use the instrument to express their observations about the world around them that has kept the guitar at the pinnacle of musical culture in the United States. This expression is the basic premise of "folk" music, and the guitar has been the primary vehicle for the expression in modern times. Set apart from those who play music for money and fame have been those who play music for its own sake. Folklorists lament the intrusion of the mass media into the ancient oral traditions of folk music, but it is undoubtedly true, as Woody Guthrie remarked, that as long as there are folks there will always be folk music. Folk guitar music owes its roots to the early black blues music, and there has been a strong streak of integrity and honesty in folk music that has weathered the Hollywood guitar cowboys, rock stars, and electronic-music revolution to remain as powerful today as ever.

The most important early figure in the folk-music movement was Huddie Ledbetter (1885–1949), better known as "Leadbelly." He was a huge and unforgettable man who played a twelve-string guitar and sang irrepressibly about everything around him. He spent much of his early life in prison, and sang his way out of prison twice with songs sent to the governor asking for pardon. He grew up in Texas and learned much of his music in the blues-rich Delta region, but his major influence on the world came from his association with folklorist John Lomax. Leadbelly's second release from prison was into the custody of Lomax, who brought him to New York, where he delighted the urban crowds with his stories, songs, and strong guitar playing. His music repertoire was vast and included blues, children's songs, new versions of old ballads and folk tales, as well as his own songs. His unique style seems to have reached more urban audiences than the music of many of his black contemporaries, and he was a cornerstone in the urban folk-music scene. His best-known songs are "Irene, Goodnight" and "Midnight Special."

Woodrow Wilson "Woody" Guthrie, although never a commercial success, became another great force in the folk-guitar tradition. A dust-bowl refugee from Oklahoma during the depression, Woody traveled all over the country, singing and writing about everything he saw. He referred to himself as a "one-cylinder guitar picker" and wrote hundreds of songs, many of which were based on earlier songs or tunes. He particularly championed the cause of the poor workers and early unions, and his musical career was severely stunted by the "communist" label given to him by enemies of the union movement. Woody was largely responsible for creating the image of the acoustic guitar as a vehicle for speaking the truth, and the next generation of folk singers, including Bob Dylan, Phil Ochs, the Kingston Trio, and Peter, Paul and Mary, owe a great debt to Woody. His song "This Land Is Your Land" has become one of the best-loved folk songs of all time, and "Tom Joad," "Pretty Boy Floyd," and many others have become timeless classics of ballad writing and storytelling.

The first "hootenannies" and many of the early labor rallies featured Woody, Leadbelly, Burl Ives, Josh White, Pete Seeger, and the Weavers, who were the first wave of urban folk musicians. Their message was that the folk music of America was not a special statement by isolated cultural groups but part of the common expression of humanity world-wide. The late 1950s saw the huge folk revival in urban and suburban areas; suddenly it was the educated middle class who began to see the whole of American folk music as its own and the guitar as the means of expression. The Kingston Trio hit the charts in 1958 with "Tom Dooley," opening the way for the very popular folk artists of the 1960s. Bob Dylan, Simon and Garfunkel, Joan Baez, and Peter, Paul and Mary reached very large audiences with their fresh brand of music. The acoustic guitar was the almost exclusive means of accompaniment; the honesty, perception, and convictions of the performers struck a nerve in American society. The guitar became, in the hands of someone like Bob Dylan, a way to speak out against the unfairness and injustice in the world, and the guitar was adopted by the antiwar movement as being more effective than a microphone for communicating the message.

The idea of the truth-seeking guitarist writing songs about his or her perception of the world was first propagated in our culture by Woody Guthrie and Bob Dylan, and continues to this day. The music of John Prine, James Taylor, Gordon Lightfoot, Eric Anderson, and John Denver, among others, is an outgrowth of this idea and has had a profound influence on our society and music. In most cases the guitar is merely the accompanying instrument in this kind of music, but it seems to have provided a necessary impetus and symbolism. Indeed, it is hard to imagine this music without the guitar.

It was the 1960s that caused a mixing of the styles of guitar music in this country, and the different threads of folk, country, blues, and rock music began to intertwine. It may have been the mass media that allowed the interaction between the culturally isolated parts of the music spectrum, since suddenly recording artists began selling unprecedented numbers of records both in this country and world-wide. The interest in guitar music was further increased when it was discovered by rock audiences that rock guitar music was largely derived from earlier blues styles. The rush to find old blues records caused many record labels to reissue out-of-print recordings, and many young listeners discovered new sounds and techniques. It was out of this cross-fertilization of guitar music styles that a movement using the steel-string acoustic guitar as a solo instrumental voice had its beginnings.

Blues players had amassed considerable guitar technique by 1930. Throughout the century there have been skilled guitar instrumentalists, but they seldom reached the ears of the mass public. Sam McGee, who performed on the Grand Old Opry almost since its inception, was perhaps the first country player to begin performing in the fingerpicking style. Merle Travis astonished audiences in the 1940s with his smooth, polished, complex arrangements of finger-style guitar. Travis, in turn, inspired Chet Atkins, who has gone on to further develop the style to include classical and pop-music sounds and techniques. John Fahey is usually credited with founding what he calls the "American primitive guitar," which features the acoustic steel-string guitar as a solo voice. Fahey combined the smooth, three-finger fingerpicking sound of Mississippi John Hurt with an almost Eastern drone sound built around various open tunings of the instrument to create his own instrumental music. Fahey's hypnotic fingerpicking originated in his early studies of rural blues guitar but soon developed into a neoclassical sound.

Mississippi John Hurt's guitar style also influenced many other players at the time. Hurt was one of the older bluesmen who had been "rediscovered" in the 1960s and who performed a great deal in coffeehouses and small clubs before his death in 1967. His uncluttered guitar sound typifies what is called Travis-style guitar, with clean melody lines played against a steady, four-count bass. Elizabeth Cotton, the author of "Freight Train," also inspired many young players to adopt the fingerpicking style (although she played the guitar left-handed and used the thumb to play the melody).

There is a constantly growing number of young guitarists who use the steel-string guitar as a solo instrument and who have adopted much of the European classical guitar tradition and have combined it with the various elements of the American folk guitar. Leo Kottke is the best known of this group. He is an unbelievably fast and creative fingerpicker who uses the six- and twelve-string guitars to create his own instrumental music. Rick Ruskin, Pierre Bensusan, Robbie Basho, and William Ackerman are others in this movement who use the guitar as a melodic instrument rather than as an accompaniment, and there are others such as David Bromberg, Ry Cooder, Jorma Kaukonen, and Doc Watson who integrate their exceptional guitar skills into structures that include songwriting, entertainment, and storytelling. Other fingerpickers have taken the foundations laid by the Reverend Gary Davis and have developed a style of ragtime guitar that is extremely sophisticated and complex. Stefan Grossman has been a tireless proponent of the style and, together with players such as Guy van Duser, Dave Laibman, Eric Schoenberg, and Leo Wynjkamp, Jr., has brought it to near perfection. The musical and technical complexity of the counterpoint ragtime piano music as played on guitar has brought it to a point where it rivals the European classical music in difficulty.

In England, there are large numbers of musicians who use the acoustic guitar extremely skillfully to play a range of music that encompasses not only much American folk music but also that of the British Isles. Davey Graham, John Renbourn, and Bert Jansch originated the British acoustic guitar style in the 1960s and launched the "folk Baroque" sound of Pentangle, Fairport Convention, and Steeleye Span. Now John Martyn, Martin Carthy, John Pearse, and others are developing a new European guitar tradition that is based more on the American steel-string tradition than on European classical music.

THE GUITAR IN ROCK MUSIC

Rock-'n'-roll music probably owes its origin to the electric guitar. Certainly no style of guitar music has come on the popular scene so quickly and permanently. The rock-'n'-roll style was originally an outgrowth of the Chicago blues sound of the late 1940s and early 1950s and first emerged in the Memphis "rockabilly" style of Carl Perkins, Elvis Presley, Jerry Lee Lewis, and Johnny Burnette. The southern white rockabilly players picked up the exciting style and were able to get the predominantly white popular-music industry interested. The black players had their own R&B (rhythm and blues) charts, and the sound of T-Bone Walker, Little Richard, Fats Domino, Chuck Berry, and other black players was new only to the white audiences.

The first rock-'n'-roll guitar players to come to national attention were Chuck Berry, Scotty Moore, who backed Elvis Presley, Buddy Holly, Bo Diddley, and Bill Haley. Bill Haley's single "Rock around the Clock" has been called the first rock-'n'-roll hit, and after its release and popularity in 1955 the way was paved for many more. The pop charts had been dominated by crooners and the mellow vocal sound of singers such as Frank Sinatra and Perry Como, and the new, exciting rock sound caught on very quickly. Much of the early rock music featured a saxophone as the lead instrument, and it was largely the invention of the solid-body electric guitar by Les Paul and the playing of Chuck Berry that really brought the guitar to prominence. The Beatles and Rolling Stones and other "British invasion" groups drew heavily on Berry's style, as did the California-based "surf"-music sound. Berry's playing style is exciting and rhythmic, using single-string and multistring leads and clever, offbeat syncopations.

As the rock-'n'-roll players got more accustomed to playing loud electric guitar music, a new, lead-guitar sound began to emerge that was distinctly different from the rhythm-and-blues–oriented sound of early rock music. There were numerous electric-guitar instrumental groups in the late 1950s and early 1960s that began to explore the use of the electric guitar as a solo voice. The Ventures, Link Wray, and Duane Eddy had chart success with instrumentals, although they were mostly still based on blues and swinging rhythm figures.

Many of the British rock players such as Jeff Beck, Jimmy Page, and Pete Townshend, who had started playing in the early rock-'n'-roll style, began to use the sustaining power of the instrument and the high-volume tone to create a different effect. Instead of the rhythmic, staccato runs of dance rock-'n'-roll, the electric guitar began to wail, scream, and cry. Eric Clapton personified the "slowhand" approach to lead guitar, where distinctively arrhythmic and atonal leads were played against a rhythm and chordal background. The players began to take long, improvisational solos instead of the four-bar breaks in pop tunes of the 1950s. Although many players were working on redefining the sound of the electric guitar, it was Jimi Hendrix who completely crystallized and popularized the sound. He used numerous electronic effects and had a prodigious technical ability and a very aggressive style of showmanship. Instead of being a conventional musical instrument, the electric guitar became a way to create and manipulate a whole new concept in sound. There was no longer a concern for the "natural" tone of the instrument, and new, electronically induced sounds became the tools of the players.

The list of rock guitarists reads like a *Who's Who* in rock music, since the guitarists were most often the group leaders and trend setters. Fusion players began to combine the screaming sound of the rock guitar with the rhythms of Latin music and complex jazz chords, as well as the basic appeal of country music. Carlos Santana, John McLaughlin, and Duane Allman all used the rock-guitar sound and took it in different directions. Santana mixed it with conga drums and infectious rhythms, McLaughlin integrated it into an experimental jazz format, and Allman launched the southern "country rock" sound.

Since the 1970s, the lead electric guitar as a focus has waned considerably, and the sound has been pushed more to the background, with vocalists once again occupying the charts. But the sound has retained a certain degree of its raw aggressiveness and permeates the popular and country-music sound. New Wave groups have begun to rekindle the energy of early rock-'n'-roll as a reaction to the "watering down" of commercial rock music, and are striving to reinject the music with the urgency and excitement that spawned it. The disco movement relegated the guitar to the background, with the drumbeat and horns predominant, and now the New Wave and "punk" music is once again relying on the "tried and true" rock-'n'-roll guitar sound that will, no doubt, remain an important part of popular music for some time to come.

The guitar is presently living many simultaneous lives. Something about its portability, personalness, and the wide range of music available to its players has enabled the guitar to exist both as the pastime and hobby of many, and as the lifetime devotion of a few. It continues to be used effectively by people of all ages and cultures to express personal emotion and experiences, timeless beauty, rhythm, and harmony, and simply to communicate to people.

Suggested Further Reading

Artis, Bob. *Bluegrass*. New York: Leisure Books, 1977.
Charters, Samuel B. *The Country Blues*. New York: Da Capo, 1975.
Evans, Tom, and Evans, Mary Anne. *Guitars: From Renaissance to Rock*. New York: Paddington, 1977.

Guitar Player Magazine Publications. *The Guitar Player Book,* rev. ed. New York: Grove Press, 1980.

Malone, Bill C. *Country Music U.S.A.: A Fifty-Year History*. Austin: University of Texas Press, 1969.

Sandberg, Larry. *Folk Music Sourcebook*. New York: Knopf, 1976.

Wheeler, Tom. *The Guitar Book*. New York: Harper & Row, 1978.

Selected Discography for Aspiring Guitarists

There are thousands of good recordings featuring guitar, but the following indicate the evolution and culmination of many of the skills found in this book.

Carter Family
> *The Original Carter Family from 1936 Radio Transcripts.*
> Old Homestead, OH 90045.

Elizabeth Cotton
> *Elizabeth Cotton Folksongs and Instrumentals with Guitar.*
> Folkways, FG 3526.

Bob Dylan
> *Bob Dylan's Greatest Hits, Volume II.*
> Columbia, PG 31120.

John Fahey
> *The Best of John Fahey.*
> Takoma, C-1058.

Woody Guthrie
> *Woody Guthrie: This Land Is Your Land.*
> Folkways, FTS 31001E.

Mississippi John Hurt
> *The Best of Mississippi John Hurt.*
> Vanguard, VSD-19/20.

Leadbelly
> *Leadbelly.*
> Capitol, DT-1821.

Nitty Gritty Dirt Band and Others (3-record set)
> *Will the Circle Be Unbroken.*
> United Artists, 9801.

John Prine
> *John Prine.*
> Atlantic, SD 19156.

Jimmie Rodgers
> *The Best of the Legendary Jimmie Rodgers.*
> RCA, AHL1-3315(e).

The Smithsonian Collection of Classic Country Music (8-record set).
> Selected and annotated by Bill C. Malone, Smithsonian Collection of Recordings.

Doc Watson
> *Doc Watson on Stage.*
> Vanguard, VSD 45/46.

appendix A
Getting Started with the Third-Hand Capo (Esus)

Appendixes A and B contain two new approaches to learning simplified beginning guitar chords. The approaches have been effective in providing both adults and children with the skills necessary for the accompaniment and singing of songs. The confidence gained from acquiring these skills transfers into more successful learning of the conventional guitar chords that are introduced in Chapters 2 and 3. Therefore, these appendixes can be used as preparatory material for those chapters. The sections "Reading Chord-Fingering Diagrams," "Strumming," and "Lead-Sheet Notation" in Chapter 2 should be studied while Appendix A or B is being covered. If a student does not have a Third-Hand capo, a conventional capo can be modified to perform the same function.

The guitar has a reputation for being an instrument that initially is not difficult to play, especially when it is learned as a chording, accompaniment instrument rather than as a melody instrument. There are a number of "easy" approaches to learning guitar that emphasize how quickly beginners can learn to play songs; however, the nature of the guitar itself is such that even the simplest and most basic chords that can be used to play familiar songs require three fingers of the left hand. For most people, these basic chords are achievable after a few hours of practice, although it may take many days or even weeks of practice or class time before a total beginner can accompany a three-chord folk song. Given the limited number of two-chord songs and the desire to play interesting music, this appendix presents a unique approach to acquiring initial playing skills that are needed to build a foundation for and provide a natural transition to more difficult techniques.

A device called the *Third-Hand Capo** (Figure A.1) provides even a beginner with an excellent way to produce full-sounding chords and accompaniments to both two- and three-chord songs. Instead of clamping all the strings, as with a conventional capo, the Third-Hand capo has six rubber discs that can be rotated "up" or "down" to clamp the strings as desired. To make your own Third-Hand–type capo, slice up a normal elastic capo or whittle a piece of wood to slip under a normal capo so it only holds down certain strings. But the patented design of the Third-Hand capo makes it useful in many different configurations and applications.

---

*The Third-Hand capo is protected by U. S. patent no. 4,183,279 and is distributed by the Third-Hand Capo Company, 716½ West Lincoln, DeKalb, Illinois 60115.

FIGURE A.1 E Suspended Configuration with Third-Hand Capo

E Suspended Configuration

With the Third-Hand capo placed to form an E suspended chord (Esus), three full-sounding chords can be produced with only one finger of the left hand (see Figure A.2).

The songs in this appendix are all notated in the key of E. Because of this, the singing pitch for some of these songs will be comfortable for some people but may need adjusting for others. The overall pitch level of a song can be moved or transposed through the use of a normal capo or a second Third-Hand capo with all of the discs facing down. By keeping the capo with the E suspended configuration

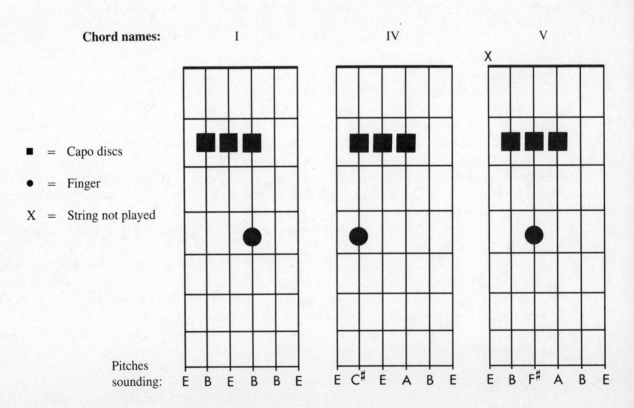

FIGURE A.2 E Suspended Configuration Fingerings

two frets above the normal capo you can play all of the songs in this appendix at several pitch levels. See Chapter 12 for a more detailed explanation of how to transpose with a capo.

"Skip to My Lou" has just two chords that can be played immediately. The song is usually performed with a quick tempo, and the chord changes should present no obstacle to playing the song at the proper speed. Attention can be concentrated on developing strumming skills. Try playing the song first using downstrokes on each beat—D–D–D–D. Then try D__ D__. When you have mastered those strums, play D–D/U–D–D/U. Note that the underlined syllables in each verse correspond to the first (stressed) beat of each measure.

2. Fly in the buttermilk, shoo fly shoo! (3 times)
   Skip to my Lou, my darling.

3. Lost my partner, what will I do? (3 times)
   Skip to my Lou, my darling.

4. I'll get another one, prettier than you. (3 times)
   Skip to my Lou, my darling.

In playing the accompaniment to "Clementine," strum a downstroke across all six strings on the first beat, and a downstroke across only two or three treble strings on beats 2 and 3. Then try D–D/U–D/U.

Clementine
(Esus)

2. In a cavern, in a canyon, excavating for a mine,
   Dwelt a miner, forty-niner, and his daughter Clementine.

3. Light she was, and like a fairy, and her shoes were number nine,
   Herring boxes without topses, sandals were for Clementine.

4. Drove she ducklings to the water, every morning just at nine,
   Hit her foot against a splinter, fell into the foaming brine.

5. Ruby lips above the water, blowing bubbles soft and fine,
   Oh, alas, I was no swimmer, so I lost my Clementine.

"Michael Row the Boat Ashore" introduces the IV chord. Be sure to play this song at a relaxed tempo. The D–D/U–D–D/U pattern will make an effective accompaniment. Experiment with other strums as you gain confidence in performing this song.

Michael Row the Boat Ashore
(Esus)

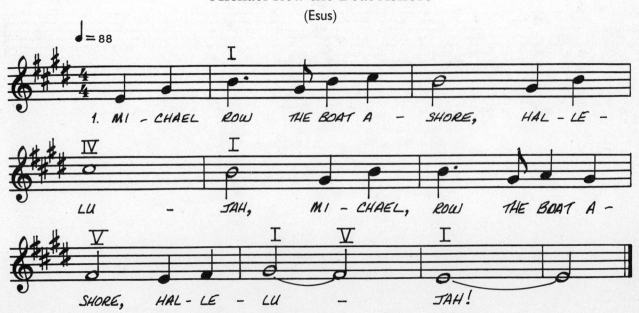

2. Sister, <u>help</u> to trim the <u>sail</u>, Hallelu <u>jah</u>.
   Sister, <u>help</u> to trim the <u>sail</u>, Hallelu <u>jah</u>.

3. Jordan's <u>River</u> is chilly and <u>cold</u>, Hallelu <u>jah</u>.
   Chills the <u>body</u>, but warms the <u>soul</u>, Hallelu <u>jah</u>.

4. Jordan's <u>River</u> is deep and <u>wide</u>, Hallelu <u>jah</u>.
   Meet my <u>mother</u> on the other <u>side</u>, Hallelu <u>jah</u>.

5. If you <u>get</u> there before I <u>do</u>, Hallelu <u>jah</u>.
   Tell my <u>people</u> I'm a-comin' <u>too</u>, Hallelu <u>jah</u>.

"The Streets of Laredo" is a cowboy song that features the IV chord only once, near the end of the verse. The color of the Esus chords lends itself very well to this song, providing a distant, plaintive sound. Begin by using a D–D/U–D/U strum.

Streets of Laredo
(Esus)

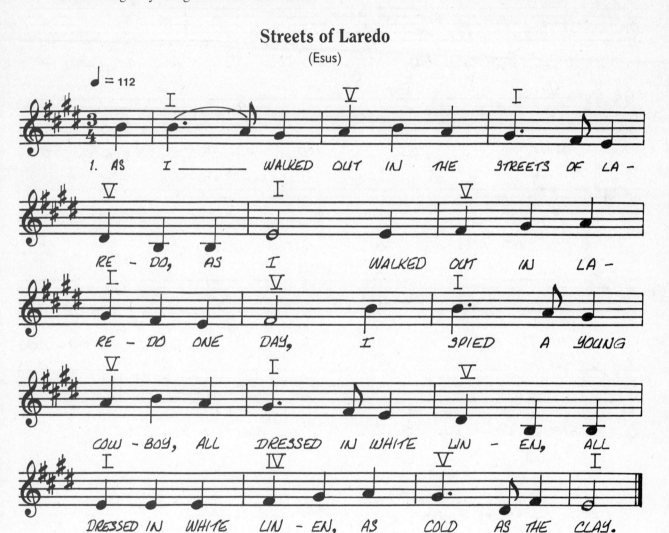

2. "I <u>see</u> by your outfit that <u>you</u> are a <u>cowboy</u>,"
   These <u>words</u> he did <u>say</u> as I <u>boldly</u> went <u>by</u>,
   "Come <u>sit</u> here be<u>side</u> me and <u>hear</u> my sad <u>story</u>,
   For I'm <u>shot</u> in the <u>chest</u> and I <u>know</u> I must <u>die</u>.

3. "It was <u>once</u> in the saddle I <u>used</u> to go <u>dashing</u>,
   Once in the saddle I <u>used</u> to go <u>gay</u>;
   First <u>down</u> to <u>Rosie's</u> and <u>then</u> to the <u>card</u>-house;
   Now I'm <u>shot</u> in the <u>chest</u> and I'm <u>dying</u> today.

4. "Get <u>six</u> sturdy <u>cowboys</u> to <u>carry</u> my <u>coffin</u>,
   Get <u>six</u> pretty <u>maidens</u> to <u>sing</u> me a <u>song</u>,
   Put <u>bunches</u> of <u>roses</u> all <u>over</u> my <u>coffin</u>,
   For <u>I'm</u> a young <u>cowboy</u> and I <u>know</u> I've done <u>wrong</u>.

5. "Oh, <u>beat</u> the drum <u>slowly</u> and <u>play</u> the fife <u>lowly</u>,
   <u>Sing</u> the death <u>march</u> as you <u>carry</u> me <u>along</u>;
   <u>Lay</u> me to <u>rest</u> and <u>toss</u> the clods o'er me,
   For <u>I'm</u> a young <u>cowboy</u> and I <u>know</u> I've done <u>wrong</u>."

6. We <u>beat</u> the drum <u>slowly</u>, and <u>played</u> the fife <u>lowly</u>,
   <u>Hummed</u> the death <u>march</u> as we <u>carried</u> him <u>along</u>;
   We put <u>bunches</u> of <u>roses</u> all <u>over</u> his <u>coffin</u>,
   For <u>he</u> was our <u>friend</u> <u>although</u> he'd done <u>wrong</u>.

"Cindy," a traditional dance tune with many verses, needs three chords for accompaniment and usually moves at a rapid tempo.

Cindy
(Esus)

1. I WISH I HAD A NICK-EL, I WISH I HAD A DIME, I WISH I HAD A PRET-TY GIRL TO LOVE ME ALL THE TIME. *(Chorus)* GET A-LONG HOME, CIN-DY, CIN-DY, GET A-LONG HOME, CIN-DY, CIN-DY, GET A-LONG HOME, CIN-DY, CIN-DY, I'LL MAR-RY YOU SOME DAY.

2. You ought to see my Cindy,
She lives a-way down South,
And she's so sweet the honey bees,
All swarm around her mouth.
(*Chorus*)

3. The first time I saw Cindy,
She was standing in the door.
Her shoes and stockings in her hand,
Her feet all over the floor.
(*Chorus*)

4. She took me to the parlor,
She cooled me with her fan,
She said I was the prettiest thing,
In the shape of mortal man.
(*Chorus*)

5. I wish I were an apple,
A-hanging on a tree,
And every time my Cindy passed,
She'd take a bite of me.
(*Chorus*)

6. Apples in the summertime,
Peaches in the fall;
If I can't have my Cindy,
Won't have none at all.
(*Chorus*)

"Oh, Susanna" can be strummed with the patterns already introduced in this appendix, or it may be played with some of the fingerpicking patterns introduced in Chapter 6.

Oh, Susanna

(Esus)

Stephen Foster

2. I had a dream the other night, when ev'rything was still;
   I thought I saw Susanna dear a-comin down the hill.
   The buckwheat cake was in her mouth, the tear was in her eye,
   I says, "I'm comin' from the South, Susanna don't you cry."
   (Chorus)

3. I soon will be in New Orleans, and then I'll look around,
   And when I find Susanna, I'll fall upon the ground.
   And if I do not find her, then I will surely die,
   And when I'm dead and buried, Susanna don't you cry.
   (Chorus)

John Denver's "Leaving on a Jet Plane" will sound nice with practically any ⁴⁄₄ strum or finger-picking pattern. Try the following strumming pattern, practicing carefully, paying particular attention to the silent downstroke on the third beat:

D–D/U–__ U–D/U.

Leaving on a Jet Plane

Words and music by
John Denver

2. There's so <u>many</u> times I've <u>let</u> you down,
   So <u>many</u> times I've <u>played</u> around,
   I <u>tell</u> you now, <u>they</u> don't mean a <u>thing</u>. __
   Ev'ry <u>place</u> I go I'll <u>think</u> of you,
   Ev'ry <u>song</u> I sing I'll <u>sing</u> for you,
   When <u>I</u> come back I'll <u>bring</u> your wedding <u>ring</u>. __
   (*Chorus*)

3. <u>Now</u> the time has <u>come</u> to leave you,
   <u>One</u> more time, <u>let</u> me kiss you,
   Then <u>close</u> your eyes, I'll be on my <u>way</u>. __
   <u>Dream</u> about the <u>days</u> to come
   When <u>I</u> won't have to <u>leave</u> alone,
   <u>About</u> the times <u>I</u> won't have to <u>say</u>: __
   (*Chorus*)

By using the E suspended configuration, beginners can accompany folk and popular songs during the initial guitar-playing experiences. For very young children, people with learning disabilities, and anyone who would like to play and sing immediately, this can be an invaluable aid. If you want to combine players at different levels of proficiency or use the E suspended configuration as a transition to playing the normal open-position chords presented in Chapter 3, then Figure A.3 will be of interest to you. The I–IV–V progression is shown at four levels of fingering complexity. One of these levels can appropriately challenge the left-hand technique of practically any player.

As you master each fingering complexity level in Figure A.3 you will be able to play the normal open fingerings for the D, G, and A7 chords. Work with this page until you can play the chords at levels 1 and 2. The chords at level 3 require skills parallel to those presented in Chapter 3, whereas the skills needed at level 4 are introduced in Chapter 9 and need not be attempted until you have played for several months. It is shown here to hold the interest of students with advanced skills while rookies acquire basic skills. All of the preceding songs should be played with the chords for fingering complexity levels 1 and 2 before moving on to Chapter 2 or 3.

Chords

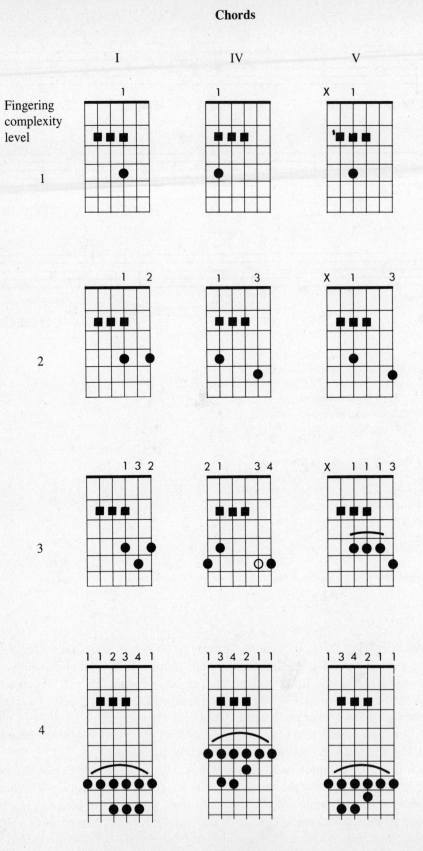

FIGURE A.3 Four Levels of Fingering Complexity for the E Suspended Configuration

Many of the songs that are presented elsewhere in this book to illustrate other skills can be adapted easily for use with the Third-Hand capo although some of them may have to be transposed to the key of E (see Chapter 12).

The Third-Hand capo can be positioned at each fret in 63 different configurations. You may enjoy discovering some of these ways to put the Third-Hand on your guitar. Don't be afraid to experiment.*

*Other easy playing techniques for the Third-Hand capo can be found in *Duck Soup Guitar,* by D. H. Canard, also available from the Third-Hand Capo Company.

SONG SUGGESTIONS FOR ESUS CONFIGURATION

Song (Composer)	Key:	Chords
Amazing Grace	E:	I, IV, V
Billy Boy	E:	I, IV, V
Blowin' in the Wind (Bob Dylan)	E:	I, IV, V
Clementine	E:	I, V
Early Morning Rain (Gordon Lightfoot)	E:	I, IV, V
For Baby, for Bobby (John Denver)	E:	I, IV, V
The Gambler (Don Schlitz)	E:	I, IV, V
Happy Birthday (Mildred J. Hill and Patty S. Hill)	E:	I, IV, V
Irene, Goodnight (Huddie Ledbetter)	E:	I, IV, V
Me and Bobby McGee (Kris Kristofferson and Fred Foster)	E:	I, IV, V
Paradise (John Prine)	E:	I, IV, V
Peaceful Easy Feeling (Glenn Frey and Don Henley)	E:	I, IV, V
Red River Valley	E:	I, IV, V
Rock-a My Soul	E:	I, V
She'll Be Comin' 'round the Mountain	E:	I, IV, V
Swing Low, Sweet Chariot	E:	I, IV, V
There's a Place in the World for a Gambler (Dan Fogelberg)	E:	I, IV, V
This Land Is Your Land (Woody Guthrie)	E:	I, IV, V
Will the Circle Be Unbroken (A. P. Carter)	E:	I, IV, V
Yankee Doodle	E:	I, IV, V
You Are My Sunshine (Jimmie Davis and Charles Mitchell)	E:	I, IV, V

appendix B
Getting Started with the Third-Hand Capo (Easy C)

Appendix A presented one way to teach guitar skills to students with little or no experience. Another effective approach utilizes the Easy C configuration. The Easy C configuration is played with the normal open-position guitar fingerings for A7, Em7, and D. However, when these fingerings are used in conjunction with a Third-Hand capo positioned as shown in Figure B.1, the resulting chords are C, G7, and F. Several benefits accrue from this particular configuration. First, beautiful, full-sounding chords are produced. Second, the technique required to produce the C, G7, and F chords is no more difficult

FIGURE B.1 Easy C Configuration with Third-Hand Capo

than that required to play the D and A7 chords (see Figure B.2)—the two chords often presented first in guitar instruction texts. In addition, playing the guitar in the key of C major, which is normally inaccessible to beginners, makes it compatible with other instruments such as the autoharp. The fingerings learned are transposed but real; once the capo is removed the newly acquired executive skills are still applicable to playing the guitar. The A7 (I) to Em7 (V7) fingerings are much simpler to play in initial playing experiences than D. Therefore, the D fingering can be delayed until the students have acquired some facility with two easier chords.

The tuning of each string is indicated below the diagram. The squares show the Third-Hand capo disc placement. Circles depict placement of left-hand fingers. Arabic numbers placed above the diagrams indicate which left-hand finger is used (1 = index, 2 = middle, and 3 = ring). An X shows strings that should not be sounded when strumming or fingerpicking.

All of the songs in Appendix A can be played using the I, IV, and V fingerings with the Third-Hand capo in Easy C configuration.

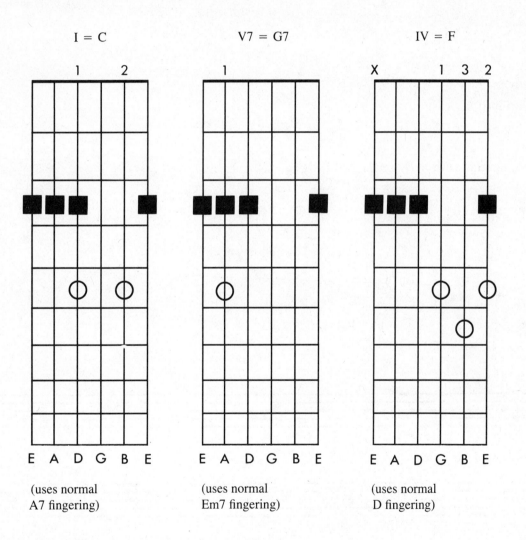

FIGURE B.2 Easy C Configuration Fingerings

appendix C
Answers to Exercises

CHAPTER 5

Note Identification

E, G, A, F, B, A, D, D, E, G, C, C, C, F

Note Identification with Accidentals

1. C, Db, Db, C#; C, A, Ab, Ab; C#, D, E, C#;
   C, A, G, Gb; C, C#, D, C#; G, F#, F#, F;
   E, Eb, E, E; A, G, Gb, F; E, A, G#, A;
   C#, C, E, C

2. B, E; G, E, B, E; G, E, B, A, B;
   B, E; B, E; G, E; G, G, F#, E, B;
   B, E; E, E; F#, E, D, B, D, E;
   G, E, G, A; G, E

3.

Tablature

316

Note and Rest Durational Equivalencies

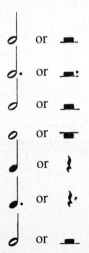

Meter

1. Number beats per measure   Note value of one beat

3	
4	
4	
4	
6	
4	
3	

3. No. "The Gambler," "Row, Row, Row Your Boat," "Stewball."

Counting Melodic Rhythm

1.

2.

3.

4. $\frac{4}{4}$, $\frac{6}{8}$, $\frac{3}{4}$, $\frac{4}{4}$, $\frac{5}{4}$

5.

Notational Symbols

A	F♯m	D	E7
A	E	D	E
A	E	D	E
F	G	A7	D7
Em	F♯m	B7	E7
A	E	D	E
A	E	D	E
A	A	G♭	A

Alternative Interpretations of Meter Signatures

2. Song   Beats per measure

"Down in the Valley"   3 or 1

"John Hardy"   4 or 2

"Oh, Susanna"   4 or 2

"Red River Valley"   3 or 1

"Shady Grove"   4 or 2

"Streets of Laredo"   3 or 1

3. Yes. Faster tempos suggest fewer beats per measure.

CHAPTER 7
Dropped-D Tuning

2. Barre chords don't work. The tonic chord sounds full with the sixth-string root bass. There is no root-position subdominant chord. The dominant chord (A7) requires an extra finger. The C, F, and Gm chords are much more difficult to play because they require partial barre forms.

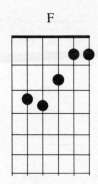

Open-G Tuning

3. Barre at the fifth fret for the C chord.
   Barre at the seventh fret for the D chord.

Open and Simulated Tunings

1. 6–D, 5–A, 4–D, 3–G, 2–A, 1–D

2.

       I   IV   V

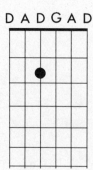

3. Probably more difficulty because you must relearn the placement of notes on the fretboard.

4. Yes, but you have to go out of first position (to the fifth fret) to play the fourth degree of the scale built on the open sixth string. With the Third-Hand capo you cannot play the second scale degree on the sixth string or the second scale degree on the second string without moving your left hand out of position.

CHAPTER 9
Barre Chords

1. G♯, Gm, Am, B7, D♯ (E♭), C, Bm, Em, D7, F7

2. B♭   = A form, first fret, or E form, sixth fret

    D7   = A7 form, fifth fret, or E7 form, tenth fret

    Am   = Em form, fifth fret

    F   = A form, eighth fret, or E form, first fret

    E♭7   = A7 form, sixth fret

    F♯m   = Am form, ninth fret, or Em form, second fret

    A♭7   = E7 form, fourth fret

    G   = A form, tenth fret, or E form, third fret

    C   = A form, third fret, or E form, eighth fret

3.

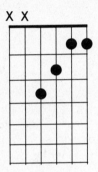

4.

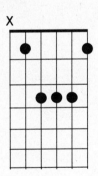

6.

Key	Chords					
B♭	B♭	F	E♭	A♭	Gm	F7
E	E	B	A	D	C♯m	B7
D	D	A	G	C	Bm	A7
G	G	D	C	F	Em	D7
A	A	E	D	G	F♯m	E7

CHAPTER 10
Playing Scales

3.
D

A

E

4.
G

B♭

5.
B♭

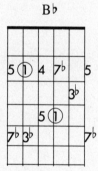

C

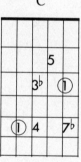

D

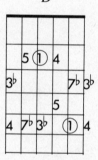

CHAPTER 11
Major Scales

2. F, thirteenth fret, twelve

3. E, E major, E major

4.

5. Eb, F, G, Ab, Bb, C, D, Eb

   Three flats

6.

7.

Modal, Minor, and Blues Scales

2.								
Ionian	G	A	B	C	D	E	F#	G
Dorian	G	A	Bb	C	D	E	F	G
Phrygian	G	Ab	Bb	C	D	Eb	F	G
Lydian	G	A	B	C#	D	E	F#	G
Mixolydian	G	A	B	C	D	E	F	G
Aeolian	G	A	Bb	C	D	Eb	F	G
Locrian	G	Ab	Bb	C	Db	Eb	F	G

3. Dorian

4. Mixolydian

5. E   G   A   B   D   E

Keys

3. One flat, Bb

4. a. G major

   b. A minor

   c. E Dorian

   d. C Mixolydian

   e. D minor

   f. C major

   g. D major

   h. D Mixolydian

Intervals

1.

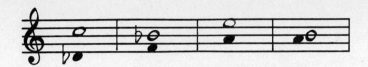

2. Yes, one half-step difference between the thirds of major and minor chords.

3. C to D

Triads

1. E or G, C, E, G, C, E

2. Third is C♯ in A-major chord and C in A-minor chord. Third.

3. E, G, B

   E, B, E, G, B, E

Four-Note Chords

1. D, F♯, A, C

   D, F♯, A, C♯

2. A7 chord: E   A   E   G   C♯   E

   G7 chord: G   B   D   G   B   F

   E7 chord: E   B   D   G♯   B   E

Seventh is on the third string in the A7 chord, first string in G7, and fourth string in E7. The seventh tends to be played on the treble strings.

Augmented, Diminished, and Other Chords

1. C   E   G   B♭   D

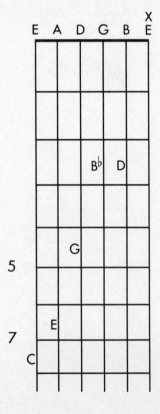

2. B, D, F, A♭

   G♯, B, D, F

   The pitches are the same in the two chords.

3. Three

   B, D, F, A♭

   A♯, C♯, E, G

   A, C, E♭, G♭

   G♯, B, D, F (repeats B, D, F, A♭ pitches)

4. Four

   E♭, G, B

   E, G, B♯

   F, A, C♯

   G♭, B♭, D

   G, B, D♯ (repeats E♭, G, B pitches)

Chord Inversions

1. Play the second fret of the bass E string with the thumb.

2.

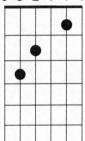

3. B7 in second inversion.   A7 in third inversion.

4.

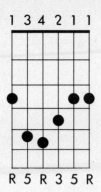

1 3 4 2 1 1

R 5 R 3 5 R

5. No.

6. First, root, second.

7. Notes of the Em chord on the guitar fretboard.

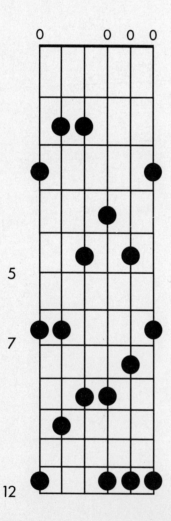

Three ways to play the Em chord while keeping the bass E, B, and high E strings open.

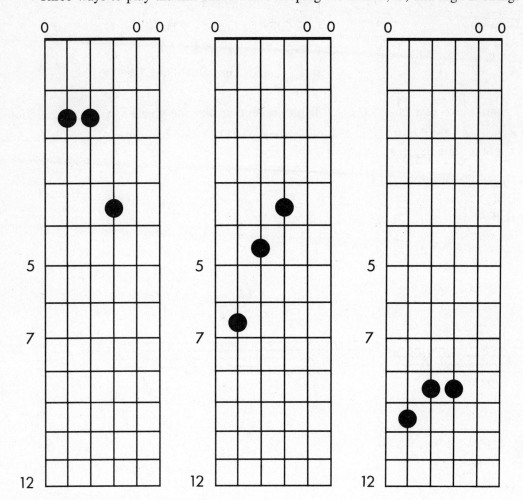

Playing Chord Progressions

1. A   /   /   /
   D   /   A   /
   D   /   A   /
   E7 /   A   /

2. A   /   A7   /
   Bm /   E7   A7
   D   Bm   C♯m F♯m
   B7 E7   A   /

(This is busy, but it works. Try other solutions.)

Harmonization and Modulation

1. D   D7   G   D   D   F♯m G   A7
   D   D   A7 A7   or   D   E7   F♯m A7
   D   D7   G   D   D   D7   Em7 A7
   D   A7   D   D   Bm A7   G   D

2. | D | D | D | D | | D | Dmaj7 | D7 | D7 |
|---|---|---|---|---|---|---|---|---|
| G | G | D | D | **or** | G/G G/F♯ | Em | Dmaj7 | D7 |
| D | D | Em | A7 | | F♯m | G | A7 | A7 |
| D | A7 | D | D | | Bm | Gm | Dmaj7 | D6 |

3. The A7 chord needs resolution. The A7–D progression creates the greatest sense of resolution.

4. The G chord provides the strongest resolution after D7. The common root movement is from the fifth to the first scale degrees.

CHAPTER 12
Counting Half Steps

1.   5   3
     7   4
     10   2

2.

Transposition

1. | A | A | E7 | A |
|---|---|---|---|
| A | A | E7 | A |
| A | A | D | A |
| A | A | E7 | A |

2. | C | C | G7 | C |
|---|---|---|---|
| C | C | G7 | C |
| C | C | F | C |
| C | C | G7 | C |

3. B♭ major

Chords in key of G: C, D7, G, Em, Am7

Capo Transposition

1. Third fret.

2. | Put capo at fret number | Play these chords | | | | |
|---|---|---|---|---|---|
| 1 | E | A | B7 | C♯m | B7 |
| 3 | D | G | A7 | Bm | A7 |
| 5 | C | F | G7 | Am | G7 |
| 8 | A | D | E7 | F♯m | E7 |
| 10 | G | C | D7 | Em | D7 |

(Notice that these solutions are in the five keys that are best for guitar: C, G, D, A, and E.)

3. Fifth fret.

   Dmaj7, F♯7, Em6, G, Em/C♯

4. Capo twelve-string guitar at second fret.

   Fifth fret. Play in G.

5. Second fret. Third fret.

6. Chords for key of A.

   For C, F, and G7 the capo would have to be placed at the tenth fret.

Two-Chord Song Index

Songs in This Text

Barb'ra Allen, 56
Clementine, 306
Deep in the Heart of Texas, 139
Down in the Valley, 26, 42
Drunken Sailor, 58
Go Tell Aunt Rhody, 124, 144, 172, 183, 187, 197
He's Got the Whole World, 31
Hush Little Baby, 36, 128, 144
Joshua Fit de Battle, 46
London Bridge, 123, 184, 186, 194
Pay Me My Money Down, 89
Polly Wolly Doodle, 24, 209
Rock-a My Soul, 154
Rye Whiskey, 47
Sinner Man, 59
Skip to My Lou, 305
Tom Dooley, 24, 131, 171, 182, 196
Yellow Rose of Texas, The, 37

Other Two-Chord Songs

Alouette
Ashes of Love (bluegrass)
Blind Fiddler
Boll Weevil
Bringing in the Georgia Mail (Charlie Monroe)
Gospel Ship (Carter Family)
Honky Tonking (Hank Williams)
John Henry
Lonesome Pines (Sara Carter)
Mary Had a Little Lamb
My Old Home on the Green Mountain Side (Norman Blake)
Oats, Peas, Beans and Barley Grow
Okie from Muskogee (Merle Haggard)
O Tannenbaum
Pat-a-Pan
Paw Paw Patch
Puttin' on the Style
Reuben's Train
Ruby (Osborne Brothers, bluegrass)
Sally Goodin'
Southern Railroad Blues (Norman Blake)
Stay a Little Longer (Bob Wills)
Tonight the Bottle Let Me Down (Merle Haggard)
Willie Seton (Tom Paxton)
You Never Can Tell (Chuck Berry)

General Song Index

General Index

General Index

accidentals, 107
Ackerman, William, 191
acoustic guitars
  nylon-string, 266
  steel-string, 267
    arched-top, 267
    dreadnaught, 267
    flat-top, 267
    metal-body-resonator, 267
    twelve-string, 267
action, 271–272
Aeolian mode, 235
amplifying acoustic guitars, 282
Anderson, Eric, 191, 299
arranging songs, 290
Atkins, Chet, 6, 266

Baez, Joan, 299
bar, *see* measure
bar line, 104
barre, 205, 208
barre chords
  explained, 205
  in rock and blues, 217
  playing, 208
barre chord forms, 205, 219
Basho, Robbie, 191
bass clef, 104
bass runs, 91
bass run arrangements, 93–99
beams, 114
beat, 112
beat groupings, *see* meter
bluegrass music, 298
"blue" notes, 222
blues, 250
  history, 295
  left-hand damping, 217
  open-D, 156
  open-G, 157
  scale, 235
  shuffle rhythm, 32, 83
  walking bass, 201
  twelve-bar progression, 250
  bridge, 3

callouses, 8

capo
  normal, 263, 281
  Third-Hand, 164, 303, 314
Carter, Maybelle, 169
Carter Family melody style, 169
cases for guitars, 270
chord diagrams, 19, 225–228
chord fingerings, 64
  A, 29
  A7, 23
  Am, 45
  B7, 48
  C, 50
  D, 20
  D7, 41
  Dm, 57
  E, 45
  E7, 30
  Em, 42
  F, 60
  G, 35
  G7, 55
chord progressions
  "drop" chord, 253
  identifying, 247
  listening for, 286
  primary, 248–249
  secondary dominant, 250
  twelve-bar blues, 250
chords, playing
  added ninth, 227
  augmented, 225
  diminished, 226
  dominant ninth, 228
  dominant seventh, 225
  fingernails, 22
  hints, 22
  major, 225
  major ninth, 228
  major seventh, 226
  major sixth, 227
  minor, 225
  minor-major seventh, 227
  minor ninth, 228
  minor seventh, 225
  minor sixth, 227
  seventh suspended, 226

seventh with added sixth, 227
  sixth, 226
  suspended, 226, 304
chord structure
  augmented, 243
  diminished, 243
  dominant seventh, 242
  major, 241
  major seventh, 243
  minor, 242
  minor seventh, 243
  on fretboard, 246
chromatic scale, 231
church lick, 71
clef sign, 104
coda, 120
compensating saddle, 272
composing songs, *see* writing songs
copyright, 294
Cotten, Elizabeth, 137, 191
counting melodic rhythm, 115
country music, 297
cross-keying, 264
cutaway guitar shape, 266

da capo (D. C.), 120
dal segno (D. S.), 120
damping
  right-hand, 6
  left-hand, 217
Davis, Reverend Gary, 137
Denver, John, 157, 191, 299
Dobro, 267
dominant
  chord, 242
  scale degree, 248
Dorian mode, 235
double bar, 104, 120
doubling in chord, 245
Dylan, Bob, 191, 285

electric guitar
  acoustic-electric, 266
  hollow-body, 266
  solid-body, 266
electronic tuners, 17
endings, 120
enharmonic, 234

About the Authors

TERRY LEE KUHN was a music teacher in Oregon for six years before earning a Ph.D. in Music Education at Florida State University in 1972. He taught at the College Park Campus of the University of Maryland where he initiated the popular Folk Guitar Class. He has been at Kent State University since 1977, and has continued teaching the folk guitar class along with courses in music research, teaching methods, and the business of music. In addition to numerous scholarly research publications, he has co-authored *Contemporary Music Education* with Clifford K. Madsen and *Fundamentals of Classroom Music Skills* with Gustav Wachhaus.

HARVEY D. REID has made his living playing, teaching, singing, recording, and writing music since 1975. He taught folk guitar at the University of Maryland from 1976 to 1979, and since then has performed extensively on acoustic and electric guitar, banjo, Dobro, mandolin, and autoharp both as soloist and with various country, bluegrass, and rock groups. He has won several acoustic guitar competitions, including the 1981 National Fingerpicking Guitar Championship.